A Feel-Good Life

The wandering, uncertain journey of a dad who loves
his kids…and sometimes his dogs…

by Dave Markwell

About the author:

Dave Markwell lives in Des Moines, Washington. He is a writer, thinker, business owner, and proud father. He believes in friends and family, and that being a little bit sunburnt and a little bit drunk, surrounded by the people we love the most in the world is a pretty good way to spend a day (photo above), and that simply being a good guy (working document) is a pretty good way to spend a life...

He can be contacted at: afeelgoodlife@gmail.com

I felt it. So, I wrote it…-Dave Markwell

My words in this book represent thoughts or feelings I had during the course of a unique period in my life. As such, they are dedicated to the people who inspired them: Aden, Helena, Genie, Mom and Dad, my brother, Mike, and countless other friends and family. I am blessed to have too many to mention here, but…you know who you are…thanks…

Special thanks to Nicholas Trahan for cover design, and Chandler Simon for making my words a book. And extra-special thanks to Scott Schaefer for too many things to mention, but mostly just saying "yes" to my "Feel Good Friday" column idea and letting me be me…

11/3/2020

Preface

This collection of stories is loosely organized in chronological order, though it does jump around a bit. The topics vary and the tones change, as such, this book was not necessarily designed to be read "front to back". With this in mind, I invite readers to skip around and taste the different flavors.

These are the stories of my life, but are likely the stories of your life, too. I sincerely hope so. My wish is that my words and experiences feel familiar and create some sense of connection to the beautifully absurd moments of which much of life consists. We live our lives in these moments and recognizing the good ones is vital to recognizing that the world is a pretty fun place to be, and the simple truth that life is pretty good...

Joan!!!
Thank you for sharing your wonderful spirit with the WORLD!!? Your unique magic is invaluable and beautiful...
Love, DAVE

Order of Stories

Beehives.

Last summer, my five year-old daughter, Helena, and I went for a walk with our dogs down to the Beach Park in Des Moines, WA, our hometown. It was a little misty and cool, a pretty standard late August morning. While walking through the park, we ran into my ten year-old son, Aden and his buddy, Elijah, riding their bikes.

For the previous three days, the boys had been scouring the town with the fairly newfound freedom of being able to ride around un-chaperoned. I remember this time in my life very fondly.

Upon seeing me in the park, my son's eyes lit up in excitement to see me. He was playing it pretty cool, but he was either genuinely happy to see me, or maybe just happy for me to see him being independent. "What are you clowns up to?" I asked, casually. "Not much. We were just throwing rocks at a beehive. Want to see?" Aden replied.

A tiny, but powerful electric impulse hit me. "Do I want to see!!?!! Of course, I want to see!!" I thought, frantically. Beehives still excite me and it will be a sad day when I pass up an opportunity to check one out. As we headed to the back of the park, I felt the rare and beautiful anticipation of something cool about to happen.

When we got to the beehive, I saw that it was a dandy! It was a big hive and the bees were thick and swarming pretty good. It hung about ten-feet high in a wide-open hole between the branches of a maple tree.

I gently questioned Aden if he remembered how it felt when he stepped, barefooted, on a honeybee in our yard a couple of weeks earlier. His scream had been heard for blocks. He responded with, "Oh, yeah!" Enough said. It was a subtle, yet effective warning; a father's duty. Upon clearing my parental conscience, I picked up a good-sized rock and hucked it.

I hit the hive hard and square, then scooped up my daughter and ran with a wild-eyed smile on my face. Just behind me, laughing the hysterical laugh of fear and fun, the boys peddled furiously. We were all laughing that laugh. We managed to outrun the bees and were unharmed. I suppose this story would not be told had we been stung, as I'm sure my wife would have made re-living this moment un-fun, probably forever.

Nonetheless, we lived to tell the tale and though there are many things that I am eagerly waiting to outgrow, chucking rocks at beehives is not one of them. I have become convinced that a small fragment of youth resides, untarnished by work deadlines and house payments, in each hurled stone, waiting to make a man a boy again.

On a cool August morning in my son's tenth year, I was able to surprise him by truly sharing his excitement and letting one fly!! From the moment the rock left my fingers, I had, in some small, though not insignificant way, changed to him. I wasn't just Dad, the rule-maker and fun-taker. He saw that I was capable of something else, something more. I had the potential to be more to him. He's not sure what yet, but I got him thinking and that's a start. It was a good day.

Bad Daddy.

In another semi-desperate attempt at being a good Dad, I have decided that my six year old daughter shall no longer be allowed to watch her favorite TV shows. While this may seem a bit oxymoronic, it is not completely without thought.

My daughter is rapidly becoming a stuck up little snot. I say this with much shame. It is my fault. I, in my own laziness and haste, allowed this to happen. This is not to say that she is a bad kid, she's absolutely not. But she's heading that direction without a little more leadership. It is time for a modest, yet painful intervention.

She enjoys "Hannah Montana", "Wizards of Waverly Place" and "I-Carly" immensely. Unfortunately, these girls are young teenagers and my daughter, as mentioned, is six. She doesn't want to be six, but she is. I, on the other hand, very much want her to be six and remain six for a very long time.

She has learned language and attitudes that she should not have learned. She has been a quick and true study. I, now, have decided to turn back the clock. I have hit the reset button and am no doubt faced with an epic battle. Some crying will be involved, probably by both parties. Some yelling and whining and foot-stomping will also occur. I am prepared for this; my mess, my broom. I will do the dirty work. I failed.

Fortunately, I am committed. Understanding that my daughter is headed in a direction that I cannot bear has awakened a resolve that lurks deep in a dad; a resolve to be better, for the child's sake. This hidden little treasure of insight is often unseen, but welcome and it's good to know that it exists when you need it. I will trudge forward against her pleas and attempts at barter, if not some flat out bribery. She will try to lure me with sweet looks and kind words. She will try to break my will. She will not succeed. I will hold my line and be strong because I must. My failure will not be hers.

A parent's duty is complex and elusive. When do we chime in? And when do we let it go? These questions diabolically evade clear answers. Having little background to draw from, we must make it up as we go. We improvise and dance and dodge. We simply do the best we can. It is delicate work, but vital, on many levels to our own quality of life, if not our sanity itself. Raising kids that will listen and respond and behave appropriately is a lofty goal, but without striving high, we are by default settling for low and low is no fun at all. Trust me on this one.

So, I will now try to get a bead on that ever-shifting bar that is good parenting. I will do the right thing that, as a lot of right things do, hurts a little bit. I will look forward to a brighter future with a hope and a prayer that I don't screw up my kids too bad and a wish that, when they reflect on their lives, they will know that I tried to be a good dad. In my faulty, goofy, dense, dimwitted, ignorant, short-sighted, ill-tempered, impatient, thoughtfully-thoughtless ways, I tried.

Daddy, I can't find my phone…

"Daddy, I can't find my phone. It fell and I don't know where it is." My six year-old daughter said. My daughter loses a lot of things so this statement was not unique or surprising in itself. What was unique and surprising was that she said it at 3:30 in the morning, waking me up from a rather strange dream involving myself, Billy the Kid and some hostile looking penguins. As I cleared my head, I brilliantly replied, "Turn your light on." Suspecting that this ingenious solution had probably escaped her sleep-weary mind. She left.

Proving once again that, on occasion, I am not completely without value, she returned to my bed with her phone and other things. For clarity, I must disclaim that I do not endorse or promote a six year-old having a cell phone. This phone was somehow one of several extra phones we acquired in an attempt to shave a few bucks off of our monthly bill. Through some cell phone company trickery or perhaps using the Bush system of "fuzzy math", it was somehow cheaper to have three extra phones that we don't use than just the ones we needed. My daughter, in another attempt to feel like a big girl, adopted one of these extra phones, which she carries around the house and uses as an alarm clock. Apparently, she must have been fumbling for it in the dark and it fell off of her shelf and went under her bed, thus the reason for her concern this late night.

As she climbed into my bed, I positioned myself firmly in a comfortable spot, knowing that it would not last. I tried to calculate the appropriate distance allowance for her shifting, twisting and kicking that would eventually force me to dangle on the thin edge of the bed without a pillow or a blanket. I'm not sure how she manages to manipulate a 200-pound man into a state of absolute discomfort so effortlessly. But she does it, regularly.

Per her ritual, she grabbed her fuzzy purple blanket and favorite doll, Mary, and slipped quietly between her mother and me and snuggled closely against my warm bare back. Some nights, it is annoying and I just wish she'd sleep in her own bed, but this night was different.

It occurred to me at this unfortunate hour that many things our kids do, they don't do them forever. We get a finite number of nights that our kids will climb into our bed and snuggle with us. I can already feel the number dwindling. Our daughter is six and our son is ten. On very rare occasions will he climb into our bed. Gradually, she will stop as well. I will be sad when they stop.

A certain duality exists is parenthood. On one hand, you want the kids to be more independent and able to help themselves. On the other hand, you want them to stay little. You want them to need you and to still be able to comfort them with a band-aid, a fudge- sickle, or a kind word.

So I tolerate my own lack of comfortable sleep and wake early with a sore back and don't get up, but lay still and watch my daughter sleep. Her fresh and peaceful face evokes feelings that only a parent of sleeping children understands.

At bedtime, they cry and whine and say "no way", but then sleep and dream and are happy. You can then remember why you love them so. It is a forgiving time. It is a special time that reaches a place in the heart of a parent that is often untouched and overlooked and probably wouldn't exist were it not for the vision of sleeping children.

While I may I complain and futilely shove her back in place, sometimes a little violently, I feel the clock ticking on her, as well as me, and I understand that this time, like all other times, is fleeting and I'd better just appreciate it, because I know I'll miss it when it's gone.

Road Trip.

This week my eleven year old son, Aden, and I embark on our annual boy's road trip around the Northwest. This event is not to be confused with "boy's weekend". Certainly, there will be much beer consumed, but most of it will be "root".

For the past several years, my son and I have taken a summer road trip exploring the little nooks and crannies around the area. We have both been introduced to some new places and some new faces. Our trip was originally designed by me as an effort to spend a little time with my son doing something we both enjoy. These occasions seem increasingly rare around home as the distractions of life and other unnamed members of the family demand other things from us. Traveling with just the two of us eliminates a lot of debates about how and what we should be doing. We can just "do", as guys will.

Being on the road is unlike other traveling. It allows for a slower pace and some genuinely peaceful enjoyment of the scenery. The inherent stress-factor of other forms of travel is not there. No airports or customs or even traffic, if we plan it right...and we do! We drive the back roads and sleepy hamlets littering the wonderful three states in the great Northwest corner. We do it with the windows down and shirts off, eating chips and drinking soda. We are unwashed, decadent explorers and enjoy it all.

I have been a road-tripper since way back. I have seen most of the continent through windshields. I've met countless fascinating people in my travels; People one does not meet at Senor Frogs in Cancun. People that have changed the way I think and the way I am. These adventures have shaped me in ways that are difficult to explain or quantify.

Little ideas or insights here and there flow freely on a road trip. My mind and spirit are alive and the soil is fertile for my best thoughts. Unburdened by other obligations, road trips allow for true free-thinking. These thoughts are the cornerstones of any good ideas I have ever had. They are my most important thoughts.

Having the opportunity to explore the dusty two-laners of my soul with my son riding shotgun is priceless and it is wonderful to know that years from now we will share these as some of the best moments of our lives. We share an armrest as our lives unfold through the bug splattered windshield. We live it together. I recognize this as precious. That's why I started it. My son does not.

He recognizes this as fun. One day he will understand and be grateful. This was not and is not my goal, but I will be happy when the light bulb clicks on and he understands how significant our fleeting time was.

So as I load the rig and stock the cooler, I look forward to the adventure and the freedom that awaits us. We will stop and swim when we get hot. We will eat when we are hungry. We will see sights previously unseen. And we will talk. We will talk about important things. We will share pieces of ourselves. We will get to know each other better. We will be what a dad and son should be, but often aren't. We will be pals with a flexible plan and the authority to change it whenever we want. We will be the co-owners of an experience that counts and I cannot think of a better way to spend a week of my life.

Performance Art.

The other night my six year old daughter and I attended a concert at Highline Community College. My ten year-old son was performing with the Parkside Elementary orchestra as they opened for a Des Moines Arts Commission Music Series show. He plays viola.

In the past few months, I have come to understand that the learning curve for instrument mastery is decidedly not steep. The slight twitch my dog, Diego, is now afflicted with, no doubt the result of the unnatural sounds piercing my son's bedroom door, will testify to this.

While the process is slow and sometimes painful, there IS progress and as the group came together and played their pieces, it was actual music and it was great. Their focused and serious faces read their music as they played powerful works. Occasionally, a shrill missed note would find its way to my spinal cord, followed by an eye-raising wince from the assailant, but overall they sounded pretty good and I was proud.

As proud as I was of my son, my daughter, on the other hand, on several occasions, narrowly avoided a very public strangulation. "Just sit still, PLEASE!", I loud-whispered, and repeated as a mantra throughout the concert.

Now, I had no illusions that bringing a six year-old to a classical music show would be entirely trouble-free, but as the bouncing, talking, swinging, fiddling, fidgeting and kicking ramped up, I was considering very bad things.

Fortunately, as it sometimes will, fate intervened. As my son's performance wrapped up, the headline group, The Sirens, came out and began to play. They are a trio who play piano, flute and oboe. I don't ever recall hearing an oboe before, certainly not like this. This woman played notes that I did not know existed. They touched me and gratefully must have touched my daughter as well. For three wonderful minutes, she sat on my lap and we listened to a song that we could feel. There is an emotion in the oboe that surprised me. The music swept over us and it was beautiful.

I looked around the room and saw my son sitting next to his buddy several rows away from us, because if there is anything un-cooler for a fifth-grader than a classical music concert, it is sitting with your dad and little sister at a classical music concert. I understood and was not hurt, too much. I enjoyed the true magic of the moment and was genuinely moved.

This was until my daughter woke up with a simultaneous flailing back head-butt to my face and swinging heel crotch-kick. The wonderful moment was over in an instant. It was just too good to last. As a stifled a yelp, I collected our things and knew it was time to go. "Go get your brother." I said as I made my way to the door and stepped out into the cool Des Moines rain.

I tipped my head to the sky and smiled and knew that the brief, pure moment was worth all of the hassle, struggle and even the crotch kick. The beauty of a single moment is worth all of it, every time.

Number 522.

Apparently, I am now number 522. For some unknown reason my stock took a nosedive today. I was up to 37, but not anymore. My seven year old daughter informed me of this. Using some complicated and mysterious calculations, she ranks me.

As she looked at me with pity and dismissal while telling me my new ranking, I shook my bowed head wondering where I went wrong. I never know what I did wrong. Her system of quantifying my value to her puzzles me. Only on rare and precious occasions do I break the top ten. I am usually deep in the hundreds. My wife remains solidly placed at number one and my son, my daughter's unrivaled nemesis, frequently ranks higher than me. I don't get it.

I am the one making blueberry pancakes that I don't eat. I construct lunches and brush hair and teeth. I play and read and talk. I say nice things. I tell her she's beautiful and smart and wonderful. Yet, I still trail an apparently large pack of others. My current ranking of 522 is strange. I don't think this little girl even knows 522 people. In this case, she must be ranking me behind people she doesn't even know. WTF...whatever...if 522 is where I am, fine.

While considering how or where she even began to think of ranking people, I had to look no further than my left ring finger. My wife, while not vocalizing my rank, wears my placement on her face. Where I stand with her is very obvious. The scale and severity of my indiscretion or error in judgment is detailed in her expression. She does know over 522 people and I am certain that I have done things resulting in a ranking below 522. I am not proud of these moments and the only explanation I can offer during these uncomfortable moments is that I am male. The degree to which a guy can screw up in the eyes of his ladies is immense. Trust me on this. I have tested it, exhaustively.

An illustration of this occurred today as my wife called me to let me know she missed her yoga class. This may or may not have been my fault. Upon answering the phone, I immediately went into defense mode by pointing out the various delays, besides me, that may have resulted in her tardiness. How well this went over became obvious after she hung up on me. It was not good. Being concerned about my new and likely deserved slide in ranking, I dove straight into damage control.

I cleaned the kitchen and swept the floor. I picked up my crap from the living room. I even picked up the kids' stuff. I, in a mild form of parental protest likely known only to me, rarely put their stuff away. I yell at them to clean it up, trying to impart some lesson on responsibility that goes largely in vain. I don't enjoy talking to myself, but I do a lot of it. The clincher on my amends making was my preparation of chicken enchiladas for dinner. Tonight was my wife's late night at work and understanding that the way to her heart truly is through her stomach. I knew that having a good meal ready for her when she walked in the door had the power to change the climate in my home.

It may not have been total magic, but it did soften the edges of her frown and she loosened the grip on her anger and disappointment. With each delectable bite, she unwound and I felt my rank creep higher. A hungry woman is an easy fix. My daughter is not so easily persuaded, but as all people do, I'm sure she has a trigger-point. I will keep searching and hoping that a soft spot is discovered. I will throw some chocolate chips in her pancakes and maybe add some whipped cream. I will scratch her back and rub her feet. I will serenade and dance. I will find her trigger...hopefully soon, because I don't know how much longer I can take being number 522.

Paradise...FOUND.

Every year my Rotary Club donates dictionaries to all of the third graders in our city. Distributing the books to the students is always a neat event. It is fun seeing all of the young faces exploring their new gift and it feels good to give this gift. This year was even cooler for me because my daughter is a third grader.

A couple of days ago, I went to the school and handed out dictionaries to her and her classmates, many of whom I have known since kindergarten. It was great seeing their enthusiasm and it was fun seeing my daughter in her school environment. I pick her up from school every afternoon, but I don't often witness her in a classroom. She was happy to see me, but also a little bit anxious as I had, the previous evening, detailed all the ways I was going to embarrass her during this event.

Waiting for her dictionary, she wore a nervous smile and begged me with her eyes to not do anything stupid. She needn't have worried. I behaved myself and was proud to be there. I did come to understand as I stood watching her interact and actually pay attention that she is a pretty good kid. It is easy to forget this.

At school, she listens and minds her manners. Things are different when she is home with me. Besides her good behavior, this experience illustrated to me that she is growing up faster than I can comprehend and is changing in ways that astound me when I catch glimpses of them.

Prior to the dictionary distribution, I went to the school office and signed my girl out of class for the rest of the afternoon, as a little surprise for her. After the books were handed out, I told my daughter that we were leaving early to meet my wife and to get some hot chocolate at Auntie Irene's, a local coffee shop. She was pleased with this news.

During the brief drive from Des Moines Elementary to the coffee shop, the radio was tuned to a country station and a song mentioning "paradise" was playing. The song referenced islands and sand and sun and it felt pretty good to hear about these things on a rather dreary northwest afternoon

At the coffee shop, I sat in a comfy chair while my wife and daughter playfully visited. Glancing out the window at the waters of my life, Puget Sound, the song about "paradise" kept replaying in my mind. The idea of paradise is a little slippery and nebulous to me. It's a "you know it when you see it" kind of thing.

That afternoon, sitting with my girls, sipping a good cup of coffee, looking out a rain splattered window at my world, I felt paradise. And it was nice.

I felt paradise, too, when my daughter was collecting her things to leave the classroom as her envious classmates returned to their school work and my girl looked at me with a conspiratorial shrug and a grin of pleasure. She knew that she was special. It's important to feel special sometimes and the fact that I made her feel special made me feel special. Paradise was found...again.

These moments of paradise are a soft-soled dance with perfection and feel good every time. What struck me and stayed with me following this insight was that moments like this happen often. Every single day we experience moments in paradise. The key to achieving them is seeing them. They are there. We just have to look.

Each day is filled with brief sparks of true moments that slow us down and baffle the noisy world we spend much of life living in. These moments are paradise. A certain peace lives in this stillness that reminds and recharges and sometimes reinvents us in ways that make us better. Paradise lives here and surrounds us always. It is in the mind and heart. It has infinite shapes and colors. And the hue is especially shiny on a dark and damp afternoon playing hooky with a happy eight year old daughter.

Banned.

My eleven year old daughter banned me from attending her "6th Grade Breakfast" event. Her reasoning was unclear, but fear and shame seemed likely culprits. Afraid and/or ashamed of what I'm not sure, probably just me, I guess.

Having attended many long-winded school functions during my lifetime already, I didn't put up too big a fight. Sure, I postured a bit, but when I'm off the hook, I don't try too hard to bite it again.

I am, however, still slightly troubled that I was actually banned. My sweet little girl did NOT want me at this event. I'm not sure what I did to inspire this action, though, if I ask (which I won't), I'm pretty sure my daughter could produce a list. I don't want to see that list. I prefer my head in the sand.

In my absence, my girl was awarded "Most Intellectual" during the little ceremony that I missed. Another parent, who apparently wasn't banned, sent me some pictures. They were bittersweet. I am a sucker for milestones. I like seeing my kids' achievements and find much joy in their joy. Like all parents, I think my kids are pretty special and it's fun for me when others think so, too. Thus, my banishment became a bitterer pill to swallow after seeing my girl standing in front of the auditorium accepting her prize.

My daughter is growing up. She is making the transition from "cute" to "beautiful". Seeing her every day, I am somewhat blinded by the close distance and sometimes miss what a beautiful and wonderful creature she is. The other parent's photos had an outsider's view; a different perspective than I am used to seeing. And it was nice.

Viewing my girl through a new lens allowed me to see something maybe truer than my own eyesight. As parents, we often get stuck in what "was" or what "will be" and overlook what "is". Our kids' moments today are special. They are special because they won't stay here for long and without knowing and seeing them as they "are", we can miss important things. Important things rarely last, which makes recognizing them while they're happening an important thing, too.

This is always the challenge: slowing down and seeing what "is"; taking a breath and observing and capturing in our minds and souls the unique spirit of our unique times. These times become our lives and remembering important things helps us remember that life is important. And, by extension, we're important, and life is pretty good.

So, while I sit licking my wounds following by daughter's ban, I will accept this goofy moment and will remember it. I will tell stories about it later. I will laugh last and hardest. Her milestones are mine and I will claim them. These moments are our life. She tipped her hand and from now on I will not be denied. She poked the bear and will suffer my attendance at all of her future events. She won the battle, but I will win the war. Though, I suspect we'll both win. She just doesn't understand that part yet, but she will...

Big Ideas.

"Hey, Dad! Check this out!!" my thirteen year old son, Aden, bellowed. Based on a rather dubious history with his exclamations, I am rarely quick to respond to these requests, because they usually result in me having to clean something up. This day, I was pleasantly surprised.

As I cautiously opened his bedroom door, he was sitting at his desk with a notebook. "So, I was thinking…" He said. Again, based on my experience with him saying these words, I was prepared for him to ask me to do something I didn't want to do or spend money I didn't want to spend. Refreshingly, neither of these things happened.

"I want to build an electro-magnetic engine." He stated. "Sounds good" was my response as I began to slowly back out of his rat-cave. "Here, look." He said, as he passed me his notebook, drawing me back into his filthy lair. He had detailed a complete materials list and a rough schematic about how it could be done. I sat with him and we discussed how viable the project might be. We determined that it was worthy of further exploration. So, that's what we're doing: exploring.

While I know less-than-jack-sh#t about how to build this thing, I like the idea of it. And, more importantly, I like that my son is THINKING about ideas like this. He is exploring the great, big potential of this world and thinking and trying to make something happen. He is inventing possibilities and inspiring himself to keep thinking. This makes me, as a dad, very happy and proud.

My daughter celebrated her ninth birthday last week. One of her presents was a grab-bag full of different fabrics and textiles. She is dreaming of her own handbag line. I am currently converting our storage room into a usable space for, among other things, a work space for her to do her thing. She doodles and makes drawings and questions different materials and designs and thinks. Again, her big ideas live with her and inspire her and make her move.

The value of a big idea is immense. It has the power to transform us; to make us better; to change us, and the world. Big ideas have moved mountains and shaped lives. This is pretty awesome.

Through my forty-three years on this planet, I have had lots of big ideas, dreams which have made me happy and given me hope. While some have worked, many have not. But the value of a big idea is not always about whether it works or not. Big ideas always succeed in making us come alive. They make us feel good and worthy and capable. And this is good.

With this in mind, I will always support and encourage any hair-brained, half-cocked, goofy, wild, insane, impossibly huge ideas that shoot across my brow or out of my kids' mouths or anyone else's for that matter. These ideas make the world better and make people better.

Everything great begins as someone's dream. This basic truth validates the fantastic day-dreamer, the wanderer and the seeker. And, while it is nice to know that, once in a wonderful while, dreams really do come true, their true beauty lies in the hopeful comfort and recognition that we are made truly special simply by thinking them.

Collision.

I am not a big Halloween guy. I don't like to dress up much. With the one notable exception in my life being my plastic Batman costume that I had as a kid and wore religiously until it finally broke, which as it turned out was past Easter, as evidenced by a picture of me holding my Easter basket in said costume. I was a big fan of this one, but in general, I am not a fan of costumes.

These days the best effort I pull off is grabbing one of two wigs I have in the closet and transforming myself into my standard "guy in a wig" costume. Not impressive. Halloween has never been my favorite holiday, but I grudgingly do what is required, especially now as a parent. As little as I enjoy Halloween, I very much enjoy that it opens the gates to the holiday season and most importantly for me, the Charlie Brown holiday specials.

As further testament to my stunted maturation, a rare yet not un-welcome moment occurred as I was watching "It's the Great Pumpkin, Charlie Brown" with my kids. I was sitting warm and cozy with my daughter in the poofy recliner. We had a soft blanket and some snacks. About the third time I repeated Charlie Brown's forlorn, "I got a rock." My daughter started laughing. I laughed, too. At this moment our childhoods collided. While she was creating a memory and a feeling that she will carry throughout her life, I was remembering and feeling moments of my own past and it was a beautiful collision.

I, like many of my generation, grew up watching Charlie Brown holiday specials. They always signaled a cool event coming up. I watched them all, every year. I would look through the TV Guide and highlight the time and channel in anticipation. At first, I just enjoyed the cartoons as I enjoyed all cartoons at this early age. Over time, the shows, while still entertaining, became more. They began to represent an age that was gone. Charlie Brown became a nice little time machine back to this time. He remains such for me.

From Snoopy kissing Lucy to Linus' blanket artistry to their teacher's muffled voice, these cartoons remain the same. Everything in my life (and everyone else's, too, I suppose) changes. It is nice to have a constant. Charlie Brown is my constant. He will always have "trouble with the scissors" resulting in a crappy Halloween costume. He will always pick the shabby Christmas tree. And he will always get rocks instead of candy. This is good to know. I'm glad he's there for me each season with these wonderful reminders of my own simpler times. I'm also glad he's there for my kids. I'm glad to share him with them.

Like nothing else, the holiday season has the unique ability to take us back. It is nice to be back once in a while. Life is busy. We spend much time in motion and less in emotion. It is good to feel our lives. The holidays allow us to feel. The various smells and tastes and shapes of this season open the door to our favorite stuff. This stuff feels good and is important and what life is supposed to be.

So this year, I will put my head down and do what needs to be done for Halloween and watch Charlie Brown and chuckle and remember and be happy and grateful. I will be grateful for another holiday season to spend with my family and friends. I will embrace the moment sitting in a chair with my daughter watching Charlie Brown get a rock......again. The childhoods in my home will collide and we will all enjoy it for a pleasant change as Shroeder's piano plays our life's songs.

Never pet a burning dog.

"Look within, Listen, Be Nice" and "Never pet a burning dog" are my two all-time favorite pieces of bathroom graffiti. These words were written right next to each other on the wall to the left of the urinal trough in the best college bar in the history of college bars, The Coug. I read them many, many times.

I was always struck by the absurdity of their connection. The duality in their relationship is not unlike many other things in life. Life is filled with light and dark, hard and soft, good and bad. They exist together. They share the same space on bathroom walls and perhaps truly need each other to exist at all. Sunny days in Seattle are always more sunny because they follow gray days. This duality must exist for us to have anything of value.

The other night my wife and I were having a very serious discussion. We were talking urgently about the usual un-fun topics of money, plans, bills, the future, the laundry list of things I was doing wrong, etc.

While deep in the heat of the intense conversation, I noticed that on my right index finger I was, not consciously, yet quite deliberately, twirling a piece of fake dog poop. I tuned out of the conversation for a moment, hoping my wife wouldn't notice me playing with a fake turd during our important talk, and pondered how life IS this duality and how sometimes, in our worst moments, we are our best and how humor and joy exist even in the most serious circumstances. I began to feel that, though our conversation about "stuff" was significant, it was not everything. Few things are everything. Family and friends are the only items I can think of, that qualify to me. Yet, a lot of emphasis is placed on things that don't and won't ever matter.

Our world is filled with bad stuff happening. We have wars, oil spills, sucky economies, and lots of bad people doing bad things. This is sometimes overwhelming and disheartening. But as I looked out my lighthouse home office window the other morning and glanced into my neighbor's yard and witnessed him dressed head to toe in his raingear, sitting on his lawnmower cutting his grass in a downpour, I was happy. He had a cup of coffee in his hand and was smiling. At this same time, I noticed his two year old daughter playing nearby with dirt in her mouth and flowers in her hair. She was wearing a pink puffy dress that she swiftly removed before she squatted and peed in her dad's freshly mown lawn.

It is very easy to get lost in all the bad news that chokes us daily, however, I think that as long as carefree little neighbor girls exist that will stand in the rain and whiz in the yard, we're gonna be ok.

Birds and Songs.

"A bird doesn't sing because it has an answer, it sings because it has a song."- Maya Angelou

Unlike human beings, the song bird is unconcerned with having an answer. As human beings, we are often focused, and sometimes crippled by the need to find answers; to "figure it out", whatever "it" is. We struggle and search and don't find. Some people spend disappointing lives looking for something that doesn't exist.

Much like the" truth", answers are where we find them. Answers are subjective. We decide for ourselves what we care about. These are the answers. These are our songs. In these songs, we find the peace and joy and beauty in our lives.

The most apt definition of "success" I have ever found is: Success is being both content and ambitious at the same time. Clear and content in the quality of its song, yet ambitious in the song's delivery, I suspect that the song bird is very successful.

Many years ago, I experienced a profound epiphany when I understood that I will never really know anything. I will know some things, but much and most of the world will live unexplored by me. Instead of being disheartening, this was liberating. I did not need to worry about what I would never know. Too much knowledge exists for anyone to know all of it. I was off the hook. I can read what I like and listen to what I like. I don't have to know it all. I believe in exploration and enjoying new things, but I am not tortured by a ceaseless quest for information that I don't really care about anyway. Living our lives true to the song of our heartbeat is the answer. The singing of our own unique song is the answer. And this is good enough for me.

Last night my daughter asked me to sit with her on the couch. She lay down with her legs on my lap and asked me to rub her feet. She then promptly fell asleep curled up in her favorite purple blanket. In this moment, I understood both the song and the only answer I will ever need. Thank you, Maya.

A Long Walk.

The other day I was tired. This is not news. I am often tired. I wake up early and don't always go to bed early. This makes me tired. On this day, I was so tired that I took a nap. This was not unusual, what was unusual was that I laid down on my son's bed and napped while he watched YouTube videos and played video games after school. It felt really good.

My son has been "borrowing" my favorite blanket for several years now and it was nice to be reacquainted with my old friend. It also felt nice to be lying in my son's room. His smelly little cave is usually off-limits to me. But, this day, I took it. He tried to harass me into leaving, but I stayed. And I think both of us liked me being there.

Rapidly approaching my eleventh wedding anniversary, I look back to "then" and see a much different life. I was different and my wife was different. "We" were different. Through struggle and stubbornness, pain and love and trying, we have arrived at this place. And it's a good place. Many honest, authentic and uncomfortable conversations got us here. We were changed by them. Thankfully.

In assessing our arrival at this place, I remember the other place. Selfish interest, pride, ego and immature ideas about what life should look like steered us down a path to destruction. We all have ideas about how life should be. These ideas are usually wrong.

Life is not a tidy business. It gets messy. "Two people becoming one" in marriage is an insidious idea. It violates our natural need for self-expression. And we need this more than we need another person. We simply need to be who we are and become better in the ways we want to become better. We need to evolve for ourselves, our own self-value, but it is a good thing when this evolution saves our marriages. It saved mine.

So, through eleven years of climbing and falling and climbing again, we are here. My wife and I understand each other better. We accept our differences and embrace our sameness. We are both free to be who we are and respect the other's need to express our unique selves. Life is still untidy, but it works.

Last week, I heard someone say, "You have to give up the life to get the life." I understood these words. Letting go is sometimes difficult. We cling to things that sometimes don't serve us well. Many years ago, I scribed a thought in an old journal, "Some things change and some things don't. Gratefully. The

24

difference is knowing the difference. And moving on from there..."
Understanding what we can and should change is important. But understanding what we can't change may be a more significant insight.

Changing and not changing allowed me a wonderful mid-afternoon nap on my son's bed. I felt close to him and a sense that soon his personal journey would be taking him out of our home. I was not sad, but felt grateful for mine and my wife's efforts that afforded me this nice moment.

Life is a series of steps. Some backwards, some forward and some sideways. The direction of travel is not as important as keeping moving. A life in motion is a beautiful life and a warm spring sun shining through the window and a stinky pillow in a teenage boy's bedroom is a fine reward for all the walking...

A Streaming Consciousness.

Some weeks, I have a lot to say and words fall like raindrops onto the page. This week I just have thoughts, random and spotty thoughts without any common theme tying them together. I suppose this is representative of my life, in that, the story is not always clear, but simply a collection of fragmented daily moments that, when blended through the magical alchemy of living them, become more than the story of a moment. They become the story of a life.

"Dad... DAD....DAADDDYYY!!!" And so begins my daily dance. I never answer the first time, because I like the fairytale idea that she might fall back asleep or forget that I am here. She never does. My nine year old daughter, Helena, persists and will persist until I move from my comfortable spot and begin my morning service.

As I enter her bedroom, she asks, "What took so long?" I reply that I was comfortable and did not want to leave my blanket and warm spot on the couch to get her stuff. I say this very sincerely, but she just rolls her eyes in disbelief. She cannot comprehend that I might prefer my own comfort over doing things that improves hers. This seems to be a common idea in my house. I am built to serve, period.

Now and then, I will revolt. I will not answer the call. I will not start the shower or make the sandwich or melt the cheese on the after-school quesadilla. Some days, I will not make coffee or breakfast or find shoes. Some days, I say "screw it". Though I think it is easier just doing it than listening to the incessant complaining when I don't, but sometimes a man has to make a stand.

My little revolutions are rare and don't make any difference in how my household is run. It is not run by me. My wife and kids rule. I understand this and they understand this. And while I may sound whiny and ungrateful for all that I receive from them. I assure you, I am not...well, maybe I'm kind of whiny...but not ungrateful.

My wife works harder than anyone I have ever known. My kids are good kids with good grades and good friends and even adults unrelated to them, like them...for the most part. This says something. I like many kids unrelated to me, but not all of them. Kids are kind of annoying, mine included, but I don't have any choice about dealing with mine. So, having kids that most adults don't mind being around is, to me, a positive. Or having friends that don't tell me that my kids are annoying is a positive. Either way, I'm protected from feeling like a bigger failure as a parent than I already do.

In our living room, we have plant. It is a palmy-type of thing and it is not healthy. The fronds are yellowing and the stalks are dry and cracked. The cause is unknown. We water it, not too much, just enough. It gets sunlight, enough, not too much. But this sucker is knocking on death's door.

The other day, we noticed some dirt in the planter had been "disturbed". Actually, my wife's little dog, Grace, had dug a big hole and we suspected she may have been peeing in this planter. My wife took it harder than I did. Grace is pretty spoiled, but my wife still takes it personally when this dumb little dog behaves too much like a dog. Normally, this involves her pooping or peeing in the house. "Correction" is swift and sure. My wife is small, but fierce, with a heavy hand.

While discussing the mystery of the dying plant my wife asked me if I had done anything to it. Due to the fact that I don't really care if this plant lives or dies, I was only half-listening and replied, thoughtlessly, "I don't think so…. I mean… I put a booger in there the other day." Following my admission, my wife looked at me, dumbfounded, then left the room to, no doubt, ponder all of the other options she had to choose from in her choice of husband.

During her absence, I understood that whoever said, "Honesty is the best policy" was an idiot of magnificent proportions, only outdone by a slow-thinking slob of a man who would first commit and then admit to such a crime. Honesty was not the best policy in this case by a long shot. Oh well, I guess breakfast tomorrow better be a good one.

Post Office.

After dropping the final kid off at school, I was ready to start my day. I began with great hope and many complicated plans that were going to secure a fruitful and most productive few hours. I had washed my hands of the usual morning catastrophes: "Dad, I can't find any socks!! *Look in your drawer, dinkus.* Oh, ok." "Daaaddd, I don't want that in my lunch!! *Too bad.* I won't eat it!! *I don't care.*" "Dad, where's my homework?!! *It's on the table where you left it..* Oh, yeah." "Daddy, how long until my birthday?!! *Ten and a half months, sweetheart.*" I was now ready to dig in earnestly.

My first plan involved the post office. I knew that this was the wildcard. The pace at which I could navigate this hill climb would determine the shape of the rest of my day. I hate going to the post office. It is never a quick trip. I have never lucked out with a short line. I'm not sure they even exist. I have tried going to the post office at all hours and it doesn't seem to matter. It is slooowww-going. I knew that hinging my day's outcome on this uncertain variable was risky, but I was prepared and gave a reasonable cushion to allow for an exceptional delay. So I thought.

An hour and a half later, I walked out the door and felt like a corpse hopping out of the coffin. The sunlight was blinding and I was nearly run-over by another post office escapee fleeing in haste towards a better fate. I was deflated, if not completely beaten. My day was shot. The domino effect of this lost time was irrecoverable. I knew it. It was a done deal. I would go through the motions, but would end the day disappointed and dejected by all the unfulfilled potential. Oh well, not the first day that blew up and not the last, I'm sure. I prepared myself to move on as best I could.

While sitting in my truck gathering myself, I looked to my left and saw a lady in a small red car, two parking spots over, crying. Now, I was pretty sad about my big day getting flushed, but I wasn't going to cry about it, though, in all honestly, I may have been close a couple of times while in line. As I cautiously spied on this poor woman, I felt bad for her, but I also felt kind of good, because for some perverted reason other people's misery sometimes can minimize our own. Sad, but true.

As I started my truck and began to back out, I glanced at this unfortunate woman again and saw that she was indeed crying. In fact, she was bawling, but she was not sad. She was laughing her head off!! She was happy!! She was

28

reading a letter and shaking and nodding and smiling with delight. She was affected. I watched her and began to smile myself. Then, I started laughing. This anonymous woman's shameless joy was contagious and I was infected. Whatever was in her letter was magic. I felt a transformation take place not unlike when the Grinch feels his heart grow, then lifts the sleigh high over his head and streaks down the hill to deliver Christmas to the Whos in Whoville. I was changed.

I chuckled and drove away forgetting about what was lost and grateful for what was gained; a new perspective about what's important. The people that write letters that can make us laugh hysterically in the post office parking lot are what matters. This recognition saved my day and I saw with fresh eyeballs all the wonderful potential that still existed. The outcomes were less important than the grin I would wear running my errands and the tone I would greet my late appointments with. My mood was lifted and that was the difference between success and failure. The smiling attitude that I met the world with was what mattered. This is true on any day. I understood then, that my day was going to be just fine and I have never left the post office feeling better.

My Sea

The other night I took the garbage out. This was not as remarkable as my wife may find it. I take the garbage out as often as necessary. Sometimes volume and sometimes smell will inspire my trip outside to the can. This night it was a combination of both. The nine o'clock sun was setting and the sky was cloudy, blue and red. It was nice. Somehow weaving its way through the stench of my trash was the smell of the sea. It must have been low tide, as I could smell the briny water and heated sand and mud and the creatures that dwell in both.

This is my favorite smell. It is the smell of my life. It is the smell of my youth and my life today. It reminds me of standing in line for the Scrambler at the Waterland Festival as a kid. It reminds me of early morning and late evening water-ski trips in high school to the sand pits hoping for some flat water. It reminds me of fishing and crabbing and sitting on a boat in guest moorage drinking beer in the sun. It reminds me of dog walks and family walks and squiding off the pier. It reminds me crisp autumn mornings mowing Beach Park and warm summer afternoons looking for spider crabs and perch along the pilings in the days when they both excited me more than they do now.

This smell and this sea is my home. It is where my Dad's ashes lie and where mine will go when the time comes. Today, my sea serves to make taking the trash out something more. Like nothing else, it has the power to give my life perspective. As I get bogged down by life's have-to-do's and running-lates, the late spring smell of my sea in the evening brings my life back in order. It is easy to get mired in unimportant things. As human animals, we struggle and chase and want. We spend an unseemly amount of time running, with tunnel vision, towards a future of more running. Sitting still, smelling, listening and feeling that life is pretty good, right here, right now, is necessary for both the piece and state of mind that make life truly wonderful.

It's a little odd to me that a fairly routine trip to the garbage can inspire thoughts like these, but maybe the thoughts needed to be found and perhaps any vehicle would do. Either way, I'll take them when they come and I appreciate them as old friends. I have a lot of great, old friends, but these thoughts and the smell of my sea are some of the best. As my wife will testify, I am not exceptionally fussy about my choice in friends. But as I have come to learn, a man can never have too many friends and I'll take all that I can get.

Frogs and Dogs

The day began with an ominous, but hopefully not prophetic, start. I, in another confounding battle with my coffee maker, entered my day by forgetting to put my cup beneath the coffee squirter spout (techno-jargon, sorry). After using half a roll of paper towels and all the swear words I possess, the mess was cleaned up and I moved on.

This coffee maker and I have engaged in some epic struggles. I have screwed up making a simple cup of coffee many times and in ways that would certainly puzzle and likely amuse the designers of this machine. I can easily imagine them sitting back, with a perfect cup of joe, snickering and looking at each other with raised eyebrows saying things like, "Wow, I sure couldn't imagine someone trying to do it like THAT." And, while shaking their heads condescendingly, "My God man, we tried to idiot-proof this thing, but you're a special breed!" Well maybe, I am. I had finally figured out our other coffee maker after six years and now this new one has me stumped, but I will fight the good fight and prevail. Eventually, I will have a delicious, grind-free, cup and I will be pleased. I, also, won't have to face any more awkward questions about how we go through so many paper towels. I look forward to this day.

Following my coffee-making snafu, my day carried on, though it was still a little shaky. My daughter reset her morning alarm for 6:15 instead of her usual 7:15. While this may not seem like a big deal, it was. I get up at 5:10, exercise, then train the 6 am class at my CrossFit gym. I arrive home around 6:45 or so and enjoy sitting and drinking/eating my coffee while watching the news and a few minutes of the "Today" show before the hive awakens.

Since, my daughter was already up and was watching cartoons, I had to play the old "catch the remote from the moving hand" game with her in order to change the channel. This is not an easy game anymore, as she is getting pretty quick. After grabbing the remote and changing the channel, my act was met with some soft-screaming and dirty looks. And in a thoughtful display of her anger, my little girl ripped up the blue construction paper swirly flower thing she had made for me the night before that had "I Love You" written in black marker. She set the torn pieces on the arm of my chair with a satisfied look in her eyes. I was a little hurt by this gesture, but since I had placed my "present" in my wallet the previous night, she actually tore up the one she had made for her Mom, so no real damage was done. At least not to me. Upon showing her my in-tact gift, my daughter made some strange noises with a mean face and stomped off, foiled again. So it goes.

The house came to life at this point with the dogs needing to go outside and my sleepy son fighting to stay in bed against my gentle, but insistent, pleas. He is delicate in the morning and requires kid gloves or a shark suit for his wake up call. I always lie down next to him and softly whisper, "Time to get up, buddy", while gently scratching his back. This seems to soothe his savage morning mood and saves me some time screaming at him for screaming at me. He was up and moved, slowly as a glacier, to the shower. Ok, I thought, things are shaping up. It's gonna be a fine day.

After making breakfasts and lunches, I began the day for real. It was foggy and as I do whenever it's foggy, I thought about a day in my life many years ago: I was probably five or so and performing my daily ritual of eating cereal with my Dad at our kitchen table before he went to work. As he opened the sliding glass door to take the trash out, I noticed that it was a foggy day and, using my hilarious, even-way-back-then, wit told my Dad, "Daddy, it's froggy out there. Don't step on any frogs!" I laughed about this one for quite a while that day and I still do, but for different reasons these days. I like the fog and frogs because of this.

Back to the present day: Before I could really claim a portion of the day for myself, I had to drop my dog, Diego, off at his buddy, Dakota's, house. They are best friends. As I pulled into the driveway, both dogs were barking and jumping in excitement at seeing their pal. Their genuine joy was a little contagious and as I opened the gate and watched them fake bite and jump all over each other, I was happy that my dog had a best friend. I am not offended that I am not his and he knows he's not mine, but I'm glad he has someone better than me to play with. Everybody needs a best friend. As I drove away, lighter in heart and head, I felt pretty good about the direction of my day. It was ordinary and extraordinary at the same time, just like most of them, and that's just fine with me.

Pockets

While doing laundry the other day, I checked the pockets in my kids' pants. This is a must-do every single time. The margin for error is thin and wrought with heavy consequence. Following an unfortunate bubble gum-to towel-to chest hair transfer some time ago, I have learned this lesson and it is for my own safety that I check pockets religiously and thoroughly. My kids have, once again, demonstrated that even in their absence they have tremendous power to disrupt my pretty easy-going life. This fact is not lost on me and I live a pretty wary existence with this in mind.

Various little minefields surround my home. From trip hazards to improperly stacked dishes in the cupboard to unsecured caps on the milk, my kids create an environment in which any lapse in my attention will be met with disaster or at least a mess that I will have to clean up. As my wife will enthusiastically testify, I don't enjoy cleaning up messes. So, I try to avoid any unnecessary spillage or breakage. I am not often successful, but I try.

The pocket presents a unique challenge in that some of the objects contained therein are pretty inexplicable. I shake my head a lot. I question why they keep some of things they do. I find candy, candy wrappers, and other random pieces of paper, jewelry, cards of some sort or another and lots of other miscellany, including on rare occasions, money. I keep the money. My son will enquire, "Dad, did you find the five bucks I had in my pants?" At this point, I will happily lie to his face, "Nope, you probably lost it", while silently burping the Jack In The Box dollar menu items that I purchased with his five bones. I have zero guilt about this, because it was probably my money in the first place and, even if it wasn't, that kid **owes me**.

While the pocket garbage is a certainly a nuisance, it is also a small window into what they think and care about. The other day I tossed out a tiny bead found in my daughter's pocket. Though I have little compunction about throwing away items that have seemingly no value, I have come to understand that I really have no idea about what has value to them. This simple, anonymous little bead apparently was a "present" to my daughter from her "best friend" and she wanted it. In fact, she *needed* it. She told me so.

As I dug through the trash searching for a stupid bead that meant everything, at least that day, to my daughter, I was struck by how little I know my kids. I often think I can read their minds and sometimes I can. They are usually pretty transparent and have no poker faces. But, as they get a little older, I see the individuals they are becoming. They care about things that I have no idea about. They have conversations and experiences that don't involve me. This is a little unsettling, but also a little liberating. I want them to need me for as long as they do. However, I also want them to evolve. As painful as it is now and most certainly will become in a few years, I will not mind not hearing "Dad, I'm hungry" fifty times a day or "Dad, where are my shoes?"

I suppose that these questions like the kids will evolve as well. I can already hear, "Dad, have you seen my earring?" and it won't be my daughter asking. I can hear, "Dad, will you drive us to the mall?" I can hear, "Dad, I'm taking the car." I can hear it all as I once said it all to my own parents. I will understand as well as I can, which is sometimes not very well, but I will try. They will outgrow lots of things including, and maybe especially, me.

They will not though, at least any time soon, outgrow the need for clean clothes and as I am the main player in our daily laundry battle, I will be checking pockets for a while. I will continue to learn things from the pockets' treasures and I will be diligent. I will stand guard and I will keep my eyes peeled, as I know what sorts of things pockets can hide. Because, as my kids don't understand now, but hopefully one day will: Once upon a time, not a long time ago, I had interesting things in my pockets, too.

Good Day

On a warm and sunny, mid-September, Tuesday evening, I sat very redneckish, drinking beer in my driveway with my buddy, Dan. We had camping chairs set up and our feet on a cooler. I make no pretense about owning even a small sense of refinement. I am quite happily borderline classless and it is very natural for me. I require very little to achieve joy. I am a simple man with simple pleasures. I might add that Dan did not look too uncomfortable, either.

I have learned many things over my years and understanding where my joy lies is probably the most valuable. I am happy in little moments. I have certainly enjoyed fairly lavish vacations in exotic lands. I have traveled and seen and experienced much. I have enjoyed the adventures and new places and faces. However, I have not enjoyed them more than sitting at my picnic table in the sun with a couple of old buddies and maybe my son, playing cribbage and telling bad jokes. These days do not require much more than a couple of phone calls to occur. No months of planning or itinerary debate, merely a small effort and fun is at hand!

Muddying the waters of my simple existence is a complex world; a world filled with nuance and expectation. I am often confounded and sometimes feel a bit out of step. I care a lot about moments and lack a lot of foresight regarding consequence. I enjoy the day and figure the future will work itself out. I am sometimes wrong and sometimes right, with no clear winner either way. This may seem a bit immature, though I make no claims to maturity and would not place a bunch of dough down on me arriving there anytime soon. I'll settle for my wide-eyed, extended adolescence and, in fact, I embrace it. I have seen a lot of very mature, very miserable people. This scares me. I am in no hurry to get there, but, we'll see how it goes. Time will tell as it always does about these things. Time always tells.

One thing I am certain of is that today was a good one and I can't imagine anything that would inspire me to alter it. We are allowed a finite number of days to enjoy and we waste plenty. When the rare, beautiful ones hit, we must take them, cherish them and live them. These are the rewards. This is life.

So, is life, recognizing the moments that count and counting them. We write our own ticket and have the absolute power to decide how we spend our time. Spending it with our friends and families and the people that create the easy smiles seems like time well spent and a guarantee that life will be good. I have yet to discover anything else more important to me. If it exists and I find it, I will be very excited, because it will have to be pretty awesome to beat a late summer day in the sun with a good buddy, drinking beer in the driveway...

A Mouthful of Bees.

When my daughter was just a baby learning to crawl, I used to sit in the corner chair of our living room and let her drag herself around the floor while I worked on stuff. One day as she was meandering around my chair, she wound up behind me. The chair had some rocking potential and being the ever-astute dad, I did not want to pinch her little fingers if she happened to put herself in that position. So, as I delicately stood up, taking great pains to not move the chair just in case her fingers were in a risky spot, I noticed her safely tucked in the corner chewing on something. Well, as everyone knows, babies put things they should not into their mouths.

Upon safely standing up, I dug her out from beneath the chair and began my exploration into what she could be chewing on. She battled me for control of her jaw as I tried to take a peek. After prying her mouth open, I may have shrieked. I certainly winced and shook and I would very much like a picture of my face at that moment in our history. Her mouth was full of dead bees.

Recovering quickly from my shock, I started digging out the shredded bees from her tiny mouth. Little crunchy yellow and black pieces fell to the carpet and the wings, lots of them, floated from my finger as I tried to end this horror. Eventually, I completed this awful job, but the horror remains if only in my memories.

Last week my little bee-chewing daughter hit double-digits. She turned 10. I was conflicted between celebrating and lamenting this little milestone. I don't want her getting older, but I am obligated to fake joy about this happening anyway. And so, as I do many things, I enthusiastically faked it.

My daughter has grown into a bright, curious, kind, headstrong, thoughtful and beautiful creature. She makes me proud and drives me crazy every single day. She baffles, astounds and confounds me. She is a lovely, messy pest of a soul and I wouldn't have her any other way. To me, she is perfect.

Last night, while performing our nightly bedtime ritual of me telling her to get ready, followed by her stalling and yelling, something strange happened: While waiting in her room for her to finish brushing her teeth, I laid down on her bed. As she walked in the room, she first glared at me and then her face changed and she crawled over me and rested her head on my chest as she pulled her blanket up.

I turned on her music and we just snuggled. It has been a long time since my daughter has cuddled with me without pinching, poking, jabbing or biting me. It occurred to me, in this soft moment, that she is still my little girl.

As the days and years pass, my daughter stretches much closer to becoming everything else except my baby girl. With her fresh-smelling hair in my face and head on my shoulder, it struck me that she still needs to be my baby girl sometimes. And as she takes her sometimes perilous journey toward adulthood, she will always need me to just be "daddy".

Through the running, growing and learning, it is easy to overlook these things. With a new sense of my place in her life, I have found some comfort. She can grow up all she wants. It doesn't matter. She will always need me as "daddy". And she will always be my baby girl with or without a crunchy mouthful of bees...

A Weird Week.

This was a weird week. At least I think it was. I'm not sure that I am qualified to determine what's weird anymore. But, the week seemed weirder than my normal weird weeks.

On Sunday afternoon, Diego, my fun-loving, oft-farting, gypsy of a dog came up missing. I filed the appropriate reports with the appropriate authorities. We drove around and recruited friends and neighbors to be on the lookout for him. And then, we just hoped.

My sadness about my missing dog was a bit surprising to me. This dog has done little but drive me crazy during his seven years as a member of our family. He has stolen food, thrown up stolen food in my bedroom, barked, scratched, crapped and licked himself, loudly and publicly. Many days, I have wished for his demise and, on more than one occasion, may have actually plotted it myself. But, after two days without this stinky hound staring at me every time I sit down, I really missed him and was sad at the thought of him not returning to his home.

As luck would have it, he was found and after a mild lecture from local law enforcement, he was returned. Diego's significance in our home was verified when I went to pick up my son from Pacific Middle School. I brought Diego with me and as my normally sullen and crabby fourteen year old boy saw his dog sitting in the front seat of my truck, he smiled. He does not normally smile when I pick him up. He was happy and relieved and our family was back in order.

Also, this week, my son had his 8th Grade "promotion" ceremony. While I am always game for recognizing life's little milestones, this event was a little much even for me. I found myself shoe-horned in a hot and crowded middle school gymnasium praying for time to pass quickly. If there is a hell for me it will involve a crowded middle school gym.

As I stood there sweating and wishing myself anywhere else, I noticed that some people actually seemed to be enjoying themselves. Lots of families were carrying balloons and flowers and smiles. Many of these families were of international descent. As I pondered their odd joy, it occurred to me that maybe I was taking for granted how cool moving past eighth grade was.

In many countries around the world, opportunities for a quality education, and thereby a quality life, do not exist. This goofy, droll and meaningless ceremony was not meaningless to the people who understood the value of opportunity. Upon this recognition, I felt like an entitled, selfish crybaby of an American ass and then enjoyed the joy of the folks who knew it was an important day.

Later in the week, another school year came to an end and summer vacation began, the globe kept spinning and my life carried on. And as I drove into my driveway following another day at work to witness Diego hunkered over with his tail pumping up and down doing his business in the yard...I felt a sense that all was right with the world...

Glassy Water.

I am a notoriously impatient driver. I am not an aggressive driver, but I know the rules and expect others to know and follow them as I do. I am often disappointed. In these moments, my expressions of displeasure range from simply shaking my head to a finger-pointing admonition or a finger-raising admonition, depending on the indiscretion. Usually, I just swear really loud.

A few years ago, when my daughter was still sweetly nestled in her baby car seat behind me, a distracted driver in front of me failed to recognize the green light and sat until it turned yellow, then bolted through, leaving me sitting through another long traffic cycle with my red light.

While waiting for my turn, I must have exclaimed a few juicy words, though I am not certain since I blacked-out in my rage. I suspect that I must have yelled some bad words, because upon leaving the stop line when my light turned green, I heard my lovely little baby girl muttering "F#CKER, F#CKER, F#CKER..." I think these were some of her very first words.

In shock and fear finishing my drive home, I contemplated first: how was going to explain this to my wife? Next, I pondered how truly our kids mirror us. This can be good or not good depending on what we do...

This idea holds true not only for our kids, but also everything else in life, as well. The face we shine into to the glassy water is the face reflected back at us. Like the water, the face we greet the world with returns to us. Some call this karma. Some call it justice, poetic or otherwise. I don't know what to call it, as its shape and form changes, but I believe it to be real.

Having the benefit and burden of our "higher" human intellect, free will is ours. With this, the ability and capacity to create is ours. This is our super-power. And it begins with the face we choose to point into the mirror.

All of life is a choice. A lot of excuses are made and justifications evoked and cop-outs copped, but when the leaves fall and the tree of life stands bare, we all have choices. These choices determine our outcomes. And our inevitable results begin with the face we point at the world: the who and how we are. We make our own weather. We put the rain in the clouds and we craft the glorious sunrise. The power is ours.

In the end, our will to choose well determines the lives we live. We own our lives. Our currency is choosing well. Being flawed human beings, though, we must take care to not be too hard on ourselves when we make imperfect choices. Sometimes these choices wind up being not so bad after all...hey...it's funny hearing a baby swear...

The Countdowns.

Well, the countdown is almost over. Next Friday ends the annual month-long trek towards summer vacation. It will begin. Understanding that summer vacation marks the beginning of nearly 3 ceaseless months of making lunches, breaking up sibling tussles and trying to entertain bored kids, I am still kind of excited about it.

Summer vacation is still magic. At least the idea of it is. My own summer vacations were filled with adventures and exploring the deep mysteries of the neighborhood. I learned to make bike jumps that wouldn't fall apart. I learned how to tie water balloons that didn't explode in my face. I learned to mow lawns and get my chores done ten minutes before my parents got home from work. I played soccer and football and fished and crabbed. I wore the tires off of my bike riding around town with my friends. I split and stacked wood and swam and spent a lot of time with my cousins and grandparents. My summers and the experiences they held shaped me. I hope the same holds true for my kids. But so far, it's not looking good.

They are already fighting and my nerves are already showing signs of wear. Not good. Nonetheless, I am excited for school to get out. The magic of the last day still lives. Few experiences in life provoke the same giddy sense of excitement and anticipation as the last day of the school year. I am glad my kids get the enjoy feeling this feeling. I am going to enjoy feeling it with them. In my own nostalgic wanderlust, I will return to my last days and remember that it was pretty damn awesome.

I will enjoy this for about a week. Historically, a week is about my threshold for having my kids around all day long fighting and needing. After a week, things get squirrelly. I yell and find lots of ways to distract myself. I will spend a little more time working at my gym than necessary. I will find excuses to just be gone. A few minutes are all I need, but I need them.

In spite of my natural desire to escape, I will not...for long, anyway. I will serve. I will find distractions for them. I will drive them to camps and friends' houses. I will set up the sprinkler and slip-n-slide. I will get smores fixins'. I will stand by the grill and cook hot dogs and hamburgers for them and their buddies. I will do this not because I must, but because I know how great a summer can be and I know I can help them. In spite of my instinct to hop the fence and keep running, I will not.

Come first light, I will make pancakes and say "What do you guys want to do today?" They will respond and so will I. A week before summer break, I am filled with noble intentions of shedding my laisse faire Dadhood and being better, more attentive and engaged. I am hopeful that we can all enjoy a summer that we will remember. Time, as it always does, will tell. But those are my hopes today.

So, the countdown narrows and next week the hurricane of summer will begin. The wind will blow and the tears will fall. We will laugh and we will play. We will smile the wonderful smiles that only live in the long days of a kid's summer. With sunburned shoulders and bare feet, we will share our summer for as long as it lasts.

In about a week, this countdown to summer will end. About a week after that, I will begin my own countdown marking when summer will be over and these fantastic, smart, creative, beautiful and interesting creatures of mine will go back to school and order can be restored.

Until then, I will ride the wave of this summer with loose hips and a grin and hope I don't hit the sometimes shallow reef.

Toys.

The other night I stepped on one of my son's toys. It was a red SUV-type truck with a surfboard rack. It used to have a surfboard, but that was lost a long time ago. I have stepped on a lot of my son's toys over the years. In fact, I have probably stepped on, tripped over, kicked, stubbed and/or somehow otherwise damaged myself on more of my kids' toys than I have not. Breaking toys is not new to me. What was strange about this incident was that I felt bad about it. I was very surprised on this day that the accidental destruction of yet another trip hazard actually affected me.

Through the years, I have been a veritable serial killer of toys and have been personally responsible for countless "disappearances." Literally, hundreds of victims have met their demise in the stinky, shallow grave of my kitchen trashcan, covered only by chicken bones and eggshells. I have been indiscriminate in my toy tossing. There has been no pattern that any expert CSI or profiler could reveal. It has been random and willful. I have been able to perfect a straight-faced response to my kids' queries into where a particular toy that I had thrown away might be. "You must have lost it, like normal." I can say without flinching or shame. Why do I do this? Simply put, my kids have too much crap and I have taken it upon myself to cull the herd. It is a lonely duty, but it is mine.

Independent of my efforts, the life of a toy in my household is a rough one. It is perpetual teeter-totter hell-ride, bouncing between extreme neglect and extreme abuse, with nothing in between. The truck that I damaged on this day had already endured several tough years. It was my son's favorite for a time and I can remember him playing with it several years ago, back when he was just a cute little five-year old boy with a baby teeth and a big head. This truck had managed to survive, when many, many others could not. While this accomplishment is worth noting, it, to me, does not explain my unusual reaction. I am a jaded and calloused toy killer and I sleep well at night knowing this. Why did I feel bad about crushing another toy that had done nothing for me, but be in my way for years?

Upon reflection, destroying the toy itself did not affect me. Rather, the toy represented something else that is both gone and leaving more every day; my kids' childhood. This stupid, broken red truck symbolized something wonderful and fleeting and its destruction spotlighted the fact my kids are growing older.

Its obsolescence hurt me, because, I know what's coming next...my obsolescence!! I am slowly and surely becoming the dusty, busted toy buried deep under the bed that nobody wants to play with anymore.

While this makes me sad, it comes with, as all downsides do, an upside. They say life begins "when the kids move out and the dog dies." I cling to this idea as a life preserver. I look forward to golfing more and people not crying in my house every day. I look forward to watching what I want on the TV with a FULL bag of Doritos. I look forward to fewer questions and less laundry.

This is where I am stuck, because these things I will also miss. I will miss the constant bickering, crying and yelling. The silence scares me. My concerns may be premature as my kids are still young and I have a few years to get over my fears and simply enjoy the screaming, fighting, inconvenient pains in the arse that are my kids. They are growing up regardless of how I feel about it and I should embrace this as a natural part of life. So....I guess that's what I'll do.....right after I fix the windshield and glue the roof back on the red truck, maybe polish it a little, and while I'm at it, I should look for that surfboard...

Go to your rooms!!!

My kids don't get along very well. To simply say this is a vast and profound understatement. They cannot be in the same room together. In fact, often times the entire house seems an inadequate space to contain their high level of disregard. Disregard might be the wrong word. I wish they would just disregard each other and pay no attention to what the other was doing. Such is not the case.

They very much regard. They cannot pass on any opportunity to comment, shove, scare, berate, leer, shout, scratch, or in my daughter's case, pinch and/or bite. They seem to enjoy the screaming, both the other sibling's and mine. I have become a key player in their sordid little game. I don't want to play, but I get sucked into their battles.

Ironically, in my persistent struggle to achieve some degree of quiet in my home, I yell. I don't want to, but I can't help it. They make me. I try to remain calm and set a nice tone and allow them certain appropriate expressions. But that doesn't work. They drive my polite bus off the cliff every day, forcing me to their level of passionate, often illiterate and borderline obscene, violent threats.

I have only my own experience to make any judgment about what is normal. Most days, I feel that my kids, and certainly I, are seriously flawed. Some little genetic code for tolerance and forgiveness and simple niceness has malfunctioned somehow, with devastating results. It is worth noting that I am always quick to pass the buck to excuses like this. Looking in the mirror makes me feel bad. But some goofy genetic defect seems like a reasonable explanation and gets me off the hook. I can get very creative in finding these excuses. They may be the canvas upon which I paint some of my best work.

As frustrated as I become by the incessant bickering between my kids, I, on occasion, have the good fortune to encounter some of my friends' kids. Last week, I picked up my buddy's three daughters from school and drove them home. The entire trip was littered with "shut ups", "I'm gonna kill you when we get homes", and one "your butt looks big", followed by "not as big as yours". These girls, aged 5, 7 and 10, took the gloves off and delivered! They were ruthless and sharp as blades with their scathing insults. My heart was warmed. I was not alone. My kids are not weird and I am not the smoking gun leading to the corpses of my kids' sad, mean, and mouthy childhoods. I was quite relieved by this and as I dropped the girls off, I looked at my buddy and smiled and thanked him as he started what was sure to be several hours of telling his kids to "knock it off" and "leave each other alone".

Again, I was touched. I had a brother-in-arms. I suspect that all parents are comrades in this war against our kids being whatever they are, unless, of course, one is a parent of children that actually get along. I have heard of them, but have never met any. I will likely be highly suspicious of them if I ever do. Something devious and possibly criminal must be to blame for children's good behavior.

So I can rest easy knowing that most, if not all, parents are screwed and I just happen to be one of them. It is an undistinguished and unsavory fraternity. But I wouldn't change it if I could. Though, in full disclosure, not a day goes by that I don't consider renouncing my membership. However, when dawn breaks, I awaken with some strange form of amnesia, possibly one that only afflicts parents of annoying kids, and begin each day with new hope and fresh eyes and good thoughts that this day might be the one that leads us down a new path. I usually end the day beaten and disappointed. Thank God for the amnesia. It may be the only thing that keeps me going.

Green Blankets

Sunday mornings are mine. I get up early, make a cup of coffee and watch my favorite show on television, "CBS Sunday Morning". This is a news-type program without the bad news. Imagine "60 Minutes" without any dark, controversial subjects. I like good news and positive stories about interesting people. I especially like them on Sunday mornings when my family is still asleep. This is my time. I don't have much time that is mine alone, so I claim whatever I can and I claim this.

Last Sunday, while watching my show, lying on the couch, I dozed off. The soft din of Charles Osgood's soothing voice lullabied me into a peaceful morning nap. I was cozy, wrapped up in a green blanket and a quiet house. It is rare that I get both of these at the same time. And, like most good things I get around the house, this was not to last.

I was awakened by my 8 year old daughter, Helena, standing over me glaring, her beautiful green eyes burning a hole in my face. She was a silent devil in pink pajamas with a loud stare. In my peaceful slumber, I felt her evil presence and awoke with a start.

My first instinctual response was to fight fire with fire. The question, "What the F*** is YOUR problem!?!" was nearer my tongue than I am comfortable revealing, but gratefully did not leave my mouth. But I thought it. Yes, I did. Instead of screaming these unrecoverable words, after my brief fury at having been awakened in such a manner, I asked, in a nice voice, "What's wrong, Sweetie?'

She continued her hard look into my eyes, though she shifted her gaze down slightly to look at the green blanket. It then became clear to me. She wanted the blanket. This green blanket is the best blanket in the house. It has a soft, white, sheep-skinnish pad on one side and a green, even softer, micro-fiber flip side. It is heavy and light at the same time and is the subject of much debate in our home. Everyone wants it. And this morning my lovely little girl wanted it so much, she angrily stood over me, glaring, until I woke up to give it to her. Which I did. I did not want to, but I knew, from my vast experience with matters such as this, that my time enjoying this moment and blanket were over. I could surely keep the blanket, but I could not enjoy it, of this, my daughter would make certain. We both knew this and so I gave her the blanket and retreated to the kitchen to make her breakfast.

The morning continued without incident. Upon reflection, the single, difference-making choice I made was my initial response to my daughter's rude wake up call. In this moment, the outcome was determined. I chose to be better than my nature would generally guide me to be. In a split second, I recognized that this response was significant and would create the weather for the rest of my morning, if not the rest of the day. I chose well. It is nice when this happens. It doesn't always.

This episode highlighted the fact that in every situation, many responses are possible. Some are good and some are not good, but always, the power to choose is ours. Choosing well creates good outcomes. Choosing bad creates bad outcomes. This is a very simple insight, but also an important one.

Basic physics indicate that for every reaction there is an equal, but opposite reaction, and so for every word we utter, a very predictable reaction is imminent. Each word sets into motion a chain of events or, at least, sets a tone for events that determine our day. Since every life consists of a string of days, whenever possible, I try to choose good words, which will, hopefully manifest themselves in good days. "Try" being the operative word here. I fail plenty, but I know it when I do it and usually try to do better next time. This idea is at the heart of any progression we attain as human beings: being better than we were before. Again, this is a simple insight, but an important one. Learning from our mistakes is a constant challenge, but it happens, sometimes in spite of us.

Recognizing the impact of our words is a powerful understanding and is a true game-changer. It determines a day and indeed a life. And, though it may not return us to a sleepy morning nap with a comfy green blanket, it is not without value. This is good to know. Today...I hope to choose well...

The Confession.

I like country music. There, I said it. I am officially "coming out" as a guy who likes country music. While this may not seem remarkable, as a fella having grown up in the age of the Scorpions and Def Leppard, this is a major leap from the closet. My awakening occurred today as I sat in my truck with the windows rolled up waiting for my daughter to get out of school. I had the windows rolled up because I did not want anyone to know I was listening to country music. The volume was low, yet I still checked the mirrors frequently to make sure none of my after-school parent pals could sneak up on me and discover my secret. While listening to the gentle twangs and homey lyrics, it struck me that, despite all of the crap country music gets, it pretty much has it right.

Each song is homage or a celebration about something important or something significantly insignificant. Rich with symbolism, stories are told and people "get it." This has appeal to me. Many things in this world I do not get, I do, however, understand stories about resilience and struggle and hope. I understand the allure of a beach and a beer. I understand love, both lost and found, as much as anyone understands such a mystery.

Country music speaks to these topics in ways that I get. I am always searching for some understanding and meaning about life. Country music reminds me that these questions are not mine alone. Others, if not all of us, have the same questions. Knowing that others struggle with finding answers is comforting. A collective uncertainty lives in country songs. Rarely, in a country song, is the answer clear, but this doesn't matter. This is more settling than unsettling. In fact, understanding that sometimes answers don't exist lifts the burden of not being able to find them. This, too, is comforting. Sometimes, I feel like I don't know what I'm looking for, but I know that it's important to look anyway.

Siddhartha said, "It is better to travel well, than arrive." Country music, and likely, most other music, too, is about a search. And the searching is the traveling. Every day, we encounter our lives. We wake up and live a country song. We sing in the shower and eat breakfast and raise families and bust our butts and have our hearts broken. And every day, we wake and do it again. We respond.

We search. And when we search, we are alive. When we don't, we slowly die with the deliberate knowledge that we could have and should have done more. The" answers" are the destination and they are less important than trying to find them. We discover ourselves during the traveling and are sometimes surprised by what we find. We are more powerful than we understand and when we awaken hopeful and inspired by our trip, our lives are truly lived.

Country songs tell these stories in a simple, yet complex and universally understood language. They strip down posture and pretense. They lie bare as a truth. The beauty and significance of the soft moments come alive and sing to the parts of us that need to hear. These messages about finding solace and comfort in our soft moments are something that we all need to hear and feel and believe in. For this reason, I complete my confession, without much shame, and hope that others, too, can find a song to sing, with the windows rolled up or down, and know that everything is going to be ok.

Empty Plate

A couple of years ago, after an evening out, my wife and I headed to Denny's for the obligatory late-night gut-bombing. Per normal procedure, my wife drove as I was, once again, over-served and not capable of operating any type of vehicle, motorized or otherwise. It had been a good night with friends and I was happy. We were seated at our table and my wife took the booth side, which she always does. I like the booth side better, too, but never get it when I am with her.

Sitting a table away was a young man. He was in his early twenties, I would guess. He was obviously in the military as his dress blues and haircut made this clear. He was sitting alone with an empty plate and a cup of coffee and the saddest look I have ever witnessed on a human face.

After a few minutes of hesitant looks over to him, our eyes met and I said "Hi". He replied with a soft smile and we began talking. He was from somewhere in the Carolinas and was awaiting his red-eye flight back to his base. I don't remember which branch of service he was in, but I remember that his grief hung like smoke in the dining room.

Through our course of small talk, I asked him what he was doing in town. He replied that he had come for a funeral. A fellow soldier and buddy had been killed in Iraq and the fallen man's family was from the Seattle area. So, this soldier and other members of his unit had flown here to honor their lost comrade. The service was held earlier that day. This poor boy had just lain to rest a friend and brother. He had spoken with the weeping parents detailing the events that resulted in the lost life of their child. He was there when it happened and witnessed it and tried to save his friend, but couldn't. His young heart was heavy and had changed.

This revelation made me want to hug this kid. I wanted to take him in my arms, like any good father, and tell him it would be ok. I wanted to turn back the clock and change the world for this sad boy. I could do nothing but shake my head and say "I'm sorry." My heart was broken in this moment. His eyes had seen things they could not un-see. The soft and hopeful part of his youth was gone and I knew that it would not be ok. It would never be ok and the life he knew before that tragic moment would never return to him.

As he looked in my eyes pleading for an answer that I did not have, we connected. I honored his duty with my own profound sadness. All I could do was be sad for him and his friend and his friend's family and the countless people impacted by the death of a single soldier. The look in my eyes said there is no answer, no truth, no tidy insight that can deliver the peace he was looking for. Perhaps it doesn't even exist.

Before leaving I paid his bill and shook his hand, thanked him for his service and wished him good, safe luck for the rest of his tour. Then, my wife and I walked to the car and cried.

I still cry when I think deeply about this poor kid. He was real. His eyes were real and they revealed the true depth of his confused anguish. It is a depth known to so many soldiers and families of soldiers. It is a place that no one wants to be, but many volunteer to go and stare it down and hope their fortune holds. Sometimes it does and sometimes it doesn't.

This Veteran's Day please imagine, deeply and truly, losing what you love most in this world and recognize that the men and women who chose to serve our great land risk losing and indeed, lose, what they love most, regularly. They do this for us. And it is with enormous reverence and gratitude that we must honor them, thank them, take care of them and do EVERYTHING in our goddamn power to keep these kids from getting killed. They are the most valuable things we have. God Bless them all...and their families...this day and every day....

Dog's World.

I woke up stealthy and ready for battle. I silently crept out of bed. My slippered feet were soundless as I slow-walked into the living room to catch my dog, once and for all, laying in my recliner. I had him this morning. I knew it. As I whipped my head around the wall to finally catch this sneaky mutt by surprise, I was greeted only by an ever-so-slightly rocking chair and Diego, his name unchanged to not protect him from anything, lying on the floor with a smirk. He knew I saw nothing.

He could not have heard me. I was the wind. I think he, by some strange dog sense, felt me. Some survival instinct, programmed in him through many generations of devious relatives, had saved him again. Diego rules the house this way. He sleeps wherever he wants. He eats better than I do and I hardly feed him. Kid's leftovers are his favorites. He will steal a few bites when no one is looking, clean up after himself and always leave enough food to create doubt about whether or not he had climbed on the counter to eat. He never cleans the plate. That would be evidence. He doesn't leave any. I know he does it, yet he knows I can't prove anything. Always, when I'm about to nab him, he will be walking the other way, licking his lips. He wins every time.

Diego's talents for deception would have him high on any CIA recruitment list or perhaps employed as a "Black Ops" operator in some distant land if he were not just a regular old snaggle-haired, relatively gassy dog. As ordinary as he seems, he is a genius in his field, which is primarily sneaking stuff when I'm not looking. He is a master. In fact, he may be the master. I think the whole "master" thing was actually invented by dogs to let us believe we have control. Not unlike wives. Though, my wife gave up the charade about who's "master" a long time ago. I am Diego's servant. He is MY master. I feed him and groom him and pick up his poop. Scraping dog-doo off of wet grass is about as low as one can get and I am there. It's a role I didn't plan on, but like many things in life, I accept.

Dogs are smarter than us. I'm convinced that the old velvet poster of dogs playing poker is an actual photo. They are probably very good poker players. Diego's face betrays nothing. He is a world-class liar. I can easily imagine him wearing a visor with a cigar hanging out of his mouth dealing cards. I wouldn't play with him.

He lies by my feet as I write and throws me a bone of affection now and then, cementing my commitment to serve him. He is a delightful rogue; an attractive nuisance. The hair on the couch and the tiny, sharp little shards of disintegrated steak bone I pick out of my feet regularly from walking barefooted in my living room notwithstanding, I am his. He's a good dog and I don't mind too much, though it does help to see other folks walking their dogs in the cold rain, and with bare hands tucked deep inside a plastic sack, fingering poop off the sidewalk, too. We are all slaves to our dogs. It is just so. It's a dog's world.

Dads.

"My Dad is the coolest dad in the world!" I thought, as I stared at my shredded jeans and, very fortunately, barely scratched thigh. I was around ten and had just suffered a could-have-been-catastrophic-but-wasn't incident with a chainsaw and was a bit rattled. My Dad told me we wouldn't tell my Mom about this little mishap. I was very happy about this.

At the time, I was relieved. Even before the saw stopped whining, I was thinking about my Mom's reaction to this episode. And it wasn't good. I felt, by not telling my Mom, my Dad was, if not stepping in front of the bullet for me, certainly pushing me out of the way. And I was grateful.

Many years later, while reliving this experience, it occurred to me that my Dad wasn't as concerned with saving my bacon as he was saving his own. My Mom might very well have fired up the chainsaw and done some real damage had she found out. But, she didn't.

Here lies a fundamental element of "dadhood": self-preservation. Few creatures in nature are more instinctually aware of potential risk than a dad. An impala in lion territory has no finer sense of danger than a dad faced with the steely eyes of an angry wife. This sense results in feverish, creative and prompt responses to circumstances such as letting your son use a chainsaw and then him nearly amputating his own leg. My Dad was quick to act and decided that telling my Mom was NOT going to happen. Thanks, Dad. I liked using the chainsaw and those days would have been over.

This incident illustrates the difference between a "father" and a "dad": Fathers warn of the risks of using a chainsaw. Dads start the damn thing. Fathers go to work and pay bills and administer the serious punishments. Dads BBQ in the rain while drinking cheap beer and smiling. Fathers dispense life lessons and sage advice. Dads give wedgies, monkey-bumps, and hurts-donuts. Fathers are concerned about the future. Dads live in the moment. Fathers instruct ethics and morals and good sense. Dads fart. Fathers ask about your friends. Dads walk around the house in their underwear in front of them.

All men with children are varying degrees of both father and dad. Both roles are vital to raising un-weird kids. Understanding when to pop into which role is important. It is a delicate balance and like fathers and dads themselves, imperfect, but necessary.

Today, as I was going through the sacred box of my kids' memories, I found my son's "Presidential Citation for Academic Excellence" certificate. I was very proud the day he received this. In the box, I also found my son's certificate of ordination into the "Church of Dude-ism". I grabbed my "minister" son's diploma and hung it on my cork board in my gym. I looked at it and smiled. I left the academic achievement in the box.

My son is a smart, good kid and will be successful in anything he decides to do. The father in me knows this. The dad in me knows that he will only be truly happy with a good dose of "dude" in him. That's why I like his "ordination" so much. The dad in me, passed down from my Dad, gave him the idea that being a dude is important. Dudes know how to do stuff and can decide and act. Dudes have good friends and good times. Dudes respond in times of crisis and times for fun. It may be the best thing I pass on to him.

In my special box of stuff, I also stumbled across an old Father's Day card from my daughter. In the card she had written in her four year old chicken scratch, "Hapy Fathers Day. Dad. I love wen you play and dance and we laff. Love, Helena." Playing, dancing and laughing are the best parts of a childhood and a life. The dad in me understands this and delivers. Like all dads everywhere.

So, this Father's Day, I say THANK YOU to my Dad. He's not around anymore. He passed away in 2002, but he lives each time I stomp in a puddle and dance in the mud or start the chainsaw for my son. Dads live forever in the lives of their kids. They live in the parts of them that don't grow up; the parts that remain as children laughing at the old "pull my finger" game. Thanks for that, Pops...and everything else, too...

Night and Day.

Last night was a blood bath. My eight, almost nine, year old daughter hit the wall, and some other things, including her brother. I saw it coming, but could not avoid or outrun the train wreck about to occur. I always see it coming. She has many tells.

When I see them, my radar chirps and I get antsy and move into damage control mode. Unfortunately, I am not the only one in my household. Other members my family are not a sensitive as I am regarding this volatile little hornets' nest. Well, the night ended with tears and screaming and me lying in my girl's bed singing corny songs and rubbing her back, trying to talk her off the ledge of crazy.

That was then. The morning, as it always does, brought a new day. She woke up with a fresh face and new attitude. I made her cinnamon rolls and brought her orange juice as she finished her homework at our kitchen table. She was happy and satisfied and quiet.

She is a dichotomy. She is super-sweet and a true monster. Her moods are unpredictable and can swing on thin, often unforeseen, minutia. Most of the time, I don't know what inspires her random outrages. But, sometimes I do. She is just tired. I know this one. I know when it is coming and I know how to respond. I like knowing how to respond. It doesn't happen very often. In these moments, I remember that she is still my little girl.

She sends a lot of signals indicating that she is not little. Not only does she say so, but she also exhibits an awareness and insight and talents that were not there yesterday. She is growing up too damn quick. I saw her use her house key today. I have never seen her use it. In fact, I forgot she even had one. This may seem like a pretty small thing, but the little things join forces with other little things to represent a big change. I have always opened the door for my girl. She has waited and yelled at me to hurry up as she stood by the door, tapping her foot impatiently, as I unloaded all of her crap from my truck to carry for her. Now, while I still carry her crap, she can unlock the door for herself. She no longer waits for me, nor even leaves the door open for me.

This is the scary and sad part for me: She is no longer waiting for me. She doesn't need me to help her with basically everything. She doesn't need me to make her lunch or fix her hair or open the door. And maybe the saddest part for me is that she doesn't want me to. She wants to do it herself. I have fantasized about this day for years and now that it is here, it kind of sucks. It is here that I am conflicted, because I am pretty lazy and don't want to do all the things she wants me to, but I still want her to want me to do them. She doesn't...at least as much.

Well, this is my life and all life and the only certainty is that it goes on. My girl is slowly, but surely crawling to the edge of the nest and will one day fly away. But, that day is not today and she will always be my little girl. So, I will enjoy the little pains in my butt that belong to her. The pains will certainly change in the unwelcome upcoming years, but they do not go away. This is reassuring. She is mine and she will always need me for something, maybe not walking her to school or opening doors. But she will need me. And I will be there singing a stupid song ready to scratch her back.

Maple Sausage

I began my day with some maple sausage. The sweet, smoky aroma drifting through my home awakened my daughter who is also afflicted with a serious jones for this delicious creation. She stood at the kitchen entry wearing her puffy, polka-dotted robe and wiped the sleep out of her half-opened eyes. She looked at me with dream-soaked love. Maple sausage is good.

Of the many things my young daughter and I disagree on, meat is not one of them. We can connect over the greasy succulence of steaks, burgers, chops, and sausage. My son like ribs and is pretty indifferent to the rest of it. He'll eat it, but doesn't need it. My girl and I need it. We are carnivores. It's how we're built. My boy likes the process. He likes standing by the grill or the smoker, stoking the fire or flipping burgers with his bare feet in the grass. I like this, too.

It is nice to bond in different ways with my kids and it is nice that the ways are different. My kids don't work well together and some separation is good every time. My son will ask my daughter how she would like her burger cooked and she will compliment his efforts. We all come together a little bit. Meat is a tasty common denominator. My wife also enjoys most meat, but likes to put strange, unnatural twists on the preparation end of things. She gets a little fancy with sauces and veggies, which, unless it's BBQ sauce, have no place on my meat plate. Good potato salad being the only exception.

Within the canon of my best days, meat is always a prime-time player, though many foods share this power. Pizza works, too. As does spaghetti. And nachos. I don't think I am unique in this. Eating and cooking provide opportunities to gather with friends around the holiday or picnic table. With a chunk of rib-eye smothered in baked beans and coleslaw stuck on our forks, we smile and tell old stories and are happy. We laugh about days long gone and we design the days ahead. Our lives unfold or are re-told in the kitchen or by the grill, and good days live here.

We eat in love and in despair. Weddings and funerals both have good food. I have enjoyed a buffet plate filled with cold cuts, salads, and pastries while celebrating fresh nuptials and while mourning a lost loved one. The simple fact is that the food is always enjoyed. It is a constant. Food makes us feel good, even on the dark days. A cupcake or a grilled sandwich or bowl of clam chowder can shave off the sharp edges of the frantic, anxious, uncertain life that most of us lead.

For this reason, upon my wife's arrival home from work at 8:30, I made her a bowl of white chicken chili. The chili was a gift from a friend. (Note: Food makes a great gift, too.) I pumped up the chili with my leftover maple sausage from this morning's feast and a dab of sour cream. She was happy and I was happy. Once again, food, and maybe especially the maple sausage, had worked its magic. Food can do this.

Life is often a traffic jam with no clear space in between the cars to move into the right hand lane. A good meal with the people we care about slows the traffic. The fellow travelers wave and smile and make room for us. Food with friends and family makes life feel rich and abundant and good, just the way it should be. The bounty is here, in these moments, no matter what's on the table.

The Dookie Chronicles (Oh, no, you didn't! Ohhh, yes, I DID!)

What began as a very safe and innocent exploration into how my relatively small-bottomed family consumes a disproportionate amount of toilet paper has morphed into something else entirely. I discovered that once I started writing about "bathroom issues", I just couldn't stop! It occurred to me that we all, as human animals, share a great number of these issues and that indeed they may be the only things we ALL truly have in common. The toilet may be our absolute lowest, yet most common, denominator. No person is safe from stomach to rear end induced anxiety, ranging from minor to major. These issues are indiscriminate and collectively feared. As such, they create both empathy and sympathy like few things in life can. A couple of examples will help illustrate this:

Example I: While inspecting a roof in El Paso, Texas a few months ago, I witnessed my buddy and colleague, Larry (name unchanged), duck-walking, quite briskly, the two blocks to our "big, blue friend", the sani-can at a construction site. I understood and rooted for Larry. With an intent stare and softly moving lips, I may have silently mouthed, "You can make it, L-Train. You can make it." He made it, but for a time, he went through a rough patch and was forced pretty consistently to duck-walk. He perfected it. In fact, his duck-walk actually became his regular walk. Over time, with the help of some dietary modifications and a lot of encouragement, Larry is walking normally, again. We're all very proud and happy for him. We all understand this urgency and will always help when we can. It could have been and has been, ANY and ALL of us.

Also worth noting, our nickname, the "big, blue friend", was not just another juvenile wit creation. It was conceived with reverence. There truly is no better friend when the need strikes. We will forsake our mother, children and God himself to find a "friend" when breathing shallows, the forehead begins to bead with sweat and the eyes blur with terror. We seek the comfort and relief our "friends" represent. They always deliver. That can be said for very few things in this world.

Example II: Another buddy and colleague, Mr. X, I will call him for his protection, was not as lucky as Larry. His episode resulted in an unfortunate late night request for new sheets on TWO queen size hotel beds. A bad cheeseburger was blamed. As disturbing as this incident was, it was met with a bunch of, "are you oks?" and, "can I get you anythings?" from a usually pretty jaded and inconsiderate group of fellas.

This episode caused genuine concern. Had he chopped his nose off while shaving, we would have called him some names and told him to rub some dirt on it. Under circumstances such as these, though, we felt for him and were genuinely sympathetic. This is a rare and wonderful thing and can only be inspired by our own fear and comprehension of the devastating events that occurred; a true, living nightmare.

These are not isolated incidents. My own catalog of "uh oh" moments is unsavory and vast. We all have a catalog. Knowing this brings us all a little closer. From the low to the high end of human status, we all share a universal worry. It is the great equalizer and indeed, may exist solely for this reason. I can think of no other good reason.

From now on, when faced with an adversary, I will try to see the softer side we share that begins with a sharp cramp, followed closely by a slight gurgle, culminating in terror and desperation. It's the least I can do.

(A side-note to the Mr. X incident was his three am phone call to house-keeping and his introductory comment, "Send someone you don't like." This is and, very likely, will remain the quote of the year for me. Thanks, Mr. X.)

Pull up your pants!!

"Aden!! Get up!!" I hollered at 6:45 A.M. My wail was answered with an impressively quick, but thankfully inaccurate paperback novel chucked in the direction of my face. My son gets a little testy in the morning, especially when he is late and forced to move before he is ready. This morning he had seven minutes to get dressed, eat breakfast, pack lunch and pee before our departure time so he could avoid yet another tardy.

The mountains were moved and the oceans were parted to make his arrival on time. And so we did, barely. Crisis avoided. The rest of the day pretty much followed suit. Urgent fires popped up requiring me, as the extinguisher, to put them out. I don't like fires, especially when I don't set them. I don't like stressful emergencies. I like control of my day and this day I had none.

Staying consistent with the "flow" of my day, I got a call from my wife about whether or not she should purchase a new dining room table. Apparently, a pretty significant sale was happening at a local department store and she saw one she liked. While I appreciated the courtesy of her phone call, I understood that it was only a courtesy and that she was going to do what she wanted independent of my feelings about it.

My wife and I differ in many ways, including the decision about a new table. I still liked our old one. It was worn and scratched and had stains and Sharpie scribbles. It was a time capsule reflecting my kids' lives. Juice was spilled on the white cloth seat covers and high chair rubs marred the table edges. I notice this stuff and I think about it. And I hate to see it go away.

But...since we ARE getting a new table, I will simply miss the old one. She was a good table.

Near the end of my wife's conversation about the new table, (I call it her conversation, because I didn't have much to say) she "asked" if I wanted to check out the new table she had in mind. I, naturally, replied with "sure", not because I was remotely interested, but because I understood that I was expected to at least act interested and she wasn't really asking.

We made a date to view the new table later that evening. Here, I was really hoping she would be too tired after a long work day to really want to slog out in the dark rain. But...she wasn't. So, we went.

When defeated, I have learned it is best to just accept it and go with it. Fighting it does no good. So, I put on the best attitude I could muster and hoped it would be a quick trip.

While in the store, we checked out the table and it looked fine to me. Deal done. "Let's go home!!" I silently screamed in my mind. But...we needed to get a "couple of things". We split up to divide and conquer this task.

Feeling slightly frustrated and impatient, I fast-walked to my item's department. Along the way, as I was approaching the frozen food aisle, I heard a loudly muffled voice yell, "Pull up your pants!!!" This was an unexpected twist to my evening and as I peeked down the ice cream aisle I saw a little boy, probably around three years old or so, dancing down the tile path with his pants around his ankles, his cartoon underwear shining for all to see. He was smiling and laughing, as was his not much older sibling. His mom was smiling and suddenly, so was I. The rest of my trip carried on without incident.

This episode made the whole trip worthwhile. A carefree, unconcerned little kid dancing down the frozen food aisle in his skivvies changes one's perspective on the world. Like me, this kid didn't want to be in the store either. Unlike me, he found a way to enjoy it. (Though it is unlikely that I could pull off this kid's response to a tough night without risking some looks that would not be smiling and/or maybe include some handcuffs.) This kid had it figured out. And he helped me figure it out, too: Sometimes, when it's raining, it's best to just tip your head up, turn your palms to the sky, and dance in the mud.

The new table looks pretty good... I think it's gonna be a good table.

Rainbow Connections.

Some things change and some things don't. I am entering the New Year with immense gratitude for both. With the notable exception of a few very old jackass buddies who will never change (thank God!!), life is in a constant vibrating, shifting and shattering state of change. Some change is massive and requires supreme reserves of courage and resolve to endure. Other change is a subtle whisper heard only by the listener. This change dances on the delicate edges of our perception and we feel it more than we see it. Nonetheless, its resonance is powerful. I am thankful for both. They remind me that I am still growing and learning and living. They give me hope.

Last night, I forced my ten year old daughter, Helena, to watch the "Muppet Movie". She prefers the new, shiny shows and usually objects to my little history lessons. When she complained that the movie was "so unrealistic", I replied with, "Yeah, they're friggin' MUPPETS! Pay attention." She did...for as long as she could. She, then, just became annoying, which is her go-to response when she's bored.

She started jumping on me and flailing around. She poked and pinched and bugged the crap out of me. During this exchange, (which wasn't much of an exchange, as I just kind of sat there and took it and hoped she would tire of my indifference and stop) I found her hair brush sitting on the back of the couch. I tried to brush her hair, which she hates, since "it hurts" when I do it. Following some yelling, I softly ran the stiff bristles along her bare arm. "Hold on!!" I could feel her say to herself. "That feels good."

I, then, began caressing my little agitated girl with the brush. Reluctantly, she complied. She turned over so I could get her back. Soft touches with a hair brush are irresistible. She lay down on my lap and allowed me some rare daddy coddling. She turned her attention to the classic "Muppet Movie" and settled down. It was during this all-too-brief respite from her growing up that I was reminded that she is still my little girl.

Watching the "Muppet Movie" as my daughter laid across me made watching the movie better than the first time I saw it. And I really liked the "Muppet Movie" the first time I saw it. Our kids have no idea how we feel about them. In their selfish, self-involved little spheres of understanding, they cannot conceive that one can love another more than themselves. It's a secret reserved for parents.

67

As most good things aren't, this gentle moment wasn't built to last. I was untroubled by this as, at this point in my life, I am beyond being too concerned about good moments lasting for long. I just appreciate that they existed at all. The good moments come and they go. Life is not lived in years or even days; it is lived one little moment at a time. And it is full of some good ones.

When I first turned on the movie, Kermit was singing "Rainbow Connection". Here, I was immediately transported back to my younger days, curled up in a blanket, watching the "Muppet Movie" with my mom and dad and brother. My own time capsule of good moments cracked wide open and reminded me that they were there. And, as I looked at my daughter, I was proud to know that they would be there for her, too...

The Dad Club (as published in Chicken Soup for the Soul: The Joy of Christmas)

The countdown is on. In a few short hours, garage floors across the globe will be littered with the greasy rear ends of dads assembling every manner of contraption the toy company geniuses can conceive. Christmas Eve is unique in its power to create an experience shared by so many at the exact same time. Since the dawn of time or at least the invention of Santa Claus, dads have been waiting for the kids to fall asleep to trek into the garage or shed or backyard to open boxes and spread out pieces and read vague directions in dim light and desperation.

Screws are turned. Fingers are pinched. Pieces are lost. Beer and blood are spilled. This is how it goes every year in countless man-caves around the world. It is a special time to be a dad. Understanding that for once, these efforts will be appreciated; Christmas morning will come and the kids will be excited. Their excitement may merely be an extension of the dads' joyful anticipation. A giddy, yet still manly, energy occupies the wee hours of Christmas Eve. Imagining surprised kids and their grateful exclamations of shock and joy keeps dads up late. The kids do not disappoint. The swearing and smiling and sweating and searching for that single, yet vital, little nut that rolled away someplace is worth it come Christmas morning when the wrapping paper starts flying.

The non-exclusive club of Christmas dads is a great organization to belong to. I recall my own initiation several years ago. It involved a complicated battery powered tractor and a trike. I spent several hours bent over or leaning on raw knees constructing these treasures which now reside rusty and broken from use and abuse and being left outside in the rain. I don't care too much about that though, because that night I joined the club. It is the club that my Dad and Grandpa and Uncles were members of. The men I loved and admired most twisted screwdrivers and got out the "magnet on a stick" to retrieve the lost screw from under the work bench for me. This recognition made me feel good and closer to them than perhaps I ever had before.

Being a dad and understanding what this means makes it easier to understand many things about my own dad that I never did before. I am glad I know these things. My life would be less without appreciating his sacrifice and efforts to bring a smile to my face on Christmas morning.

So, this Christmas Eve I will renew my membership in the club. I will follow the directions step by onerous step. I will peel off layers as I heat up and I will stretch my sore back. I will say, "No, thanks" when my wife asks if I need any help. She will close the door and walk away relieved, as the ream of paper from the instructions and the too-many-to-count pieces sprawled across the concrete floor can be overwhelming. I won't mind. This is my time to be a good dad and I will be my absolute best at the false dawn when the final bolt is tightened and the last decal goes on. It is a special time and I will pay my dues to remain in the club.

In the morning, I will sit red-eyed and oily, smelling like anti-freeze and lawn fertilizer. I will have a cup of coffee in my hand and a grin on my face. I will fake surprise at the gifts I assembled and I will be pleased. When my seven year old daughter asks why I have band aids on three fingers, I will produce a beautiful little lie to her pretty little face. And when she follows up with, "Does it hurt?" I will reply, "Not much, sweetheart, not much." And this won't be a lie. I'll be too happy to hurt.

The System

While sitting on my couch one day, I glanced to my left and saw my six year-old daughter two knuckles deep in her right nostril, digging for gold. I winced and watched. She pulled out a nugget and opened her mouth. "Don't eat that!!" I screamed. She looked at me sympathetically. Then, she ate it. With the dark green fleck stuck to her front tooth, she turned her head and grinned at me. I shook my head and smiled. Being a reformed booger-eater myself, I knew that long-term damage was improbable, but I was still slightly queased.

My daughter is a contrarian. I say, "Don't". She does. I say, "Do". She doesn't. It is a very simple and predictable system. This has been a curse to me for as long as she has breathed air. Being resourceful and certainly familiar with bad juju, I began concocting a plan to remedy the impact of her obstinacy on my quality of life. I am not interested in justice. I simply want compliance. An idea began to emerge, an idea with power. Evil power. I could get her to do anything by simply telling her not to. With this, I could do some serious tide-turning!! This was genius!!

I enjoy making my kids do dumb things. Two problems exist for me. One, my kids don't listen to me. Two, my wife does not enjoy it as I do. In this idea, I saw a solution. By telling my daughter NOT to do something, she would do it. Also, if I played it right, I could be off the hook with my wife. I would give her my normal blank, nobody's home look and she would buy it. I could exclaim, "I told her not to!" which technically, I had, and I was safe. This revelation felt like Christmas morning. A new world opened up for me. Gratefully, my daughter's awareness of my manipulative powers are not as sophisticated as my eleven year-old son's. I could ride this wave for a long time. I could have anything I wanted. I had to be smart about it, but this wonderfully despicable system was nearly fool proof.

My "system" in action: Last week, my daughter asked me if she could have a soda. I said "no", with a knowing certainty that she would get the soda anyway. I sat on my living room couch with my feet up and continued watching Sportscenter. When she entered the room carrying the soda, I, looking outraged, exclaimed, "I thought I said no". "Aww." She replied. "Give it here." I said and I now had the delicious refreshment that I had wanted and I had not moved. It was nearly flawless execution on my part, the puppet master at work, a true maestro.

I enjoyed this fabulous system until my son began getting suspicious. As the men in the house, I thought, foolishly, that we had a deal. It turns out that Benedict Arnold Markwell seems to enjoy my floundering as much as the rest of family and would forsake our man's club for his own pleasure quite readily.

While employing my "system" to receive a much-deserved foot rub from my daughter, my son took it upon himself to begin asking questions. These questions went to the heart of the system itself. "Helena, do you know that dad just tricked you into giving him a foot rub?" he said, out loud no less. I gave him the "shut up" eye, but he continued. "He always makes you do stuff and you don't even know it." Good God, man, I thought we were a team. She looked at me dubiously, then looked at the traitor and stopped rubbing my feet.

It occurred to me, upon reflection, that I have no team. The boy I thought I could count on, very happily betrayed me. I had no illusions about my wife or daughter. But my son... it hurt. I am now back to square one, trying to devise an even more clever and deceitful method of achieving something resembling control in my house. I will do this alone. As noted in the greatest movie of all time, "The Hangover", I am a wolf pack of one. So be it. The wheels are turnin', kids. Beware.

Sick and Tired

My household is sick, most of it anyway. My son and dogs seems to have avoided the bug. Ironically, these creatures take the least care about whom they interact with and/or what they put into their mouths. My wife, the chiropractor, would assert that we are not "sick", but we are simply expressing health. This may be true and it is nice to think of it this way. But, the sweating, snotting, and sleeping still seem pretty sick to me. And some of the "expressions" don't feel too healthy. We are running low on tissues and toilet paper. I guess we must be getting better with so much health being expressed. And, we are. Slowly, but surely.

Being cooped up this week, I had the opportunity to watch a lot of TV, perhaps too much. This being election week, I have been able to catch lots of coverage, again, perhaps too much.

I am often awed by some of my Facebook friends' (who, in most cases are ACTUAL friends, too) posts about the election and what it will mean for the future of our country, etc. I am not indifferent to this future as it is MY future, but I don't really understand the outrage on any side of the issues. I would classify myself as a moderate...everything. I like many of the Democratic Party ideas and ideals and I like just as many of the Republican ideas and ideals.

At this point in our history, it seems like the Donkey's ideas are more suitable and pragmatic. While I love the concept of "trickle-down" economics, I think this concept relies on a certain amount of integrity on behalf of the "tricklers", but with bail outs and record profits being recorded and still pretty flat job growth, I don't see integrity existing in the culture of our big businesses.

A key talking point by the Elephants is entitlements. Huge payouts to executives and the expectation of tax breaks and incentives and subsidies seem to be pretty significant "entitlements", just as the welfare, unemployment benefits and other social programs designed to help those actually needing help are characterized by the complainers. During this time of such need, I lean towards supporting programs which fund programs that help regular folks and I don't believe that everyone needing help is trying to escape actually having to work for what they get. I believe that most people, if given a choice, would rather have a decent job than government assistance. I believe this as strongly as I believe there are good corporations trying to do right.

I believe that I, and indeed, we, can only control our own lives. Trying to control others is effort wasted. I believe that we have a responsibility to be informed and engaged in the system, such as it is. But, I also believe that outrage makes good TV and doesn't represent, in most cases, the true sentiments felt by either the politicians or their constituents. I believe that Americans love this country. I believe that accepting this as true would make coming together a little easier. Allowing that a contrary opinion is being offered by a kindred soul softens the debate. And I think this is good. We are not red and blue states. We are red, white and blue. Period.

While watching too many pundits over the past couple of days, I have struggled with the notion that maybe I am the crazy one. Seeing such passionate vitriol, I wonder if I am missing something or if I am too naïve or dense to understand all the anger and fear. I have come to the conclusion that if I am crazy, I will take it. I would rather be crazy than bitter and angry and afraid of circumstances either beyond my immediate control or whose impacts are pretty nominal upon my daily life. Perhaps this perspective is inadequate and immature and lacks a certain broader responsibility, if so, I don't really care.

I have a sick little girl who needs me. This is what I care about. This is what I am focused on today. Tomorrow will present its own new challenges that will be mine to deal with. I don't have time to be pissed off or scared about what may, or most likely, may not happen with the rest of the world. I will not be swayed by phony outrage. I will not be convinced that the left is right and the right is wrong. I don't have the time to be convinced, so I will just trust myself about these things, and, then go get my daughter some more ginger ale.

Mirrors.

I had the unfortunate experience of passing a mirror the other day. I did not look as good as I felt and it made me mad. I felt like the mirror was tricking me, because in my head, I looked much better. I had witnessed myself looking better many times. I was sure of it. What was this stupid mirror's friggin' problem!?! I wondered.

After some soul searching and kicking my dog, I came to the conclusion that mirrors are both criminally deceptive and warmly reassuring. They are both tremendous liars and unbearably honest and it really depends on the day as to which I prefer. It depends on whether the lie or the truth makes me feel better. Usually, I suspect, it's the lie.

This mirror passing incident inspired much thought about how we look. I mean how we REALLY look. It seems that how we look changes all the time. Some days, I look in the mirror and think, "Not too shabby, Markwell. Not too shabby." Other days, I see a thin-haired, rather Shrek-ish creature unworthy of even a cross glance in my direction. I don't know if my looks really change that dramatically or not.

However, I do notice that sometimes other peoples' looks do indeed change. I can look at my son one day and see a fine, handsome, and intelligent kid capable of capturing the heart of the fairest maiden in the kingdom, otherwise known as the hottest chick in class. Other days, I look at him and see a creepy, hairy, little rodent complete with the big teeth and yellow eyes and I am sad with the understanding that he is going to die lonely. I love him either way, so don't judge me here…and it's unlikely that he's really that ugly anyway, even on a bad day, but here lies my question: What do we really look like? Are we our best or our worst vision of ourselves? And what determines which look we see?

Many factors, I'm sure, shape our perception, but I think the most urgent one is simply how we feel. When we feel good we look good, even to ourselves. It is impossible to look bad, feeling good. I have known plenty of average, if not outright ugly, people who look beautiful, because they are happy. Likewise, I have known many of pretty, but ugly folks as well. Beauty is an illusion. It is a magic trick. It is not a "look" and cannot be seen. It is felt. Beauty is a personality and has its own life. It lives in an easy smile and a kind word, a hearty laugh and a genuinely concerned frown. It is that which connects us as human animals on our deeper levels.

Our judgment of beauty is sometimes primitive, largely banal and usually involves unseen elements of character which sway the eyeball one direction or another. I believe, though, that we will always recognize and appreciate a truly beautiful soul, sometimes even our own. With this in mind, I will not call my son ugly just because he invents, on a daily basis, new ways to shave time off of my life. I know, more than anyone, how truly extraordinary he is.

And if the mirror is unkind to me, I will simply shine a casual middle finger in its direction and move on with my day. A mirror can't feel the minute variations in a heartbeat or see inside a soul and that's where everything important and truly beautiful resides.

Home Improvement.

Last night, my wife cussed at me. It wasn't a big cuss out, but it wasn't small, either. An "F" word was involved. We were working on a little home improvement project and, as usual, we had different ideas about how the work should be performed. Our difference of opinion provoked some sarcastic comments from me and then the resultant, not unexpected, "response" from my wife.

This is a fairly typical exchange whenever my wife and I work together on projects. She is very linear and organized and focused. She finishes starts and finishes one project, without deviation, and moves on. I do not. I flit from various stages of projects, moving with, to her, a chaotic and illogical order. My contention is always that my order is not illogical. It just seems that way.

No one wants to finish any project more than I do. And in my urgent motivation to finish work, I like to take big bites and understand that leaving some crumbs for later will allow me to get more done, quicker. This does not make sense to my orderly wife. I will disclaim here that sometimes I move too hastily and screw up and, in these exceedingly rare cases, she is right to question me.

Following our exchange, the weather in our household turned cool. I didn't want to watch her show on TV and so I went to bed. I wasn't angry, but slightly annoyed and didn't feel super cuddly. I woke up this morning feeling mostly the same.

As I made a mental laundry list of the things I need to do today, writing a letter for my father-in-law as he appeals to the Veteran's Administration for a PTSD settlement is near the top. While thinking about my letter, I got sad. My father-in-law is a terrific guy. He served in Vietnam while he was a young man and it affected him. (No duh)

Last summer, my family and I witnessed him having a nightmare and it was scary. He shook and screamed and cried. This moment changed me. I hope it changed my kids, as they will be responsible for determining which wars we choose to fight in the future and a clear understanding of the cost of these wars is important.

My father-in-law's service to this country cost him dearly. It cost him his youth and his piece of mind and it is a bill he is still paying on and will continue to pay on until he dies.

While thinking about this, my wife's and my tiff didn't seem so important. More than anything, I just wanted to hold her and let her know how much she means to me. Life is funny and marriage is frustrating. There are no easy answers to the complicated questions of both. Having some perspective on stuff that matters is a key to enjoying anything in life or marriage.

With this in mind, I made pancakes for my kids and served them in their early morning sleepy beds. I hugged my wife and very deliberately moved through my day with a right mind. "What's important?" is a moving target and getting a bead on that sucker feels nice once in a while.

Through our lives, we get pulled and pushed in many directions, many of which, that are not ours. We compromise and we concede and we forget. Now and then, a cold hard fact will smack our heads' straight. Remembering my father-in-law's struggle shaved the hard edges off of my own battles and put things back where they belong. It is too easy to forget, but very important to remember what's important. Few things matter, but some things matter very much. And I will choose an "F" word (or two) from my wife over the infinitely worse challenges faced by too many. It's a small price to pay for having so much and I have happy to foot the bill.

It's a small world.

Three days after my Disneyland "experience", I am still waking up humming "It's A Small World." This does not evoke the pleasant feelings of nostalgic joy which one might think it would. It is more of a haunt than a hymn. I suspect a rare type of hopefully short-term, post-traumatic stress is to blame for this morning mental serenade. This, too, shall pass, I remind myself with as much optimism as I can muster.

I loved sharing Disneyland with my kids. I loved their wide-eyed marvel at all of the fantastic attractions. Disneyland really is a tremendous monument to the incredible power of the imagination and it is pretty amazing contemplating the great, detailed care given to each and every feature. It is impressive and not-a-little mind-blowing imagining the mass of minds which must have been involved creating such a spectacular unnatural phenomenon.

It is only by being a few days removed that I can write affectionately about my experience. My threshold for dancing, cartoon-costumed oddballs and too many damn people is about five hours. We were there for nine and a half. After five, things got squirrelly.

Gratefully, supporting me around every corner, were the weary and frustrated faces of my fellow sufferers. I needed to look no further than the nearest male face to feel a little better. I probably made them feel better, too.

My own disheveled tension shone as a beacon to help guide my other listless and weary dads through the fog of fried dough concoctions and singing animals. With sunburned bald spots and sore feet, we persisted. For the kids.

While I personally knew no one, I knew them all. We shared a day, a great day that our kids will remember for the rest of their lives. We battled our worse demons and won. We said "Yes" to a seventy minute wait for a ride when we really wanted to say "No".

We shared a collective understanding that this day was not about us. We were patient and kind and smiled through a grimace with the knowledge that the day was an important one. We were helped, too, by the understanding that the day would, mercifully, at some point, end.

Upon reflection, it was worth any suffering I experienced and it may be thinly analogous to childbirth in that, following the trauma of a day's events, we are stricken by a gratuitous form of amnesia which allows us to remember things fondly. This is good.

When I scratch a little deeper, I am happy I was there and know that I only survived because I was not alone. Fellow dads were there. Unknown and anonymous dads walked the good walk. And though, we did not know each other, we did, reinforcing to me that people in this world are more alike than different, independent of race, color or creed. We are the same and on a sunny Friday in Anaheim, California we were one. It truly is a small world. After all.

Last Dance.

I was thinking about death the other day. I was thinking about my brother and Dad and grandparents. I was thinking about how I missed them and how my life changed when they passed. What was weird about these thoughts on this day was that they were not somber or melancholy. They were more practical and reflective.

As I pondered this normally depressing topic, I noticed that it was a truly beautiful day. While I was picking weeds from my planter beds in shorts and no shoes, I thought it seemed rather odd to be thinking such usually dark thoughts on such a nice day. However, this day, these thoughts didn't diminish its beauty or make me sad. More than anything, they made me mindful and very grateful to be able to enjoy such a day.

I sat on my knees and picked weeds in the bark as the late summer sun shone high in the sky. My daughter rode her bike around the yard and up and down our long driveway. My father-in-law, who is visiting us from New York for a while, puttered around singing Donna Summer's "Last Dance" in his own very "special" way. I smiled and shook my head and was happy to be able to enjoy such a fine day.

This morning my wife and I walked our daughter to school for her first day of fourth grade. I love this walk. I forget sometimes that life is moving. On a daily basis not much changes, at least very obviously to me. Little mileposts like first days of school remind me, sometimes harshly, that life indeed is moving.

My son started eighth grade. How in the hell did this happen? Where did that time go? I remember very clearly dropping him off for his first day of kindergarten and crying like a baby when I got to the car. I knew then that life was changed. Our kids grow up and in their growing up perhaps we do, too. As their view of the world changes, so does ours. We are always changing, sometimes not quickly enough for SOME people (no names mentioned), but we are changing and are changed by entering these new phases of our kids' lives.

Through our life and theirs, our dreams and worries change. We care less about some things and much more about others. I care about my kids' todays and tomorrows. I care about my wife's love of her life. I care about first days and last days and all days. I care about a moment of simple clarity that shines its precious light on my often murky horizon. I care about a fine day sitting in the sun, pulling weeds from a flower bed, thinking important thoughts and hearing Pops belt out "Last Dance." I think these are good things to care about.

An Important Thing.

Each weekday at 2:10 pm I pick up my fifteen year old son from high school. He opens the truck door, throws his back pack on the floor and climbs in. Then, I start asking questions: "How was your day", "Anything interesting happen?", "Do you have any homework?" He responds with one-word answers and grunts. We do this dance every day.

Something different happened the other day: We had a conversation. He told me a story about a guy who suffered a bad concussion and came out of it changed. He suddenly became a math and physics genius, but lost his ability to connect, socially, with people.

Prior to the accident, the man had lots of friends and family and was not particularly "mathletic". Following his injury, his life was vastly different. This story inspired me to ask my boy which of the two qualities he would prefer: solid social life or high-level math function?

He responded without hesitation: "Social skills. I think it would be very hard to happy when you're alone." I nearly drove off the road. My pride and relief at this answer was profound. My kid "got it." I was not an abject failure as a dad, in spite of much evidence to the contrary. My son understood the key to a happy life: people.

In a life filled with stress and stuff to do, having a solid foundation of good friends and family makes it all worthwhile. They are what's important. We are reminded of this when we need to be reminded. In times of struggle and worry (which is much of the time), a note, a call or a beer with an old buddy reminds us that life is still pretty good.

Life is not an easy business. Bills, work, kids require something of us. Our friends require nothing...at least the good ones don't. They require nothing except being a friend in return and this is easy to do. They are vital any joy we achieve. They are the real or fabled "meaning of life". A conversation with a friend is all we need to step back off the ledge and feel pretty good about the world.

I'm very happy my son understands this mature insight. As a dad, I spend plenty of energy concerned about my kids' futures. I don't really care about what they do or where they live. I care very much that they are happy doing it. Having a healthy store of good relationships is at the heart of this joy. This is true for all of us. When we have friends, we have everything we need. I am relieved to know that for all the things my son doesn't yet understand about the world, he understands perhaps the most powerful thing there is to understand about life. I have not completely failed!! Yippee!!

In the early morning hours of my birthday, while I was fretting over much to do, I received a couple of texts from an old buddy. "Happy Birthday" was the first one, followed by "Jackass". I felt loved. In the complex language of old friends, love and hope and connection and history were conveyed. And I got it. And it's the most important thing to get.

The Phone Call.

Twenty-four years ago on Halloween day, I received a phone call that changed my world. I was in college and had just returned home to my apartment from my early morning classes when the phone rang and my roommate, Sean (aka, the Grasshopper), answered it and said it was for me. "Hello", I said. My dad answered, "Hi….Mike died this morning." Mike was my little brother. He was sixteen and I was nineteen at the time.

These words still remain clear, yet surreal and I can still feel the shock of them if I think hard about this moment. The power of certain words is immense. These were those kinds of words. The rest of the conversation was foggy, but I remember I told my dad that I would be home that day. I then walked, dazed, into my bedroom and fell apart. The "Hopper" came in to see if I was going to my next class, as we usually walked together.

I, then, said the words, "My brother died." We both broke down and the reality of the day struck. Saying the words made them real. These are words that one hopes to never say nor hear. The significance of hearing and/or saying them changes people and I was changed forever in this moment.

As the years have passed, I have struggled to make sense and to define what truly matters in my life. I have challenged convention and sought to find my own truth. I have been reluctant to simply accept life as ordinary. I have battled myself and others in this quest for meaning and value. As a result of this event, I take little for granted. This experience taught me that nothing is a given and that the world can and does change in the beat of a heart…or when one stops beating.

I don't think of this day very often, but it lives with me all the time. It has shaped me in ways that I try to understand, but cannot. I hold my relationships stubbornly and fiercely. I do not suffer drama, bullshit or fools. I am very clear about the things I value and I cling to them as a life raft. I question and am impatient with "systems" that lack efficiency or humanity. What is "right" is usually pretty clear to me, so I prefer to just do "that" and not spend a lot of time discussing it. Time is valuable. My time is valuable. I understand this and I value others' time. I live with a sense of urgency to be happy.

More than anything else, my brother's death inspired me to try to live a life of my choosing and to find joy anywhere and at any time that I can. I try to very hard to achieve this and I can find happiness in some strange places. This awareness is the legacy left me by my brother and, during this month of Thanksgiving, is what I am truly thankful for. I recognize and appreciate simple and pure moments. These occur all the time and I am happy to see many of them.

Ironically, I don't think I would see them were it not for the worst phone call of my life. To me, this again illustrates one of life's confounding truths: nothing makes sense and everything makes sense. But with eyes wide open and a grin, the world is a pretty great place to be. And I've learned that it is best to carry the grin through all of it, because the phone could ring at any time....

Dog Dish.

"Why didn't you clean out Diego's bowl before you fed him?" my wife accusingly inquired. "What???" I responded with my usual mix of confusion and outrage. The reason I say "what??", as if I don't hear or understand the question, is to imply "what the hell are you talking about, you crazy woman??" The right tone is the key. Sometimes this will annoy her enough to stop the questioning. This day it did not. She deemed it quite urgent and necessary that our dog, Diego, have a clean bowl from which to inhale his food. I disagreed.

"He licks his butt for eight hours a day. I don't think he really cares about a dirty dish." With this remark, my wife left the room and I returned to my peace.

Our dog, Diego, is a slob. He digs, scratches, eats anything and craps prodigiously. He tracks mud and hair to every forlorn corner of our home. No place is safe from his tell-tale black dust bunnies. He's pretty hairy, but I am still always puzzled by where all the hair comes from. I brush him from time to time and it doesn't seem like he should be able to disperse the vast amounts of fur throughout my household that he does. Keeping up with it is an impossible task. So I stopped trying very hard.

While he is a slob, he is a happy one. He always greets me with a wet nose to the crotch as his hug. He gets excited to see everyone and is a pretty all-around good dog. He doesn't bark or nag or bite anyone. His biggest liability may be his live self-sex shows he seems to enjoy performing for the slightly shocked, perversely curious audience he attracts which is usually my kids' friends. I am certain he has inspired a few unwelcome and premature "birds and bees" chats between the friends and their folks as they left our driveway.

My wife's fascination with Diego needing a clean dish inspired me to clean it to see if it made any difference. I did this without her around, so as not to create any false expectations. I was just curious to see if he maybe did prefer a clean bowl.

As I suspected, he couldn't care less. I don't think he tastes his food anyway. I'm pretty sure it doesn't touch his tongue, except when it is used as a spoon for shoveling copious amounts of Purina down his throat.

For the most part, he's a good dog. He's also my dog. I don't know how I got him. I didn't want him. I really didn't want him. When asked several years ago, "Should we get a dog?" I said, "NO." Nonetheless, consistent with the value of my vote on such matters, "we" got him. It was cute for a while. The kids helped out and my wife would bathe and brush him. Those days are over.

The only meaningful attention he gets is from me. I feed him and brush him and play with him. I make him feel wanted. He rides around with me with his wet nose sticking out my truck window. And he lies by my feet as I write this. He's my buddy, whether I like it or not.

As with many of my buddies, timing is the key. I don't always want to engage, but as good friends do, Diego has a sense about when to just sit near, but don't bug. He also senses when I am open to some play or I just need to get outside and throw the ball for a while. He, like a human friend, understands the power of the right proximity and rarely crosses the line at the wrong times. I sometimes wonder what he would be like as a human. I think we'd be buddies then, too.

I'd buy him a beer and I imagine he would have some interesting things to say. I like to think he would buy me one, too and I would accept...so long as he didn't try to impress me with his "show"....

Dreamers.

My daughter had a bad day. And when she has a bad day, our household has a bad day. She is a powerful nine-year old. Her moods are unpredictable and tempestuous. While my hope is that these traits will delay the inevitable "boy" stage of life, I suspect they will not. She is also beautiful and beauty will make even the most unfavorable personality characteristics highly negotiable, especially to a young boy. But, I suppose this truth carries on in later stages of male-dom as well...so, I'm told...

When she is afflicted with a bad day, I go into damage control mode. I serve her and dote and laugh and dance and sing. While my singing often will not please her, I think she likes the effort. As she has grown older, different mood-lifting techniques have evolved. Her mind is rich with fantasies of a life she doesn't currently have.

She wants to live in San Diego and design "fashion". She wants to go to Paris and explore different cultures and eat cheese and bread, I guess. In response to her "moods", I have begun asking her about these things. I enquire about what she will do there, where she will live, what her days will look like. Her mood brightens when we discuss these things. She looks forward to this life and in doing so, she forgets about how "crappy" her regular life is. And this is good for her and me and the rest of the family.

While contemplating how this works, I came to the simple conclusion that · dreams make us feel good. Jolly fantasies of a life filled with wonderful experiences and good weather can carry us through our dark days. Dreams are hope. And hope is what stirs the blood. Hope fills the sail with a stiff, warm breeze and moves us forward. Hope is a universal magic-maker. Hope is as right as rain and as necessary as air.

The other morning, I stopped by my buddy, Dan's, business for a quick visit. Dan is a very practical, structured, yet still fun guy. He is quick with a smile and his wit and I always enjoy our chats. On this day, Dan wore a special gleam in his eye. Having known Dan for some time, I have learned to be a bit wary of this gleam. He is not afraid of a bad idea and as I had a lot of stuff to do with my day, I did not want to be tempted into a bad decision. I need not have worried. Dan's gleam was from a new idea. He explained his dream and it was contagious. I was infected by his enthusiasm. His dream lifted him above his regular work day. He was elevated and so was I. The morning turned from ordinary to extraordinary.

Such is the power of a dream. At any and all ages, dreams have the unique ability to elevate us. We can leave our ordinary, mundane lives and become more. We can become super-heroes. We can don our capes and fly. Our dreams, and the hope they give, are life's color. They can transform a sad and mad nine year old girl and they can make a fifty year old man feel like a boy again. They are the well from which the fountain of youth springs. And we can drink from this well anytime we want. Within us all lies a dreamer's heart whose beat brings us alive...and makes it all worthwhile. So...dream big and often and always. It's what we're meant to do and from where our greatness takes its shape...it also feels pretty damn good...

Two Best Days.

"No one remembers their best day watching TV" was the caption I read beneath one of the thousands of Facebook memes that drift daily through the ether of the internet world. Some of these memes validate my faith in the good people meandering this planet with me and others diminish that faith. Some provoke a grin and others moisten an eye. This one did both.

With a photo of a young boy sitting on a dock with his dad fishing, the simple yet potent words reminded me of a couple of my best days. Both involved fishing and fellas I love.

Last summer, my 14 year old son, Aden, and I took our annual boy's road trip around the dusty farmland towns of eastern Washington. We have been doing this for a while and try to visit new places. For reasons unknown and borderline inexcusable, we have not spent much time at the Potholes. I grew up fishing the various shorelines, drainages and seep lakes of which this mecca of freshwater fun consists. In high style, I made up for this oversight. We stopped and absolutely clobbered some fish. We nailed perch and bass and some lunker catfish, a few sunfish and an odd crappie or two. Each cast was met with action. It was awesome!!

With the hot August sun on our shoulders and our feet cooling in the water while standing on the concrete slabs of an abandoned boat ramp, my boy and I cast our lines and filled our stringer. Watching my son refine his technique and hook-set timing was beautiful for me as a father. Understanding his excited anticipation on each strike and knowing the hopeful bend of the pole, it was with great pride and joy that I saw him appreciating this day as I did. It was a rare day of stinky, bloody and scaly perfection.

While standing on the alkaline stained rocks with my fishing pole in hand, I felt my history coming around to greet me. Many years ago, I stood on these same shores with my grandpa. We took a couple of trips each year to sleep in a travel trailer, as compadres, and fish all damn day.

One day lives as exceptional. We could not keep the fish off our hooks. Cast after cast, we reeled those spiny ray little devils in. By the end of the day, we had nearly ten gallons of fish. As exciting as the catching of the fish is, the cleaning is another story and as I watched my grandpa saunter into the trailer to read some Zane Grey and take a nap, I knew that I was on my own.

As the soft spring sun wandered below the horizon, I sat on a sharp rock filleting our fish. In the dim twilight, I ached and smiled and bled. It was a day unmatched. I didn't even care that my grandpa stuck me with the crappy job. I was used to that part of our arrangement.

When I finished in last gasp of dusk, I entered the trailer to my favorite smell in the world: yellow perch fried in butter with cornmeal, flour and some salt and pepper. I mowed into my plate with my tired, bloody, cramping hands and laughed at how perfect the day was. I will enjoy the thought of this day forever.

Many parallels can be drawn between my day with my son and my day with my grandpa: Both will live with me until I die. They both remind me that sometimes in an imperfect life, days come around to confound this truth. Spending time on the water, catching fish with people you love is about the best thing there is. Another parallel is that both times I wound up cleaning all the fish. Next year, I'm callin' BS. Next year, that little cockroach kid of mine is gonna stand for two hours carving those babies…I'm taking a nap…then, I will remember that day as another one of the best ones…

Fishbowls.

The front windows of my little CrossFit gym in Des Moines, WA look out upon a busy street. I see many things through these windows. I see friends driving by. I see walkers and talkers and people scooping up their dog's poop from the sidewalk. I see kids riding bikes and skateboards and scooters. I see young mothers pushing strollers and old mothers pushing walkers. I see my neighboring business owners cleaning their windows and sweeping the parking areas in front of their stores. I see life.

Through the cold glass of my silent fishbowl, I see the world spinning and human beings engaged in the acts of living life. It's a unique perch from which to view the world. As a non-participating voyeur, I enjoy imagining the conversations and destinations and the day dreams of the day-dreamers who travel past my window. It's fun to see all the ants marching, dutifully and skillfully, navigating the world's potholes. It makes me proud to be a part of the human race.

Looking out the fishbowl of my home, I have seen many things as well. I have seen my son as a little boy playing with his toys in the yard, making noises while crashing his Matchbox cars and digging holes for no reason. I have seen my baby daughter toddling in the grass, tasting a night crawler before getting run over by our dog, Diego. I have seen friends laughing and my wife lying back in a lounge chair reading a book. These things I have seen have brought me smiles and occasionally a moist eye.

Taking a moment to simply observe our world, we see important things. While engaged in our own hustling and bustling, it is difficult to see much at all. Stopping is the key. Stopping and watching and thinking and dreaming our own dreams and seeing that many of the things in our dreams we already possess is necessary. A fishbowl provides a good spot from which to take stock of life.

Our culture tends to support action over observation. I think we need both. Stopping and recognizing the wonderful, goofy, perfectly imperfect world we live in makes our journey outside of the fishbowl a little more fun. It puts some gas in the tank for our journeys and allows us to share our good bits with our fellow travelers. This is not wasted time.

The Sound.

In the past few months, several of my buddies have become Dads. They have either joined or re-upped their memberships into the brotherhood of fathers. Though, I have, in each case, been very happy for their inclusion into this non-exclusive club, I have also been very happy that it was them and not ME.

Babies are hard work with little return. They are cute and smell pretty good, except when they don't, and it is neat to see them make their little progressions into actual human beings. But, they are also inconvenient. They operate on THEIR time, not ours. When they are hungry or tired or bothered by some other unknown problem, we must jump. We jump to stop that sound, that shrill, spine-piercing sound that they emit.

If this sound could be bottled and marketed, it would be a "million dollar idea". It would make even the laziest man quite productive. Efforts to stop this sound are delivered with an urgency and efficiency rarely seen or affected by regular folks. This sound, either the prevention of or elimination of, is a true motivator. We will stop whatever we are doing and ACT!! Few things on this earth can inspire motion like this sound. Just the thought of it makes me want to stop it NOW and I can't even hear it!!

However, as our babies grow, new issues arise. The mouth that delivers "the sound" begins to learn words. These words grow into complaints, demands and whiny pleas for unnecessary and impossible desires. There is probably no sanctuary for a dad to hide from his children's voices, except perhaps the grave. I say "perhaps", because I am not sure that my kids' persistent questioning and "suggestions" on how best to do things won't follow me there, too. I am anticipating an eternity spent hearing my son's "recommendations" and very helpful insights into what I am doing wrong. I signed up for it and I will accept it as gracefully as I can, which is sometimes pretty ungraceful and it is only by the slimmest of margins that my school-age kids avoid "shaken-baby" syndrome.

As a Dad, I struggle to maintain even the illusion of a low form of intelligence. My kids often think I am an idiot. Sometimes I am, sometimes not. They don't know the difference and this creates awkward moments. When I try to explain, as a dutiful dad, the pitfalls of a plan they have devised which I can tell will result in breakage of either bones or something I own, they look at me with concern and pity. They don't understand that I tried that plan and broke something. I have a perspective that they do not, and though I have never been

94

a quick study, some things make an impression that even a moron can't ignore. But, we all have to learn in our own way. I have never listened to anyone else in my life and suffered the consequences. My wife and mom will happily verify this. It seems that the fruits don't fall far from the tree. So, I do what I can do and sleep well after the emergency room visit.

I have, in speaking to my prospective "dad" buddies, described my kids as the best pains in the butt I will ever have. Parenthood is always frustrating and painful. It is also, always, great. Caring for something more than ourselves is liberating in ways unknown to non-parents. We will move burning buildings and the earth itself to protect our kids. We will compromise things previously thought uncompromisable and sacrifice the most sacred parts of our souls to make our kids happy or at least good people.

This is not easy, but it is worth it. The results being the subtle, yet rare, looks of reverence and awe; the understanding that Dad does know something and is more. These are not our goals, merely by-products of our very aware efforts that what we do as parents matters. It is a challenge to consistently maintain good parenting, but we do the best we can, because it is right and important and maybe... just maybe... it will STOP THAT FRIGGIN' SOUND!!!

Rubber Snakes and Fake Dog Doo

While in El Paso earlier this year, I was working with my buddy, Brad, who, on one of many fairly mundane days, found something to get excited about. He was inspecting a roof and discovered a rubber snake. Brad is a pretty easy-going fifty-something kid and as he climbed into our truck I could sense his excitement. "Check it out", he said, with a slightly devilish smile on his face, as he produced the nice-sized green and black rubber snake. I was interested by his find, but not overwhelmed, until he told me his plan.

"I'm gonna hide it under a towel on Larry's bathroom floor." He smiled and might have giggled a little bit. I laughed at the thought of our pal, Larry, moving his towel and shaking in start at the snake. I still smile when thinking about it. Brad's stock is always pretty high in my book, but it experienced a little jump that day as we laughed like a couple of twelve year olds at the beautiful potential of this shabby little rubber snake.

A couple of nights ago, my daughter was getting ready for bed with all the usually hubbub: pajamas on, teeth brushing, me yelling, potty, hugs and goodnight wishes. I noticed a strange nuance to her behavior. She was a little too happy. She usually mopes and complains and stalls, but this night she was more or less on task and had a peculiar way about her. I sensed something different, but couldn't identify what it was.

After she was in bed with a smile on her face, I retired to the living room to do whatever I do before I go to bed. A couple of hours later, I went through my routine, and got ready to hop in bed. While climbing into my bed, I noticed, perched as a trophy right next to my pillow, a marvelously realistic chunk of fake dog poop.

My sweet, clean, pure, little six year old daughter had placed this fake turd and had snickered herself to sleep thinking about how funny it was to "get" dear old dad. I felt at the moment a profound joy. I know how good it feels to "surprise" someone and I was relieved to realize that this simple little joy would not be lost on her. Her vehicle may not have been my first choice. However, I've learned to take what I can get. Her brother, on the other hand, I would expect no less from him. Understanding how to have fun and how to make fun is a valuable lesson and I am glad that she is developing a sense of "humor", such as it is.

A sense of humor is a marvelous thing. It certainly takes many shapes, but is important to any joy I have encountered in this life. Laughter truly is the best medicine. It keeps life in its proper place. It reminds us that though struggles exist and daily battles are waged, a smiling peace rests nearby in the unfortunate minds of fifty year old adolescents and sweet six year old little girls. It is everywhere and makes life the grand adventure it is. Having quality people providing life's comic relief is necessary and wonderful. We all know them and they are the best things I can think of to have.

Arrivals.

My father-in-law came to town last week. He flew in from upstate New York on Saturday and will be here for a month or so. It's always an adventure when "Hurricane Bob" hits town and my family looks forward to his visits.

While waiting for him to deplane and meet me at the "arrivals" area outside of baggage claim at the airport, I sat in my truck and watched people. I was uncharacteristically early and had some time to kill listening to the radio and watching travelers.

I always enjoy watching people. On this day, I loved watching people. The "arrivals" area at airports may replace Walt's Magic Kingdom as the "happiest place on earth".

Sitting in my vehicle with the music low and the windows cracked, I saw beautiful things. I saw smiles and hugs and kisses and love. Reunions between older dads and sons and daughters and mothers and grandparents and husbands and wives and their kids were magic.

Genuine and heartfelt smiles littered the breezeway as these strangers to me embraced and laughed and connected. In pure and honest moments, human beings of this earth reminded me of our collective meaning of life: the people we love.

Serious looking men in business suits jumped out of their driver's seats and jogged to hug a thirty-something son, both men with smiling eyes and joy on their faces. Middle-aged women in yoga pants opened trunk doors and stood holding elderly mothers with gentle arms and the love that only mothers and daughters can share. Little kids ran up to grandpas and leapt into strong arms, laughing the laughter of children.

I watched these reunions and was moved. In a world of much disconnect and judgment, the truth of humanity was revealed: we are a good, kind and loving species. In spite of much evidence to the contrary, at our cores, we are creatures of love. A clear example of this occurs every hour of every day at the arrival zone. People of all shape, size, color, and creed wear their enormous capacities for love on their very human faces. A more pure representation of true love would be hard to find. It's a beautiful thing to see...

Investments.

Today, as the morning fog drifted delicately above the saltwater, and the mountains above the sea shone red and orange from the sunrise, life felt pretty good. I looked out my living room window and felt peace. This does not always happen. Life is a funny business.

Yesterday, I woke up before my alarm in a frenzied state of worry. My mind buzzed with unlikely fantasies of bad outcomes. I was stressed and worried and felt no peace. My life has changed very little during the twenty-four hours in-between my mornings, which begged the question: If nothing was different, why was everything so different?

In pondering this likely eternal question, I have no good answer except to say that, I just felt different. How and why was this so, given that no precipitous event occurred? Well, hell if I know. I wish I did. Unlocking this mystery, I suspect, is the key to unlocking many other mysteries.

Perhaps the only answer is that we have good days and we have bad days. Life may be like the stock market, in that we have fluctuations. We invest our days into our lives and, provided we keep showing up, contributing our good bits, caring and trying and keeping some faith, we wind up with a rich portfolio full of funny stories and sweet memories. The key is not getting too bound up by the down days. They happen. Applying more weight to them than they carry only taints our good days. And this is a disaster.

Today, I can playfully argue with my daughter about breakfast options. Yesterday, the argument would not have been playful. The ripple effect of our moods is powerful stuff. This little girl that I love more than any other left the house with a head-shaking smile. Yesterday, she would have left with a scowl and tears in her eyes. Such is our power to affect others. We can the break the hearts of those whose hearts we care for most. So, while each day we invest in our own lives, we also invest in the stories of our kids' lives. And, for any parent, this story is far more important than our own. That's why it's important to let the bad days go...quick.

So, after shaking the dust off of a sucky day, today I see glowing mountains and potential. It's all perspective. It's always all perspective...

French Toast.

It was a morning of much to do. Contemplating the shape of my day with a sense of urgency and intention was happening. I had a long list of stuff I wanted to get done. Successfully completing these tasks was going to require some planning. And that's what I was doing when my daughter woke up.

She stood at the banister at the top of the stairs and with her sleepy eyes and sleepy voice, hoarsely whispered, "French toast". I knew what this meant. Each night, while I tuck her into bed, she details her/my breakfast plans. She is a planner. She gets this from her mother. I take no credit or blame for this. I can plan when I need to, but it does not come naturally.

Hearing my girl's reminder of my breakfast duties, I began trying to get out of it. "How about a bowl of cereal?", I responded hopefully. I really did not feel like cooking. "Nope", came the predictable reply. "How about some toast?" Thinking toast from a toaster, easy to do. She said "Yes, toast, dipped in egg with some cinnamon and vanilla, fried in a pan." She then turned her back and walked away. I could tell by her wiggly ears that she was smiling and proud of her wit at this early hour. Crap. I was doomed to follow through on my obligation.

Each night, in my desperation to get her in bed and out of what's left of my hair, I make promises that I hope I may not have to fulfill. This doesn't work very often. Nonetheless, I try. I tell her what she wants to hear, hope for the best and deal with the consequences later. Later has come. I cease serving myself and get up to do my duty.

While preparing the French toast that I didn't want to make, I took great care in making it good. Perfectly browned with the proper ratio of cinnamon and vanilla, I plated it and topped it with some boysenberry syrup and a sprinkle of powdered sugar. If I had to make it, I did not want to hear any complaints about it, so I did what I had to do.

Mid-way through my breakfast making operation, still annoyed and distracted by my own obligations, I recognized that making French toast when I didn't want to was pretty representative of many things in life. We are often faced with responsibilities and duties that we don't want to do, but must. Life is filled with jobs that simply need to get done. And someone has to do them. And we all do.

The lists change and inspiration is fickle, but duties remain. It is in the diligent, sometimes frustrating and annoying follow-through that stuff happens. This stuff matters. Our word matters. Doing what we say matters. Always, this is true. It is not easy, but it is true.

So, on a day when making French toast was near the bottom of my list of things I wanted to do, I did it. And while the pan was still hot, I made my wife some steak and eggs, too. I figured I might need some wife credits for stuff I was planning on NOT doing for her that she wanted me to. Hey, sometimes not doing stuff is important, too...

Ungrateful.

Well, summer has finally arrived and as I formulate the various ways to create a fun vacation time for my kids, I wonder to myself, "Why?" Those ungrateful dipsticks deserve nothing. I would think, apparently errantly, that with so much at stake my kids would be a little more diligent in their efforts to impress. Much like around Christmas time when their rooms remain relatively clean and their shoes don't sit in the middle of the living room floor for days. But such is not the case. My kids will shamelessly ignore, dismiss, and/or flat-out betray my pleas for help.

Help me clean the house. Help me pick up their stuff. Help me feed the dog. Help me mow the lawn. Anything at all...just help. I don't require much, but these lazy stiffs are wily and quite creative when it comes to avoiding work. In fact, they work harder at avoiding work than the actual work would require. They make excuses and busy themselves, dutifully, doing anything but what I request of them. They are geniuses of distraction and disguise. They mask their blatant disregard of my requests with false concern and falser promises. "I will...right after"...fill in the blank.. is my favorite. I bite like a hungry carp every time. I trust them. This is my fault. They are liars and I should know this by now. They play me like a dime store kazoo.

I probably shouldn't blame them as I am the parent and, supposedly, should know better. So their behavior is not entirely on them and perhaps would not bother me so much if they didn't want so much. They are completely without compunction when asking me for stuff, even after I have begged them to do something that they, once again, did not do. I am a great believer in the barter system. Some reciprocal back-scratching is nice once in a while. Again, such is not the case, my kids only want their backs scratched, often, and with the correct touch too, not too hard, not too soft. They are takers. They take and don't give. Something is very wrong with this system. It is broken and I don't know how to fix it. I yell and threaten and take stuff away. They are immovable. They are stronger than I am. This is just the way it is.

So, today, I will take them on the boat. I will run through the sprinkler. I will make what they want for dinner. I will play games with them that I don't like to play. I will let them watch their shows on TV. And I will enjoy it, because it is summer time and even a couple of ungrateful twerps cannot put me in a bad mood. They are made their way and I am made mine. Summer is my season. A

102

little sunshine and heat heals all that is broken in me. I am tan and tolerant. I will give what I have to allow my perfectly flawed kids a glimpse into life's summertime potluck of fun and I will not hold any grudges...lucky for those eggheads.

Sand dollars.

Last night, I had an opportunity to tell a story. It is a story that has been often told and has different versions, but resonates with me every time I hear it. Here is a version of the story copied from somewhere:

"A young girl was walking along a beach upon which thousands of starfish had been washed up during a terrible storm. When she came to each starfish, she would pick it up, and throw it back into the ocean. People watched her with amusement.

She had been doing this for some time when a man approached her and said, "Little girl, why are you doing this? Look at this beach! You can't save all these starfish. You can't begin to make a difference!"

The girl seemed crushed, suddenly deflated. But after a few moments, she bent down, picked up another starfish, and hurled it as far as she could into the ocean. Then she looked up at the man and replied, "Well, I made a difference to that one!""

The context of my conversation involved a chance meeting with a young girl and her Dad as they ate dinner at a local restaurant. Andy, the dad, earlier that day, was inducted as a new member into my Rotary Club. During their meal, he and his daughter were having a discussion about the value of service and he was trying to impart a lesson on how important it is to help other people. She, being a young girl, maybe 10 or 11 years old, was somewhat lost and slightly defeated by the volume of people needing help and if it really mattered, since so many people would still need help.

I told her this story, except with sand dollars instead of starfish. As she listened, looking as bored as only a young girl can, I saw the beautiful little light bulb begin to shine in her mind as she began to understand on some level that she could make a difference.

This brief and spontaneous moment demonstrated to me that, once again, it matters. What we do, what we say, the choices we make, matter. No kind gesture is too small to not matter. They all matter. This lesson is an important one to learn and remember as a small girl eating dinner with her Dad, but also for everyone else doing anything else. It is a universal lesson with no protocol or parameters. Doing something is the only requirement. Our world is better for it and we are better for it.

The Rotary motto is "service above self". This is a little misleading. It implies a certain martyrdom or sacrifice. What is lost is that serving others, serves us. Serving makes us feel good and feeling good is the basis of and reason for any good things that we achieve or enjoy in life. We are richer, smarter, wiser and better. This is possible all day, every day.

No gesture is too small not to matter and since they matter, we matter. It is nice to remind ourselves of this from time to time. Facing the daily punches to our gut this world delivers, it is very easy to feel unimportant. Creating a smile on a stranger or a light bulb moment in a thoughtful little ten year old girl can remind us that we matter and are important. All of us matter and are important and can change the world... one sand dollar at a time.

Selfish.

Tonight is a quiet time in my house. The dogs and I don't make a lot of noise. My wife and daughter are gone for a week. My wife is at a "retreat" with a bunch of women. I'm not sure exactly what they're retreating from, but I don't ask too many questions for fear of the potential answers. My daughter is spending the week with my mom. So, she's happy with some grandma time. My son is sailing. Thus, my house is quiet.

Sometimes, this is eerie. Tonight, it is not. It is a time of reflection and contemplation for me. I can listen to the music I want without complaint. I can have the favorite blanket and sit wherever I choose with it. I made dinner already, so my boy is set to go when he gets home. All the chores I am going to do today are done. The time now is mine. And I will take it.

As the buzzing bees shifting the commerce of the world, human beings get trapped in action. Always something needs to or should be done. We live with a sense of urgency and tension about the undone. It is troubling. This is called "stress". This burdens the peaceful existence that I strive for. As such, I am not a fan.

Much of our time seems to be spent running on others' clocks. We have to be "someplace" to do "something". Often the "someplace" and "something" are not preferred by us. This is called life, I suppose. And, I accept this as the toll for my travel pass, but it does feel nice to sit quietly, without obligation, and write and think. All by myself.

When my family is home and I try to enjoy a little "retreat" by myself, either on the deck, the couch or simply in bed, I am perceived as being selfish. When I don't feel like getting someone a snack or playing a game or talking about my day, something must be "wrong". I'm crabby or moody or unsupportive. At these times, I am usually none of the above. I just happen to be supporting myself: my need to sit and think about things.

This is an important time for all of us. My family needs me to have this time. I am better for it. All people are better for their own version of this time. Sometimes we just need to take a breath, reset, look back and look forward. Our lives change during these times. We filter our truths through the thin mesh of silence and thought. When we return to the busy world, we are better. We are rejuvenated and reborn with a faith that it will all be ok and that our world is a good place to be. Though it is difficult sometimes, it's important to remember these things.

Well, my son just returned home and began telling me what I "need" to do. In response, I told him what HE could do. I'm not going anyplace. I'm taking this one. He can fend for himself. I've done my job and I am now paying myself for it. And if this is selfish, then so be it. I deserve it and he deserves the outcome of a better me.

Sometimes being selfish is a benevolent act of service and love. And is not selfish at all. And we all deserve it. I trust this to be true.

Places.

Driving through my hometown of Des Moines, Washington with my son the other day, it occurred to me how differently we experience the same place. It is his hometown, too, but we have very distinct impressions of the same streets and all that occupies them. I see a lifetime of my memories and understand the heartbeat of the asphalt uniquely.

While cruising past the various bars and restaurants, I see some beautiful bad choices and many, mostly legal, adventures. At the marina, I see a seventeen year old boy sitting with his best friends in a guest moorage slip, drinking Strohs and listening to Bon Jovi. When I see the pier, I remember riding my bike on cool Sunday mornings, hauling my fishing pole and crab trap, to catch some rock crab and flounder, both of which I used to actually eat.

I see my life on these streets and no one else sees them as I do. We all see the same world differently. Pondering my son's future memories, included certainly will be sailing from the marina with our buddy, Nick. Riding his bike and long board to ABC Grocery, chatting up Yoon, and getting a "Mexi-coke" will be in his bank of fun stuff which will connect him to his streets. Eating ice cream bars at the Dog House with Tami will also hold a nice thought. He is creating memories that he will come to love.

A place is an inert, lifeless, dull thing until we apply an experience to it. It, then, becomes special. We carry the special places with us everywhere we go. And when they leave, though we may miss them, they don't really leave. They exist forever in the fond recollections of a life lived. And we can return to them anytime we choose.

This thought comforts me during times of great change. I see my hometown as a shell of its former self. I see businesses closed and the life I knew growing up gone. I suppose this is true of every place, everywhere. They change. Sometimes for better, sometimes for worse, though what is "better" or "worse" is a subjective judgment. And this judgment relies on our experience of a place. This is how we come to love places. We feel them.

As I lament the passing of some of my places, I need only enter Des Moines Drug to enter a time machine and travel back to the days when my dad would shop at Johnny's and I would cross the parking lot to go read wrestling magazines from the rack. The building is the same. The front doors remain as they were back then. And the sweet aroma of soaps and oils and medicines take me back to a special time.

What I will not lose in this experience is that ALL times are special. Yesterday was special. Tomorrow will be special. And today is perhaps the most special of all times. Things change and have always changed. Our memories don't change. They remain and are available to take us back to our wonderful and important places and times.

So…right now…I'm heading down to the marina to have a few beers with a couple of old buddies and listen to some 'Jovi…if only in my mind…but the mind is not a bad place to reside. In fact, it may be the best place there is and it's the place that lasts the longest…This is a good thought…

Ice Cream.

The softness of the morning melted like ice cream throughout the rest of my day. And like melted ice cream, once it was gone, I was left with a sense of loss and a longing for some more. The day became hard as my obligations steered me in many directions, most of which I did not feel like travelling. Some days are like this.

In the morning, a slow and thoughtful awareness of each minute of my life was laser focused and clear. This does not happen very often and when it does I recognize it as precious. Usually, my mind drifts and flits and floats to the various projects and responsibilities I live with, never finding a place to land and sit for a while. This was the rest of my day. With a stifling logjam of obligations, I felt overwhelmed by their sheer volume. My to-do list seems to grow exponentially every day. I can't keep up with it. This troubles me much of the time.

Except this morning, when the sun was low in the eastern sky and much of the world was still asleep. I felt like I had a secret. I was content and connected to the good parts of my life. It is easy for me to stumble into life's potholes and skin my knees on my daily challenges. I guess these thoughts were still asleep, as well. The softness of this peace was nice and probably necessary.

The rest of my day bordered on disaster. Once my peace was gone, it was gone for good. I was stressed and uneasy and uncertain. The pullers pulled and I resisted. That was my problem. I didn't feel like being pulled. Life always pulls and we can choose to help navigate the course it pulls us or we can fight it. Life doesn't care. It is going to pull anyway. We cannot change this. We can only choose our response. Today, I fought. And I lost.

I lost a beautiful day filled with potentially powerful moments of brilliant ideas and rewarding exchanges. I did not seek nor welcome them, so they were lost to me. I did not allow myself a chance to win. I manifested a loser, a dud, and a day of my life wasted by me not wanting to be a part of it. I blew it.

But, as all days do, this one ended. And in the smoky twilight, sitting in my house occupied only by my dogs, a football game on TV, country music on my I-Pod, and me, my morning returned. My family went to a movie and I had the house to myself. Rarely does this happen. It was quiet and felt like a secret, too. No longer burdened by the day that wasn't, I fell into the easy steps of being that I had chased away all day. I let my feet go and danced with the moment.

Sometimes spazzy and awkward, sometimes poised and smooth, this dance is a choice. The music is always playing and we decide to share it or to sit on a chair by the punchbowl and watch our ice cream melt. Melting ice cream happens in spite of our will to save it. As I sit on my couch with my dog lying at my feet, I understand that this is so and tomorrow when my ice cream melts, I will lick it off my fingers or go to the fridge and get some more. I can have ice cream any time I choose. I have a lot of damn ice cream.

"Sir!!!"

My friend died last week. It was a tragedy on a scale not yet invented. Its impact on his family and friends cannot be measured. The value of a single life is often overlooked and taken for granted, until it is gone. Only then do we REALLY know what it meant. It meant everything. Every person means everything. There is nothing more important than a single person.

Each day, death lines the middle pages of newspapers and statistic forms as a tool to inspire readership or funding. The face of death has become faceless. We have become numb to what it really means. Until a late night phone call changes everything after it and a world that once was, will never be again.

A lot is made of "just causes" and "higher purposes", but they are all bullshit to the people left behind to sleeplessly wander the wee-hours, wide-eyed, searching for answers that do not exist. These people know what matters; another day, another moment with the lost one, to embrace, to share a birthday or watch a game. They would pay or trade all that they have for one more moment. These moments cannot, however, be bargained for. They exist for as long as they do and no more. It is just so, for all of us. One never knows when a life that was will no longer be. The phone could ring at any time for anyone, without warning or even a tiny hint.

Death, though, in a peculiar irony, truly shines a light on life. We gain a greater understanding and appreciation of life's fickle impermanence and the urgency to live it how we want and with whom we love. This is little solace, but it is not nothing. Viewing the world and the people we share it with, with a more loving, less critical, more forgiving eye seems a pretty thin reward for the loss of someone we love. I would not trade for it, but I will take it. This may be a final gift bestowed upon the survivors and we are changed because of it.

Many things live in the eye of grief's storm. Many are bad things, but not all. Friends and family live here. Stories of a life live here. And, hidden in the swirling, dusty wind and dark clouds, tomorrow lives here. Some weak thread of hope lives even in the most violent swells of despair, this hope is tomorrow. Today will end and tomorrow will come. This is hope. Hope that it will get just a little bit better. Sometimes it does and sometimes it doesn't, but there is always tomorrow and maybe it could be the one.

Another "benefit" of death is the gathering of family and old friends; the fond remembrance of past days; the smiles and belly laughs, bad puns and tasteless jokes. Food and wine and perhaps a little Mac cement the remaining relationships forever. A moment shared. We are reminded of the connections we have and of the people we love and that love us. This is a great reminder: People love us as much as we love them. We don't give this much thought, but we should. As strongly as we love, we are loved by others. This is true and should not be overlooked. We matter very much to those that love us.

It is said that "friendship multiplies joy and divides grief." I hope this is true, because Brian's family has a lot of friends. Many people are suffering with them. This loss is a shared one, though a parent's grief perhaps is without any measure of depth and may possibly be indivisible. I hope this is not true, but think it probably is. Nonetheless, I will pray and hope for some small salve to calm the burning sting and place a weak shroud on the vast hole left by this event. It is all I can do. I wish I could do more. We all do.

Tomorrow will come as it always does, but it is diminished by the passing of a wonderful guy. Brian will be loved and missed forever. The best people always are.

Todays and Tomorrows

Well, life moves on, but doesn't. Last week, we lost a friend and this week we begin to live life without him. The world is not the same, but the sand continues its trek through the hourglass and doesn't stop for want or need or even death. Life moves on. It's just what it does. The world spins and we must spin with it. We do, however, have some control over where and how we rotate and how we feel about it.

Watching the sun come up over the mountains this morning as my CrossFit girls were doing overhead squats, I felt encouraged and inspired and understood that good things still exist. They are all around us, all the time. With eyes opened a little wider following last week's tragedy, the crisp morning air smelled a little sweeter and the moments of reflection scratched a little deeper into the heart of what matters. Moments matter. This morning mattered and tomorrow morning will matter. The day after that will matter, too. Each day and every moment matters. In time, they become the sum calculation of our lives and the utility and value we place on these moments is our box score.

After the usual morning battles of finishing homework, cooking breakfasts that weren't eaten, searching for socks and shoes and making lunches that I will get complaints about later, this day moved on. As I look out my office window and decide my day's path, I realize that these insignificant choices are in fact, quite significant and that this is a prized day, an award winning day!!

The sky is clear and wind is light. I have lots of work to do and will do it. In between this, I will live. I will talk to friends and have lunch with my wife. I will mow my lawn and produce outcomes that will allow me to sleep well tonight. This day will not be wasted. Some days are and that's a shame. With the ever-increasing speed of my life's time passing, an urgency is taking hold and an intense, almost desperate, need to "get there". I don't know where "there" is. Though, I am not sure this is very important or if "there" even exists, but I believe that trying to get there is very important.

We all have things we want to do and ways we want to be or become. This quest is personal and is perhaps the best reason we have to do anything. With this in mind, I will continue to explore and seek and try. In my previous travels through this world, I have a decent understanding of where "there" is NOT. Knowing this helps shrink the field and maybe narrows the focus a bit.

While what I want to do and/or be may not be super clear, I know very well what I don't want. Sometimes it is easier to define the negative. Eliminating things that we don't like or that make us feel bad seems a good place to start. Also, adding more of the stuff that we like helps. Doing more of what we like and less of what we don't changes us. Attitude is everything and nothing changes our attitudes more than joy. It is contagious and permeates a day. Beginning a day with joy makes it nearly impossible for it to suck. It just can't. With this in mind, I will remember the things I enjoy and do some of those things in the midst of doing the stuff I don't like, but have to do. That should make it all a little easier. And that, to me, is the point.

Life should not be hard. It should be easy. Only when I have to do things that are inconsistent with my natural order or aptitude is it crappy. One of my favorite quotes is, "Don't ask yourself what the world needs. Ask yourself what makes you come alive. Because what the world needs is people who have come alive." Today, I will be alive. We'll see about tomorrow when it gets here, because good Lord willing, it will.

The Marine

"The soldier has come to believe, and with considerable reasons, that those who talk about ideals do not fight for them, and that those who fight for them do not talk about them. The soldier knows that when the nation fights for freedom in far-flung areas of the world, he must lose his freedom, his comfort and even his identity for the duration of the conflict. The ideals for which he is fighting can have little meaning for any soldier so long as the war lasts, while for those who die and for many of the wounded they can never have any meaning at all. He knows that those who speak so glibly of ideals have no conception of what the process of enforcing those ideals means in terms of pain and starvation and death and horror."-written by Willard Waller, WWII Veteran in 1944

Several years ago, getting ready to return home from a visit to my wife's family in upstate New York, I had a not a-typical airport experience. My mother-in-law had driven us to the airport and we were surprisingly early. Our kids were much younger then and, in a semi-desperate plan to avoid them having to spend any more time sitting around in an airport than absolutely necessary, my wife and I left them with her mom while we went to check our bags and get some of the airport hassles out of the way without the burden of fussy kids making it worse.

While at the check-in counter, it was discovered that one of our bags was overweight and this would require an extra $35 fee. This was annoying, but not a huge deal. It was not a big deal until I discovered that I had left my wallet in my carry-on bag that remained in the car with my kids and mother-in-law. The car was not close and the line behind us was starting to stretch to an uncomfortable level. Faced with a long walk back to the car and a long wait in a line that I was already at the front of, I was agitated. Not overwhelmingly so, but I really wanted some other solution to arise. With none in sight, I prepared myself to take the trip I did not want to take.

Apparently, my situation was overheard by a nice gentleman and his wife. As I was getting ready to leave on my journey, they stepped up and offered to pay for the overweight bag. They had kids, too, and though the children were now grown-ups, they remembered the days. I politely refused, but they insisted. I relented, tremendously grateful for my saviors.

Following the transaction, I asked for their address so I could send them a check to repay their generosity. They politely, but adamantly refused. The man said, "If you want to repay me, anytime you see a Marine in a bar, buy him a beer." I was struck by his request, but took it seriously. He was kind and nice, but also serious. I told him I would do so. Then, we all left to live our different lives.

I have and will never forget that day when my wife and I were saved a tremendous hassle and inconvenience by a Marine veteran and his wife. And I have happily and gratefully bought many, many beers over the years. I have met men and women I would not have met otherwise and my life is better for it and this Marine's gift remains one of the best I have ever received.

This Veteran's Day, I remember this Marine and his contribution to my life. Though, it was small, it was not insignificant and, for me, really represents the character and grace and kindness this country's Marines, soldiers, sailors, and airmen embody. This recognition has changed my life and how I perceive our military men and women. Before being soldiers or Marines, they are people. They are fathers and sons, mothers, daughters, brothers, sisters, and friends. They love and are loved. They have fears and doubts and they smile and are funny. They are us.

While our views of wars are as different as we are as people, I believe that a collective and universal respect, admiration and appreciation of our military men and women transcend our political opinions. This is important. All that we possess in this great country was traded for the blood of our soldiers. Anything we have, are or will be is a gift bestowed by the men and women serving or having served in our armed forces. Nothing is free and our way of life is expensive. The debts our young men and women have paid on our behalf is incalculable and worthy of note on this Veteran's Day and every day. So this day I will salute and say a heartfelt "thank you" to our service people and remember the soldiers that gave all they had for us. I will remember the families of our lost soldiers, who gave all they had, too. And if I see a Marine in a bar, I will buy him a beer, today and forever. It's the least I can do.

Thunder Rolls

In another harried race to get my daughter to school on time the other day, my stress and frustration was running high. My motor generally runs pretty cool, but for some reason this morning it was kind of hot. I had a lot to do and any delays were going to exponentially screw up my day. This made me anxious and tense. I felt trapped under the weight of my busy life.

Fortunately, as life will sometimes deliver, a surprise was lurking in the shadows and my mood was changed in a drumbeat by a song on the radio. The song was, "Thunder Rolls", by Garth Brooks. From the first rumble of thunder in the beginning to the final note, my mood shifted. The day's need-to-dos and have-to-dos lost their power to determine my state and/or piece of mind. This song is pretty unremarkable as far as songs go, but to me, it is special.

In 1992 or '93, during a two month road trip around the U.S. with a couple of my best buddies, Jason and Scott, this song was played many times over the course of a several hour late night trek from Albuquerque, New Mexico to Corpus Christi, Texas. I recall this as vividly I remember anything: I was riding shotgun. Scott was driving and Jas was lying down in the back of the van. Scott was a very proud and vocal country music hater, but something seemed right about listening to it while driving through West Texas in the middle of the night. So we listened.

I believe we played the entire tape five or six times, with Scott picking up new lyrics each time. The last time the tape ran, "Thunder Rolls" cued up and he started singing it. He not only sung. He laughed. We both laughed. Jas told us to shut up, but laughed, too. As we dodged the swarm of suicidal deer lining the interstate far away from our lives and homes, we laughed the hysterical laugh that can only come with the sleepless adventure of cross-country travel and youth.

At our top speed of sixty-five miles an hour, we had a moment. We knew it then. We were shoeless and shirtless and the windows were down. The hot breeze blew and we were alive. Life was at its absolute best. We were free; free of clocks and calendars and jobs. We were broke and happy. We owned our days and understood, even then, that this was rare and beautiful. I took a picture of my bare foot on the windshield and it remains one of my most valuable treasures. The moment was captured.

Even if I did not have the photo, the moment was captured in this song. I had heard this song many times before the "moment", but it was never that special. In the years following, this song has a tremendous power to remind and rewind. It is nice to go back to a moment that was perfect. In a world and life of much less-than-perfect, a truly perfect moment is very welcome and I never change the channel when I hear this song. It represents a time that was wonderful and pure and ours.

And as my life today careens down its many uncertain paths, it feels good to turn back the weighty hands of time and sit, again, in the sweaty passenger seat of my 1986 VW Vanagon and let the hot wind blow the dust from the page and the magic notes do their thing. It feels good every single time.

Serf's Up.

"Dad, you need to make my sandwich", my twelve year old son, Aden, informed me this morning. And so began our daily dance. Every single day, we both don't want to make the sandwich, so every single day we bob and weave trying to avoid it. His strategy is to dink around and stall for twenty minutes collecting his school stuff and falsely searching for his shoes and socks until I have to make the sandwich.

My strategy is less sophisticated: I sit on the couch drinking coffee and yell at him to "hurry up". This doesn't work. He screws around until I am faced with the choice of making his stupid sandwich or wasting a half-hour of my valuable morning time driving him to school because he missed his bus. I always make the sandwich. I hate making his sandwiches. I have made hundreds of them. I used to enjoy it. I used to feel dutiful and loving and proud while making his lunch. I don't feel this way anymore. In the past, I would sneak a secret treat into his lunchbox to surprise him. I would imagine him finding my gift and declaring to all his classmates seated near him in the school cafeteria that he and he alone, had the best Dad ever! I don't care about this anymore. Now, I just want him to make his own damn sandwich.

I'm not sure when this changed, but I suspect it has been a progression. I recall no definitive moment standing as a benchmark between times. It just happened. Somewhere along the way, things changed and the doting, ever-concerned father was replaced with a somewhat indifferent and passive man bearing a rather eerie resemblance to my own Dad. It is happening. I am becoming my Dad. I swore I never would, but it was inevitable, I suppose. We become our parents, just as they become theirs. And so it has been since time began.

As I ponder this phenomenon, the only conclusion I can draw is that all kids possess a diabolical power to transform their otherwise reasonable, rational, thoughtful and intelligent parents into mindless and shameless servants. They need things that only we can provide and we have a duty to provide these things. They know we have this duty and so, they manipulate our sense of this duty to turn us into resentful, yet still compliant lackeys placed on this earth to serve only their needs. We are mobile, but beaten robots. We are the defeated.

Since the dawn of parenthood, kids have been screwing over parents exactly this way. It's what they do. Our job is to take it. It's what we do. I say this without ill regard or malevolent intent. It is just so. It doesn't bother me all of the time, just most of the time. I have become a servant, a serf, whose purpose is serving my kingdom's masters. The masters happen to be a lovely, slightly snotty, eight year old girl and the aforementioned too-smart-for-his-own-good twelve year old boy. They direct my day, hour by hour, minute by minute. They own me. I say this without complaint, only somber resignation. It is what it is and I signed up for it.

"DAD!! DAD!! DAD!!, Diego threw up in my room. Come quick!!" my girl bellowed from the hallway just as I sat down on the comfy couch for an afternoon snack. I didn't want to clean up dog puke. But I did. I didn't want to scrape the still warm and soft, half-digested Purina off the carpet. But I did. I did this and I will do this for some time, I suspect. I am here to serve whenever and wherever directed, including and probably especially, on the super nasty jobs. So it goes.

Good Wins.

I started writing today about lots of bad news. It seems that horror stories have dominated the headlines recently. Terrible tragedies and bad people doing bad things are the big stories. Intolerant churches thinking that protesting gay rights at a funeral for two young boys horribly killed by their own father is a proper idea outrages me and makes me question much about this world we live in.

Questions about "how?" and "why?" and "what does it all mean?" confound me. As I began writing and thinking about these bad things and my lack of understanding about them, I was awakened to the fact that no one else understands them either. This made me feel better. It made me feel better because I realized that I am in the majority.

Most, if not all, people are outraged by outrageous acts. This is comforting. More people are good and reasonable and tolerant and simply sane than are creepy weirdoes intent on evil-doings. This is good to know. It is reassuring to me. All good people feel bad when the bad people do their bad things. The good people are us. We are the dominant force of the population. We are the strong and there are a lot of us. This is something to feel good about. We have little control over the bad people doing their things. These things can make us cry and break our hearts, but they should also drive us to be even better and do more good and show more kindness, more often, because we need to and it is the right thing to do, every time.

With this in mind, I will be sad for the poor boys and I will say a prayer for the church crazies, instead of wishing they were attending their own funerals, which is a very easy emotion for me to find. I will do this because I am one of the good ones. Just like everyone else, with a very few awful exceptions.

Today, I will be grateful for what I have and proud of what we have together: a world filled with good people. In spite of our differences: gender, race, religion, ideals, we all share a common underpinning of humanity which binds us: We care about each other.

Where the rubber hits the road and hope is lost... hope is found. We are of one single spirit united in grief and in a profound conviction to help each other. This matters and cannot be tainted or stained by the bad people. We are too damn strong. Good wins.

Thinking these thoughts, instead of lingering in the haze of anger and hate, changed my day. Pessimism about the future of our world was replaced by optimism. With so many good people, life is still good and it will always be good.

Tomorrow morning, my wife will wake next to me and I will bring her coffee. I will make my daughter's breakfast and my son's sandwich. I will say "have a great day" and "I love you" as they walk out the door. This matters, too, and it matters most. We all have these things and they all serve to make us the good ones. With so many wonderful people surrounding us every day, filling the world with uniquely fascinating and kind spirits, we are going to be ok. Good wins.

Fried Trout.

On a mostly sunny Monday morning in a hotel room in southern British Columbia, I remembered my Grandma. I had just made the resort supplied coffee in a little tin pot contraption. As I went to doctor my morning Joe appropriately, I noticed the hotel had "Coffee Mate" powdered creamer in a little packet, along with various forms of sugar.

Coffee Mate creamer always reminds me of my Grandma. The color of the packaging and the fine, white powdered goodness is her. I witnessed her, my whole life, scooping or shaking this marvelous little invention into her coffee countless times. And when I see it, I think of her.

It's oddly poignant that my Grandma, who passed away a few years ago, now lives in Coffee Mate creamer to me. My Grandma also lives in rainbow trout fried in cornmeal and butter. In an old cast iron skillet, she lovingly cooked these trout for my favorite breakfasts. She always perfectly browned the crispy skin, which I loved and still love, though I have never been able to prepare them quite as tasty as my Gram.

She also lives in huckleberry pie, which was also my favorite. Anyone who has ever had someone hand-pick wild mountain huckleberries in a quantity sufficient to satisfy a solid pie can be quite assured that that person loves them very much. Those berries are small and it takes a LONG time to pick enough for a pie. My Grandma picked them for me.

As I reflected on these things while sitting on the little balcony overlooking the glassy lake, I felt very grateful to have been reared by this woman. Her fish and pies made me feel special. As a young boy, and maybe forever, it is important to feel special sometimes. My Grandma understood this.

My Grandma understood a lot of things. As special as I felt while thinking of these things, I realized that I felt exactly as special as the rest of my cousins and my brother felt. My Grandma made everyone feel special. Each of us had our own sweet spot and favorite things. She knew them and made efforts to serve them. As life gets busy and challenging, the thought of a plate of fried fish will always cheer me up.

In our lives, many people pass through and all leave an impression. The remarkable ones are the ones who make us feel remarkable; the ones who create the idea of possibility. They are the heroes, often unsung, as their deeds lack flash or pomp. They are simple acts of kindness and love. These acts shape futures. They are immensely powerful and are truly responsible for any good that exists in this world.

While unloading a box of books this afternoon, I placed my bible on the book case in my bedroom. Many years ago, all of my cousins and I received bibles from my Grandma for Christmas. These bibles were inscribed with our names. I have travelled many miles and lived many lives since I received this gift. It is always on a book shelf in my home, no matter where that is. And it always will be.

From fried trout to huckleberry pie to my bible, my Grandma's legacy lives in my mind and heart and on my book shelf...and it even lives in a little white dish at Harrison Hot Springs Resort in British Columbia serving Coffee Mate creamer...original flavor...It's a big legacy.

Fuddy-Duddy

I am approaching "old fuddy-duddy" age. Next week, I will turn 45. This seems to have happened rather suddenly, though I have no big feelings about it, except that I'm glad I made it. (NOT a jinx!!) Through the years, I have changed and not changed. The obvious signs of my trek toward fuddy-duddy-dom include: ear hair, complaining about politics, a strong affinity for a recliner and a marked indifference towards the things I don't care about. I can't even fake it anymore or don't care to.

Indicators that I haven't yet arrived at grouchy old man status yet include: LOUD-Red Hot Chili Peppers and old-skool gangsta rap, a still-creative use of swear words and the ticklish joy I get from scaring my kids and pets. I believe I've got some time before these things fall off my radar.

Reading an article about how our "joy" changes as we age, I was moved by its truth. When we are young, we search for impactful and extraordinary experiences. We look for the "big" things. Monumental challenges inspire us. We are driven to explore, test, experiment all the world has to play with.

Looking back on my years, I see this as true. I tested and tried lots of stuff, some of it really stupid. I had lots of "experiments" blow up in my face. But, I also discovered what works for me. Sometimes, we find what we like by understanding what we don't like. With so many options, it is necessary to narrow the field and the only way to do this is by trying different stuff. This is a necessary step in any successful life and cannot be avoided. We must discover what we value. The real or fabled "mid-life crisis" is a testament to this idea. So, I am glad I did it when I was younger, because I've already got a trophy wife and I can't afford a corvette.

During this search, we are collecting data. This data points us in the direction we should travel, if we pay attention to it. We define our values: what's important to us. As we get older, with our values clearer, we find our joys in the more ordinary life experiences: Time with friends and family, reading a good book(in a recliner), a good meal, mowing the fresh, spring grass and on and on...I no longer need to go fast or jump off of high places. I'm cool if I never climb a Tibetan peak or leap from a speeding boat again. These days, I like simple...mostly.

As the years pass and the hair on my head continues its migration to other parts of my body, I worry less and less about "stuff". We can control few things.

However, these few things are important things and we should take great care to nurture and protect them. We can control ourselves and our relationship with the world and the people we care about in it. These are really the only things that truly matter.

At some undetermined time, we all end up as dust. The legacy of the lives we led is carved by the days we live. Today is one of those days. Carve well. Pay attention to the details, the soft nuance of a word or a smile. Our legacy is built on how we make others feel. And when the sun rises be grateful for the day, only a finite number them are allotted. They are precious.

Music Man

Last night, I had the pleasure of attending my eleven year old son's band concert. I am not using the word "pleasure" sarcastically...this time. Many times, these events are somewhat underwhelming and, if not disappointing, not tremendously inspiring either. Last night was different.

My son sat in the front row of the band with his oboe and nice shirt. He needs a haircut, but, otherwise, he looked pretty good. He sat in his chair, paid attention and played music. Actual music. It was great. I hear him practicing on the rare occasions that he practices and I was a little apprehensive about this big performance. I was wonderfully surprised.

The band played together and sounded good, with no screeching or honking mistakes that stood out. I was proud and happy to be there and was somewhat changed in my opinion about these experiences. I am usually pretty supportive of any interest my kids have, but this doesn't always mean I am interested myself. Seeing my son as a talented young man and witnessing him becoming more than just my little guy trying new stuff draws a line that is nice to be on the other side of. I am getting true glimpses at his dawning future and it's a good picture.

Many possible, but uncertain futures await our kids. With daily choices and the inevitable results, the efficacy of our parenting is called to the mat. It is nice to feel that, at least in a few ways, I haven't screwed my boy up too bad yet, and I have reason for optimism.

Perhaps last night's most significant moment, for me, occurred when Mr. Fosberg spoke. (Note here that Mr. Fosberg has been teaching music for a long time. So long, in fact, that I was in his guitar class in 1982 or '83 at Pacific Middle School. One of the few highlights of my junior high years happened during this class: Sebastian, an "interesting" kid, in a not-uncommon tantrum, hit hot girl, Leslie, with his guitar. It was beautifully outrageous; the stuff of legends.)

I remember Mr. Fosberg fondly, the way one remembers an eccentric uncle or family friend. He had crazy blond hair and wore some funky suits. He was, even then, passionate about music and teaching music. While, unfortunately, his bug did not really bite me, it bit many others and, after seeing him last night, I feel like I missed something very cool. His love and passion has inspired and enriched the lives of many, many kids and continues to. The world is better because of this and I am happy that people like him exist at all. They are important people and the world needs them and probably many more of them.

During his introduction speech last night, he spoke of the kids and music. His love, commitment and genuine interest in both of them took over the auditorium. Passion sells. And he sold it. Speaking of how music awakens the souls and lives of kids and creates collaboration and opportunity and joy, Mr. Fosberg lit the fire. Kids come alive with music, he said. He told us to appreciate the sometimes strange noises coming from our kids' bedrooms in the evening. They were our kids' spirits and dreams, as sound. His plea to recognize, support and encourage music programs in young lives was inspiring and real. He was not faking it. He felt it and believed it. It was the truth and he made a believer out of me and likely many others. The value of this truth cannot be overstated.

The value of the truth is responsible for any achievement or success anyone ever attains. In our persistent search for this elusive treasure, we often find something less, but we keep looking anyway. I witnessed it last night in a crowded high school auditorium. The truth is alive. Once in a while, we encounter these beautiful reminders that truths live. Not often enough, but on a rare and beautiful occasion, a hero will speak and when this happens, it is good to listen. Not only to the message, but to the heart speaking it. The truth lives here and even though it sometimes seems hard to come by in our daily lives, it is, I believe, important to see a truth and to know, without doubt, that it exists at all.

Old People.

An old man died this week. Probably many old men died this week. I only knew one of them. This old man lived in my hometown of Des Moines, Washington for nearly 50 years. His contributions to the community were, if not unmatched, certainly uncommon. My city is better because of him; his ideas, efforts and his commitment to service. We were very lucky to have had him as a citizen.

In the later years of his life, as his health diminished, life got hard for him. Driving, walking and many other of the much taken for granted ordinary tasks of living became difficult and frustrating. He lived a tough time of life with all the dignity and humanity he could muster. All pretense was stripped raw.

I first saw Clark in an old black and white newspaper clipping in a photo album my mom kept. He was sitting next to my mom at some type of civic event organizing meeting. He wore a smile and hair. The picture was taken in the mid-1960's.

In high school during the mid-80's, I remember, with no fondness, his early Saturday morning weed wacking outside of my buddy, Dan's, bedroom window. Clark was Dan's neighbor and as I often stayed the night at Dan's house following our teenage adventures, I was a sleepy and hung over victim of Clark's diligent adherence to his weekend chores. I did not like Clark on these mornings.

Later, I joined the Rotary Club and Clark was a fixture. While his health was poor, his presence was strong. He was a guy that had "done it". He did not need to prove anything to anyone. He was much admired and loved. In his last years, he was still highly respected and relevant. His life was one worthy of high regard and lives as a model for me: a bit disheveled, not giving a crap about what anyone else thinks, kind and still relevant is a good way to go...I think...

Over the past few years, Clark could often be seen shuffling around the Marina, moving slowing behind his walker, his hair a mess, stopping only to take a sip of his Jack in the Box milkshake (chocolate, no whipped cream, no cherry). I imagine what the kids gathered around their cars thought as Clark strolled by. It is likely they thought little of this slouched, saggy old guy moving slowly with his milk shake and sweatpants. They missed it.

We all miss it. The kids had no idea of this man's gifts, his service, his deeds, his bright mind, his big heart and big contributions to the very lives they were able to have because of him and people like him. They only saw what they saw.

They missed it. Overlooked was Clark's impact on the world. And it was a big thing to miss.

Clark's waning years told a story, but not the whole story. I think this is true for many old people. They get defined as old and we forget they were young. We forget that they built the roads we travel on. They fought the wars, created the businesses, defined the policies, had the ideas and DID IT long before we did. They lived it and DID IT!

As I get older, I find my grandparents words ringing more and more true. In my youth, back when I knew everything, I politely listened to their words then, discarded them. I had it figured out. They were old and didn't "get it". I was wrong. They got it. I didn't get it. I don't think many people get it and maybe we can't get it until we're old. This may be a curse. We have much to learn from our old folks. They are the back bone of our world. They created the framework of our lives.

Today, more old people will die. But, some will die tomorrow. With the time they/we have together appreciate them a little more. Listen to them. They can still teach us valuable lessons. We owe them, and ourselves, this and so much more. And we should aspire to grow old, perhaps a bit unkempt, funny and impatient, but still very alive and still relevant. Like Clark did.

My kids hate my music...

My kids hate my music. They hate all of it, across the board, from Buffett to Springsteen, from Bowie to Strait. They hate it all. They are indiscriminate in their disdain. They don't understand that with each note, the soundtrack of their lives is being written. These songs that drive them to say mean things to me will one day, not a long time from now, remind them of a gentler and simpler era.

I, most fondly, recall from my childhood, sitting at our kitchen table, eating Frankenberry cereal, while my Dad drank his coffee and did crossword puzzles before going to work at the water district. Every morning, KJR was tuned in on the little clock radio and DJ, Gary Lockwood, played the music that created my soundtrack. The Doobie Brothers and the other 70's stars sang through the single speaker and defined my childhood. The soft, sleepy moments eating sugary cereal sitting with my Dad in the mornings before school are what I remember best. Those moments are relived today whenever an oldie hits the air.

Hearing a favorite song is a mood lifter and day changer. We remember and feel what we felt, then. Life is and has always been, for the most part, GOOD!! Music, like nothing else, transports us to our best memories. It is a time machine or a plane ticket to where we were or where we want to be.

Music says things we can't. It is expressive and inspiring and describes thoughts and feelings better than words. Chords strike deeper than words can reach. "Hey, Jazzman, play me a serenade in a deeper blue... than you're playin'... in your brain..." The Boss reaches the dark, rarely seen, but often felt, fathoms that we all have and need. The deep blue is felt and understood and where the glory, absurdity and beauty of life reside as real and clear and relevant. It is hope.

For these reasons, I battle the "Not agains!!" and "This song sucks!!" and smile at my poor, ignorant kids who don't get it, but one day will. In a future nearer than they can imagine, they will have their own favorite songs and some of them will be mine. I will proudly gloat, "I thought you didn't like this song?" They will smile and I will know why. They will feel their life and enjoy it. Songs will remind them of their youth and their brief time sharing it with me. We will be eternally connected by melodies and guitar solos.

One day, when they hear American Pie and the words, "I was a lonely teenage broncin' buck, with a pink carnation and a pick-up truck..." they will inform their kids that, "This is Grandpa's favorite line in any song." They will be right and these words that now make them cringe and wince will sing to them something else. They will be my words and like all things parents pass to their children, they will become theirs, too.

Until then, I will play what I want and suffer the insults and hurled objects. My kids will complain and whine and I won't care. They cannot, as I could not, conceive of the notion, that Dad actually had a few things right and my Dad WAS right, "Benny and the Jets" is a damn good song. Thanks, Pops.

Nicks.

My son is embarking on a weekend long sailboat race with my old neighbor, Nick. He's excited. Nick's excited. And I'm excited. As a legitimate crew member, my son is learning about team work and contribution and sailing and fun. I could not be more pleased about this.

Nick is the hinge pin in this operation. He is a forty year old fourteen year old. He is a fun-loving, kind and generous adventurer. When I lived next door, I would often find Nick tinkering with some interesting contraption in his garage. He has a mad scientist mentality, always on the lookout for a good time. He carries a rare and beautiful enthusiasm for living life with him everywhere he travels. And he travels many places. His unconventional, yet wonderful zest for life is infectious. And I am happy that my son is getting some exposure to this contagion. It's a good bug to catch.

My boy is running for sophomore class president and while discussing his speech I was proud to hear that his "platform" foundation involves creating more vibrant high school experiences for students. Participation in clubs and sports and anything of interest shapes these experiences. My son understands the value of "doing stuff". And this is a good thing to understand.

"Participation" is the key to a good life. Actively exploring the big, bright world IS living. With eyes open and feet moving, we journey through our years. The wider the eyes and the more deliberate the foot falls, the richer the life. This is an important, yet sometimes difficult thing to remember. Our days are often filled with responsibilities and obligations which limit our capacity for exploration. Making time to enjoy and explore deserves a higher spot on the shelf and serves to reframe how we see the world and our lives. We see more. We see possibility and the truth that the world is a pretty cool place to be.

So, as my son sets sail on his adventure, I am happy to know that he will write another entry into his log book of fun stuff. With salt water and wind and friends, he will know that the world is a good place. He will carry this knowledge back to school on Monday and he will be changed in small or big ways. He will change the world with the ways that he has been changed by his fantastic experiences. A marvelous ripple effect is taking shape.

The "Nicks" of the world are necessary. They are the mystical gypsies with smiling eyes and awesome bad ideas. They make taking the risks worth it. We need our Nicks to remind us that age is but a number and we still possess the joy of children. We can laugh and try and fall and still laugh. Life is a serious business that should not be taken too seriously. We need our Nicks to remind us that world is worth exploring, being a good dude matters, and a windy day on the water with friends is valuable and necessary. We need our Nicks to shine the light of their gloriously unkempt spirits on our paths...and I'm glad my son and I have ours...he shines a bright light...

Ship building.

"If you want to build a ship, don't herd people together to collect wood and don't assign them tasks and work, but rather teach them to long for the endless immensity of the sea." –Antoine de Saint-Exupery

I read this quote the other day and began to think about it. I'm still thinking about it. I read a lot of words and many slip in and out of my mind with only a brief glance. I have a lot of short-term love affairs with words. These words remain with me. I may love them. It's still early, but we might have a future together.

These words inspired me because they tell the truth. In looking around my life for places that this idea might fit, I find that it fits everywhere. The truth does this.

While attempting to navigate a path through the wheel barrow load of shoes lying in all corners and non-corners of my living room, I began to ponder an application of this idea. How can I inspire my little piglets to put their crap away? How can I connect them to a larger vision of possibility that will make their small efforts a joy? How can I shape a message that will resonate and create a tidy and yell-free household?

Well, I have no idea how to do this. But...I still think it's worthwhile exploring it. Like many good ideas, it exists as both clear and nebulous at the same time. I "get" it, but am not sure how to apply it.

It's an idea about constructing a culture of "creation", instead of simply "work". This is a powerful culture that relies on a strong "why?" instead of "what?" "Why?" we do something is always the more important question than the "what?"

Having some clarity on our mission goals, intentions and vision is vital to establishing a potent sense of purpose. This is our "why?" Being clear on this first, makes everything easier and more authentic, thus more effective that follows it. It's a beautiful idea that I have experienced at different times in my life.

Several years ago, I worked for my local city park department. We built and maintained parks. It remains the best job I've ever had. Our crew was inspired by our work. We took pride in what we created. We had a sense of purpose and understood our role in making it so. We also had a great leader. Our boss, Rick, led well. He made us feel important. He helped us recognize the larger value of our efforts. It was a powerful lesson and one that I carry with me today.

This experience illustrates that, fortunately, it's possible. Inspiring cultures can exist...anyplace. And we can all be great leaders. We can shape cultures through our spirits and words. We matter and it matters and all oceans are ours to explore. It's a big, beautiful world filled with the magic we create. Why create this magic?...because it's what we're here to do...

Full-circle.

While hanging out at my buddy's house many years ago, I stumbled into helping his mom with some yard work. I recall trimming back various trees and shrubs, all done very delicately. She was quite specific about NOT cutting too much. Being a bit of a pruning bully, I did my best to accommodate her wishes, but could not help getting a little aggressive with my loppers from time to time. She gently "corrected" me and, as far as frustrating afternoons go, it was kind of pleasant.

One technique in her landscape management repertoire which I could not comprehend, nor endure, was chopping each clipping into a two-inch chunk to be deposited into the yard waste bin. I had no patience for this. It seemed like a tedious waste of valuable time. So, I left her to this chore and went about doing the super-important nothing I had to do. But, this experience stuck with me.

Well, life being life, things have changed. The other night while hacking away at some errant blackberry vines creeping out from laurel hedge, I found myself standing over my yard waste barrel clipping the pointy tendrils into bit-size pieces to maximize spatial economy. During this process, I remembered the day many years ago when I could not tolerate this idea, being is such a big hurry to get nowhere.

Standing in my yard performing the exact same act which so repelled me many years ago, I was reminded of "mom" and I smiled. With my face pointed toward the late summer sun, I enjoyed taking my time nibbling these vines with my shears. It was quite meditative. I was simply happy. And I "got it".

I have spent much of my life in a hurry. My tires spin fast. However, the problem with spinning tires is traction. I tend to rush from project to project, idea to idea, without allowing them to gain traction. Good, valid and important ideas litter my history and lie in the mud, wasted by my haste.

Trimming my blackberries, slowly and deliberately…and enjoying it…I hope represents a shift; a slow-down. Life is busy with infinite possibilities distracting our attention. Each possibility excites us and pulls us towards it. The problem here is that we can become so busy hopscotching through ideas that we never allow any to fully develop. We move and build and think, but don't create anything except for rough drafts and incomplete structures. This is a sad fact.

Gratefully, time is sometimes kind. The unfortunate time it takes to recognize this necessary fact is followed by a time to remedy it: A time to do something different. This is a new possibility, one full of hope and the lost optimism of youth. We still have time. Today, we have time to change what we see needs change. By taking our foot off the gas, we can gain some traction and clarity about what matters to us and move our lives in the direction we were born to travel, which, I believe, is what we are here to do...

Misfit Toys.

Last night while sitting at my local bar surrounded by a mismatched collection of friends, it struck me exactly how diverse my catalogue of acquaintances is. I suspect that I am not alone in this. Age, economics, personal philosophies, bodies, hairlines and personalities are just a few of the distinct characteristics defining each person as different. I love these differences.

A teacher, an engine fabricator/mechanic, a commercial diver, a booze distributer, a project manager, a health care professional, a house painter and a naturopath all sat around me telling stories, smiling and laughing. Unique perspectives were shared and for all our differences, we were much the same in our shared love of the moment.

I love the misfits. The simple fact that we are all misfits makes it very easy for me to love many people. We all have a story; a uniquely interesting tale to tell. People are fascinating. Compelling stories of near-misses, direct hits and lives lived keep me intrigued by human beings. The scratches in our paint jobs, dents in our doors and dings on our bumpers are what make us wonderfully special. We are a flawed humanity and beautiful in our imperfection.

This is a fact often lost in a culture where the emulation of homogenous sameness is lauded. I cannot support this. I don't like plastic, cookie-cutter, unoriginal ideas or people. I like the oddball, goofy, independent thinking that comes from the weirdoes. I think the un-pretty, weird ideas progress us further than the ones neatly packaged in a box with a bow.

Often, "celebrating our differences" feels more like a public service announcement, than a legitimate goal. Watered down versions of copycat ideas litter the information highways we travel. It is refreshing and necessary when an alternative thought pokes us awake to the possibilities. These are the golden tickets that make a life worth living.

These golden tickets are printed by the misfits. And we're all misfits. This earth we share is the real "island of misfit toys" of "Rudolph the Red-nosed Reindeer" fame. Acknowledging this and, indeed, being proud of our collective misfit-ness is a concept worthy of considering. And if "Charlie-in-the-box" was bellied up at my local watering hole I would by him a beer.

"Were it not for the presence of the unwashed and the half-educated, the formless, queer and incomplete, the unreasonable and absurd, the infinite

shapes of the delightful human tadpole, the horizon would not wear so wide a grin." –Frank Moore Colby

Contemplating my own eclectic collection of friends and family, I can rest assured that originality is not lost. It lives in every one of us. And as I reverently celebrate this, I find a grin on my face as wide as the horizon's...

The Truth

Today was a good day. I knew it would be. Some days you just know. Some days you know are going to suck. Some days could go either way. And some days are just good ones. This morning the sun was out and the breeze was cool, but warming. My dog wore a smile and my kids weren't fighting. My spirit was high and my soul was aligned with its proper place. This was a day of much to do, but also much possibility. Work would handle itself, but the variable of how to best spend the free moments was a deep consideration.

Much of my joy these days involves a peripheral sliver of my kid's fun. Their joy is mine, some of it, sometimes. I made omelets with my six-year old daughter. She likes omelets. Eggs, cheese and sausage are her favorites. I kick in a little tomato and avocado for myself. My crazy-haired son ate cereal on the couch in his underwear, shrouded in his favorite blanket while watching his favorite cartoon, some weird Asian space show that I don't get. Nonetheless, the morning was virtually conflict-free, a true oddity in my home.

Next, we went to my wife's office where I have a little landscaping project shaping up. I am removing and resetting the paver entry path. It is the perfect sized project for me. I tend to suffer from some type of adult ADHD when it comes to projects. I tire of them quickly and they become onerous and un-fun for me. This was a two-dayer, perfect. I had my son removing stones and my daughter cleaning them with the garden hose.

In another unheard-of development, my daughter did not "accidentally" spray my son with the hose. Here, we avoided an epic screaming match and potentially some serious pick-axe threats on my daughter's life by my son. It was smooth and everyone seemed to enjoy their contributions. This, too, is exceptionally rare. My kids were content and peaceful in their efforts.

Later, we had lunch, which included ice cream cones. Nobody, in their over-eagerness, licked too hard and had the scoop drop on the floor. This is, again, pretty uncommon. My kids like ice cream and will dive into a waffle cone without regard. They understand the consequences of this, but they don't care. They don't care if the ice cream falls on the floor. They will pick it up or, more likely, my wife or I, will pick it up, shave the dirt off with a napkin and set it back on the cone, always within the "five-second rule" window, of course.

In the evening, I invited a couple of buddies and their families over to barbeque. I love barbeques. I love standing at the grill with a beer in my hand

and smoke in my eyes hiding my tears of joy at how good my chicken and sausages smell. In the background, through the delicious meat sizzle, I hear my kids playing with my best friend's kids. They are going to be life-long best friends, too. My wife makes a salad with friends, smiling the entire time. I hear a couple of other old buddies smack-talking during a cribbage game. This false conflict is a ritual that I have both witnessed and participated in for nearly thirty years and a cribbage game between old friends would be less without it. My buddy, Dan, takes alternating turns spraying the hose at the swing set slide creating a redneck waterslide for the kids and spraying, my dog, Diego, in the face. This is Diego's favorite thing in the world. It is a bizarre fetish, but it is his. The kids cannot get back in line quick enough for another run down the slide.

As I look around and see all that I love standing in my yard or sitting at my picnic table, I am, very simply, happy. The sense of peace and joy and my contented arrival at the place that matters defies words or I am incapable of expressing them clearly enough to define all of the nuance and implication that this moment deserves. The depth of sentiment runs deeper than my mind can dig for explanation. This being the case, I will simply call it, the" truth". It was a good day, indeed.

A Perfect Ten.

Ten years ago, my wife and I were married. Ten years is both a long and a short time. Some days, it feels like a blink and some days it feels like geologic time would better suit its measure. It really depends on the day.

Through the years, much has changed. Our life and our lives have changed. A couple always consists of two individuals and here is the magic of a marriage that survives ten years: the individuals remain as such. WOW!! This is a globe-rattling idea!! It is true. "Two becoming one" is BS. For any marriage to last, the two people must remain true to who and what they are. Certainly some compromise is required as well, but this compromise cannot compromise one person's sense of self or their ability to express that which is unique to them.

While this may sound a little heady, it is not. It is very simple. It involves forgiveness and concession and a stubborn will to remain together. It is the gentle acceptance of the other person simply because you value them. This is not easy, but it is I believe the key to any "success" my wife and I have had in our journey thus far.

"Listen, you married me AFTER I peed in the oven. " was a common cop-out to my bad behavior early in our marriage. Here, I tried to shift the blame from myself to my wife. This did not work as well as I would have hoped. I still was blamed for the stuff that I should have been blamed for. When I was selfish and/or over-indulgent, my wife called me out. She expected and demanded more from me. This was not bad for me. It was good. It forced me to raise my own expectations of myself.

Through this I have changed much, but not all. I am still capable of doing some tremendously dumb things, but the frequency of such actions has been curtailed to a mostly acceptable level. I haven't peed in the oven for a long time. I should say "allegedly", since the initial oven whiz was never actually proven. The case was highly circumstantial, though very little "reasonable doubt" existed, certainly in my wife's mind.

The years have changed us both. Time and experience do that. My wife and I remain very different in the "process" of life, but are committed to the same goals. This, I believe, saves us. We trust that the other is heading the right direction, even if we drive in different lanes of travel. She is a fast-laner, while I prefer the second lane with a little slower pace and my head shifting from side to side enjoying the sights. She wants to get "there". I do too, but I also enjoy the ride at a slightly different pace. We have come to accept this as "how we are" and more now than ever, kind of enjoy these differences. These distinctions make my wife interesting to me. I am able to see the world differently through her eyeballs. This different perspective opens up many things that I would not have otherwise seen. And this, too, is good.

Raising kids and owning businesses and dealing with the inevitable challenges of life has strengthened us. While this has not been easy, it has been worth it. Today, I love my wife more than I did. I value her and respect her more. I truly admire and revere the person she is. The struggles and battles and the scars of both were not in vain. The scars serve as reminders of a life lived and shared. And I would do it all again.

After ten years of marriage, I would marry my wife again. This idea stands as a testament to her place in my life. After all the ups and sometimes REALLY DOWN downs, I would do it again. Nothing was in vain and it was all worth it. I will stand on this as the anchor for our next ten years together…though, I'm not counting any chickens yet…the oven is sometimes a tempting mistress…

Sidenote: Alas, my wife and I did not make another 10 years. That said, I would not change the time we did have. As evidenced by many of my words in this tome, we shared much and I wouldn't change a thing and remain eternally grateful for our time together…

The Dump.

I love going to the dump. I have always loved going to the dump. Some of my earliest memories involve climbing into the back of my Dad's old Ford truck and "helping" him unload various manner of debris. I enjoyed tossing many items into the hole, but I especially enjoyed this when something broke.

As further evidence of my stunted evolution, a few weeks ago, I hucked an old toilet onto the concrete deck at the bottom of the dump pit and it shattered, big-time. I carried this small thrill with me for the rest of the day.

Yesterday, I went to the dump again. I was met with mixed emotions as my dump had changed. A large and complicated renovation has been in the works for quite a while and is now complete. "Out with the old and in with the new" is the way of the world. I understand this, but still feel a little sad knowing that I will never again stand on the same worn and chipped slab that my Dad parked our truck on so many years ago.

Well, as I always do, I got over my melancholy and saw the tremendous opportunity in this new facility. It has separate recycling, scrap and yard waste areas. I like this. I always feel a little guilty throwing known recyclables into the trash. However, my guilt is always overcome by my laziness. My new dump will allow me to recycle and still be lazy. This is good.

As I drove into the new building and pulled into an empty stall, a dump worker came over to my vehicle. This has happened before and, in my experience, it is never a good thing. This day was different. He inventoried my load, which was mostly grass and grape vines. He asked if I had any garbage mixed in. I did not. He then directed me to the new yard waste area and informed me that it is cheaper to dispose of clean yard waste than trash. He then took the extraordinary action and called the lady dispatcher in the cashier shack and informed her of the change in my load status.

I was awed his gesture and began to really embrace this new dump. I have come to not really expect much in the customer service department from dump workers, but this guy was awesome. He was genuinely helpful and took ownership of his job, and by extension, my experience. And, if I were ever so inclined to actually hug a dump worker, it would have been him.

I left the dump happy on several levels. Firstly, I am always happy having disposed of some baggage and the cleansing that comes with that, and this was achieved. Secondly, the new dump allows me to also cleanse my conscience by not chucking my recyclable goods straight into the landfill. Thirdly, my new dump showed me that human goodness and integrity exists in any and every field of vocation. This lesson is often challenged, but my hope in this idea always lives and was indeed confirmed by a simple gesture by a guy in an orange vest.

Inspiration and faith in the value of a common humanity has many shapes and wears many differently colored vests. But, it is as simple and obvious and evident as a walk down the street or a trip to the dump. It lives wherever we live. We give hope life by being hopeful. And we give faith life by being faithful. We create the world we live in. So...create well...like the guy in the orange vest did...

Mmmmm....Dobie...

While eating dinner the other night my annoyingly picky son was questioning the taco meat. He questions everything we eat. I, in my usual fashion, avoided his queries with "Just eat it!" He did and was not displeased. The meat was elk and it was good.

At the meal's conclusion, he continued his probe into what the meat was and I, again in my usual fashion, lied to him, because I knew the truth would not be well received. I impulsively told him it was Doberman.

I didn't think much of this exchange until sometime later when I checked Facebook and saw that he had posted about this. He actually BELIEVED I had served him dog meat. Here, I was not displeased. Rarely do my kids believe me when I tell my tales and it is kind of nice when they do.

I tell a lot of tales to my kids. My wife is not always a fan of this. But, sometimes I just can't help myself. Following my bride's disapproval I will occasionally ponder whether she may possibly be right and that my way is not always appropriate. But, as mentioned, sometimes I just can't help myself.

This episode inspired me to take a broader look into why we do what we do, especially when sometimes it does not serve us well. Canons have been written about this and I am distinctly unqualified to discuss the psychological complexities regarding human behavior...but...umm...I think sometimes we just can't help it.

In evaluating my own track record of bad behavioral choices, my big mouth holds all of the top spots. I have said some remarkably stupid things. I have hurt feelings and I have changed relationships due to my inability to hold my tongue. When I think about this, I feel bad. My intentions are rarely bad. It's my judgment which betrays me.

While my big mouth has led me to say things I regret, it has also allowed me to express myself in good and important ways, too. Few of my friends don't know how much I care about them. My family understands how much I love them. I am free with a kind word or encouragement or condolences. I feel things and I say them. This feature is not altogether common in the humanity that I know and I like this side of my big mouth.

"Be careful, lest, in casting out your demon, you exorcise the best thing in you."
-Friedrich Nietzsche

It would be easy to see only one side of the coin. I think, being the uncertain and insecure human beings that we are, we often emphasize our worse demons and undervalue our good ones. We don't see that sometimes they are the same demon or at least they live on the same street.

Sometimes our curse is also our magic. To me, this softens the impact of my less-than-perfect moments. The things we trouble ourselves trying to change or that burden our self-esteem are our super powers, just sometimes in disguise. We all have unique and powerful characteristics which drive us, and sometimes our loved ones, crazy. These also make us great and define us as special.

I can easily imagine my good and bad demons sitting as friends, chuckling about my "Doberman" comment, shaking their heads, proud to be a part of me. They coexist because they must. And since they must be together to be at all, I may as well embrace both of the little devils. Such is this crazy, wonderful, confounding and confusing, frustrating and beautiful life.

Moms are mean.

Moms are mean. That's right. I said it. Moms do the majority of the yelling, spanking and band aid ripping-off. As a small child, my dad never made me lay on my back with my pants down and legs up and stuck a greasy, icy thermometer in my rear end. Mom sure did. I remember it well. Too well. I remember meeting my dad's eyes while in my compromised position. I remember his shrug and smirk and him leaving the room. Mom stayed in the room. Moms always stay in the room. This is frustrating. They don't leave us alone.

In my current house, while God has proven his existence with the advent of digital thermometers, my wife, as mom, still strikes fear in the hearts of my perfect children. They KNOW they do not want to mess with mom. She will make life miserable. She will not tolerate any BS excuses or lies. She's a tough crowd of one.

While I do some yelling and have certainly delivered a swat, I am a pretty kind dad. This is where I'm confused. No matter how sweet and generous I am, my kids still love their mom more. And she's mean. I don't get it. They enjoy her attention more. They accept her hugs. They listen to her words. They miss her when she's not around. As a dad, this is confusing. As a son, this is not.

Moms, for all of their emotional incongruences, have our backs. We know who will starve for us or kill for us. Moms will. They will jump from a moving vehicle or run into a burning house for us. Through no spoken words, we understand this. This is reassuring. No one loves us more than our mom.

After the yelling, we get a hug. After the spanking, we get a Popsicle. They give us what they have. So, we can't help forgiving them for being human. Lessons in love, compassion, kindness, charity, and all the good things about the world are delivered by our moms. They are the foundations upon which our lives are built.

So, while moms are mean, they are allowed to be, because they are so much more. They are who we call when we are sick. They are our "chicken soup for the soul." In lives filled with stress and strife, fear and tragedy, thoughts of mom are a safe place. We can always travel back to a peanut butter and jelly sandwich with the crusts thoughtfully trimmed. We can enjoy or remember a gentle, yet strong embrace and know that true love exists. We are validated.

Moms make us feel important. This may be the most vital of all of moms' virtues: the power to make us feel important.

We could live many lifetimes and not be able to express in full measure their value and impact on our lives. They made us and they protected us and they showed us. They let us stumble and learn and picked us up when we fell. They dried our clothes and our tears. They loved us and will love us no matter how poorly we behave. They know what we need even when we don't. They see our goodness when we don't. They are the magical clairvoyants scribed in fantasy works. They understand our spirits and know our heartbeats. And even when they're mean...they're not that mean.

From our first breath to the last days, moms are there. They don't leave the room. They may be the only "sure thing" in the world and they are with us forever. This is a comforting thought. For these reasons and many more, we love them and we honor them and we forgive them for their imperfections...and we even forgive them for the frozen thermometers...they are perfect to us.

The Buzzard.

"Dad didn't do it." My traitorous vulture of a thirteen year old son chimed in, accusingly and unsolicited, to my wife's query about whether or not a certain project had been completed. I looked at him with a furrowed brow and shook my head. He smirked, looked at me and shrugged, and then left the room satisfied.

He does this often. He circles around like a buzzard waiting for me to screw something up then joyously informs my wife of my failure. He takes much pleasure in this, too much as far as I'm concerned. He never steps too far over the line risking his personal safety, but he certainly achieves being annoying, if that is his goal, which is the only reasonable justification for his behavior that I can find. It is a little disheartening that my son so relishes any opportunity to throw me under the bus, but he does, indeed, enjoy watching me squirm.

As I seek explanation for his Benedict Arnoldian conduct, I need look no further than the mirror to find my answer. My son is a reflection of me, though with furrier eyebrows. He reflects both my beauty and my ugly. I am proud when he says something clever or does something thoughtful. In these moments, I take full credit for his goodness. When he is snide and sarcastic or quick-tempered, "I don't know where that came from" or I blame my wife. It is painful to admit that I am screwing him up. But I am. It's what parents do.

Parents create human beings. And, since all human beings are screwed up, it is our job to make sure our kids are sufficiently flawed. Mission accomplished in my household and my own parents may have over-achieved.

Understanding that perfection is vastly overrated and magnificently irritating, parents must delicately shape the proper imperfections. This is a complicated duty, but an important one. Making kids that can thrive in an imperfect world is the objective. This is often unstated and sometimes unintentional and it may be a little unsettling to confess this, but it is also true.

Standing out while blending in requires a fragile balance. Being able to flourish while still maintaining piece of mind, and friendships, is a challenge. Compromise is necessary sometimes. Not compromising is necessary other times. The defining metric of success is how many people one pisses off. If you don't piss off at least few people, you aren't trying hard enough and will get nowhere. If you piss off too many people, they will stop listening to you and you will get nowhere. Honing the proper ratio of folks to piss off is the key to achieving success and joy in this goofy world.

If my theory holds true, then my son is set up for a pretty good life. He annoys me and his mom and sister, but is also kind and has many friends. He can be useful and gracious. I actually saw him help his little sister the other day and this single, simple action certainly improved his life by possibly allowing him to KEEP it, because I am pretty sure she was plotting to kill him. He is beautiful in his imperfection and I take complete ownership over this. He is my son in his beauty. The other stuff...I don't know where that came from... I blame his mother...

Hour of Whispers.

Tonight I am sitting on an airplane flying over the vast nothing of the Pacific Ocean travelling from Hawaii to Seattle. My son lies next to me with his head on this fold down tray. My wife and daughter sit across the aisle, restlessly trying to find a comfortable position to sleep.

We are flying the red-eye from Kauai to home during the hour of whispers. This is a time usually, and rightfully, reserved for other things besides sitting in a cramped chair for five straight hours watching strangers sleep with their mouths open. Though mildly amusing, my alternative preferences would be many.

The hour of whispers is a solemn time of soft tones and touch and sacred conversation. It is a healing time...unless you're on an airplane flying over the ocean. Then, it's something else. However, since I'm returning from a warm weather vacation, I can't complain too much. In my world, vacations are rare. Thus, they are valuable and I do not take even a long, dark plane ride for granted.

For a solid week, my family and I swam and ate and played cards and explored the ins and outs of a new place. In damp trunks and flip flops, we cruised the island at a pace of our choosing. We were deciders. We could do or not do. And it was nice.

It is rare to have such control. Perhaps this is why we value vacations so much: we have total sanction over our hours. This feels good. It is necessary and right and reminds us of a deeper connection to the larger world and our place in it. In all of us, buried in some deep pocket of our characters, resides an ancestral nomad intent on seeing the world. Most of the time, this neat little dude or dudette suffers in silence as we go about our business, marking time for someone else. That's why it's fun to let this little feller out once in a while. We are reminded that he/she exists at all.

As I glanced out the window past my son and a large stranger, I caught a wonderful shot of the moon. Low and bright over the wing of the aircraft, for a brief moment, the moon was mine. And we travelled, as explorers have since the dawn of time, in a necessary collaboration of spirit and light. Then, the moon moved to someone else's window. Though the moment was brief, it, too, reminded me of great mysteries and fantastic wonders of this world and made me appreciate the ones I love sitting near me, sleeping with their mouths open on an airplane over the ocean...

154

Shotgun riders.

Halloween each year marks an anniversary of the day my little brother died. He was 16 years old. I was 19. Though many years have passed since this event, it remains likely the single-most defining moment of my life. It changed me and continues to change me the more or less I come to understand life. We all have events like this that shape us in ways we may or may not understand.

Prior to my brother's death, I had a pretty clear vision of my life's direction. A scripted and well-defined path to the "American dream" was being paved before me, by me. After his death, I was armed with more questions than answers. This legacy of questions remains. Questions about "purpose" and "meaning" haunt me.

All of the things that were so clear became muddy and for a long time, this left me unsettled. Through the years, I have become comfortable in the mud. I don't think many true answers exist. Life is life and joy is joy and time passes until it doesn't any more.

Understanding that my questions produced only more questions and not the answers I was hoping for, I let go of the expectation that genuine clarity would reveal itself to me and now mostly enjoy the peace in my uncertainty. Great humor and love lives in the absurdity of our human spirits. Our world spins on laughter and tears and a touch. These are things I KNOW and I am happy I know them.

For all the questions that will remain unanswered, a few diamonds of truth have been found. I am crystal clear on a very few important things. I know what and who I value. Though I may not always know where I'm going, I know who I'm traveling with. This may be the only important thing there is to know.

Our companions in this life are what matters. They are the "what" and the "why". The people we share a windshield with as we navigate the roads we travel are the truth. The ones that stand the tests of time and circumstance live as the truest of truths and are the most valuable answer I have found.

Life is a zero-sum game. When we lose something, we gain something else. I lost my brother, but I gained an appreciation for things I would not have had before. My entire value perspective changed and this changed everything else. And I wouldn't change this. It allows me to be kind, to care about things that deserve my care, and to not care about things that do not.

With the quiet fierceness of conviction, I stubbornly drive my vehicle wherever my heart says to go. And as my shotgun riders crack another beer, I smile and turn up the radio and know that life is just life and a moment on a dusty backroad with a friend or a family is the only answer that makes sense. And I'm ok with that...

Touch and Die!!!!, Love, Dad

"Hey, Aden, do you know where my drill is?" I asked my 13 year old son. "No" came his predictable reply. We both knew he was lying about the whereabouts of my drill, but we also both knew that his personal safety relied on him lying about it.

My kids take my stuff. They take it like it is their stuff. The only distinction being that they actually take care of and don't lose their own stuff. They reserve my stuff to bust and lose.

In high school while over at a buddy's house after school, we found a note from his Dad on the kitchen counter that said, "Don't touch my f***ing stuff!! Love, Dad". We found another note in the stereo case that said "Touch and Die!!" referencing the father's CDs.

At the time, I found the tone of these notes to be a bit abrupt and unnecessary. That was then. I now understand the frustration which motivated the Dad to write those notes. We took his stuff and broke it or lost it or left it outside to be ruined. I'm sure he asked us about his things and I'm sure we lied. Well, the circle is now complete and JK can rest assured that payback is in full swing.

Rarely a day passes that I don't KNOW with certainty that a tool or my i-pod or something else I want or need, and actually OWN, will come up missing. I know where it goes. We all know where it goes, but nobody is saying. Self-preservation is a powerful instinct. My son understands this, as does my daughter, to an extent, but she's a little more shameless and cavalier in her attitude regarding my things.

I think she actually believes my stuff to be hers. I will enquire, "Lena, have you seen my notebook?" And she will respond with "Yeah, it's in my room. I'm using it." I then go retrieve my notebook and find that she has doodled and scribbled and otherwise destroyed this book which I use regularly to record important information or just thoughts for this goofy little column I write.

When I express my displeasure for her desecration of my holy book, she acts like I'm wrong. She is outraged by the fact that I might not want her to touch my stuff. As far as she is concerned, it is hers, too. She gets quite indignant and is usually successful in making me feel like an ass for not enjoying her ruining my things. It is an illogical, but not uncommon phenomenon in my household which usually manifests itself in the relationships between the men and the women.

Once in a while, fate will throw me a bone. The other day my son asked me where his headphones were. It is worth noting that he has some pretty nice, noise-canceling, comfy headphones, while I have cheap, hard plastic buds which make my ears hurt and sometimes bleed. This is the part which really puzzles me about why my kids take my stuff. They shouldn't. They have better stuff than me. My only guess is that perhaps the forbidden fruit is simply the sweetest.

Anywhooo...back to the headphones...when my son asked me if I knew where they were. I said "No."

I did, in fact and of course, know where they were. They were in my truck tucked away, hidden from him, because I wanted to use them. He walked away knowing I lied, but resumed his search anyway. I felt good. Zero guilt. Less than zero. I felt like I won a rare victory. I felt redeemed....and then I went to look for my drill.

Avoiding and Outwitting.

"I understand that inside of me is a guy who wants to lie in bed and smoke weed all day and watch cartoons. My whole life is a series of stratagems to avoid and outwit that guy." –Anthony Bourdain

This is perhaps the purest and most honest interpretation of the battle between the contrasting angels in our human spirits that I have ever encountered. This battle is at the heart of our successes and/or failures in life. While we all have our own versions of "that guy", he exists and can exert some powerful influence from time to time. He is one to be aware of.

At the beginning of each New Year, many folks set out to make "resolutions". They declare a new path. They will do better and more. It is here that our insidious little "that guy" can derail our aspirations. He drives our bus back into the well-worn ruts of behaviors we don't want. He tells us how warm our bed feels, preventing us from going for a morning run. He tells us that one bite won't hurt, when we know that it will. He tells us we can't...so why try? This rascal costs us money and friends and time. He can bring hurt and disappointment and shame. His voice tells the lies which undermine our potential. In short, he can be a real bastard.

On the other hand, we need this guy. We just need to understand him. He can work for us or work against us. Significant to this understanding is that we truly do NEED this guy. Opportunities are often shaded by risk. In these moments, we need our devilish little archangels to push us into experiences that will enrich our lives. Playing it safe all the time is not a very fulfilling life. Sometimes we need a daredevil to help us take that leap which will change our lives.

"Be careful, lest in casting out your demon you exorcise the best thing in you." — Friedrich Nietzsche

"That guy" is, also, a necessary piece of our unique characters. He picks our clothes and tells the jokes. He is not ashamed to cry or laugh. I enjoy some order, but a world full of well-groomed but, achingly dull folks is no place I care to spend much time. I like the odd balls. The world needs its weirdoes. They provide color and light and art and the things which make life worth living. "That guy" does this, too.

So, in 2015, I will keep a sharp eye on my "that guy". I will only listen to his voice when he pushes me where I wish to go. I will avoid and outwit, except when I should listen to him.

And, while I enjoy turning the calendar's page and try to do better each year, I am not a big "resolution" guy. However, one idea I recently stumbled across struck me that, if it went "viral" or somehow planted itself in our collective consciousness, would change the world.

The idea is to think of two solutions before expressing a complaint. People are very free with criticism, yet stingy with remedies. This solves none of the world's many problems and, in fact, likely makes them worse. If folks turn their complaining energy into solving energy...man...what a difference it would make: A world of solvers instead of complainers...wow...powerful. This seems like as good a resolution as anything else I can think of...have a fantastic 2015!!!

Green Lights.

Stepping outside into the early morning fog, the moon peeked through a thin hole in the cloud layer and cast its warm, bright light onto my path. I was pleased by this. It felt deliberate, as if the stars had conspired to make a special day for me.

The rest of the morning was pretty typical. Fun conversations with the folks at my CrossFit box, my son nearly late for school, my daughter a little moody and my wife lying in bed awaiting her coffee were ordinary events and foretold of no fortuitous happenings. It was altogether a regular morning in my life, with exception of my moonlit driveway.

As the morning carried on, an odd sense of peace followed me as a small child wanting some attention. I turned my gaze to look upon the needy little sense of peace and realized that I was the small child and the peace was actually leading me. Standing as a sentinel, my peace guarded the soft spots in my heart from the various challengers placed in front of it by an uncertain world. This recognition was significant.

Understanding that my peace was always with me, protecting and guiding me through my confusion and frustration was quite liberating. Knowing that peace is always accessible is…well…peaceful. And this is good. We often live our lives at odds with our peace. Mudslides of doubt and sometimes avalanches of fear block the road to our peace.

Here, we miss the point. We think our peace is a destination to be arrived at and that we must travel a road to get there. This is wrong and in our search for this peace, we find everything but. We manufacture false worry. We forsake our own simple peace chasing ghosts. We construct a holographic life largely consisting of crap that doesn't matter. We do this to ourselves.

"Some things matter and some things don't. The difference is knowing the difference and then moving on from there." I stumbled across these words in an old journal of mine written many bright moons ago. I don't know if I understood the words then as I do now, but I am happy I wrote them, even if I was drunk at the time.

A clear understanding of what matters IS what matters. And on this day with a well-lit path, what mattered to me was clear. Some clarity is nice once in a while.

In the afternoon, I drove to the hardware store for some supplies for a project I am working on. While traveling the three mile trip, I hit every green light. As further evidence that my peace was telling me something, a particularly troublesome light by the highway which has always been my nemesis stayed green an inordinately long time allowing me to pass through. It was as if it knew I was coming and was happy for me. The green light had some cosmic dialogue with my peace and let me pass without even turning gas-pedal-mashing yellow. I held magic.

Some foggy morning moon-shine and a few green lights will make a guy feel ok about things. A couple of little things going your way establish a sense of trust and faith that things will work out. They always have and they always will and, in this recognition, lives peace. This is a good thing to remember.

Seagulls.

While sitting in my truck down at my Des Moines Marina, I was writing a different column in my notebook. As I pondered important words and profound thoughts, I watched some seagulls sitting on the old, abandoned "touch-n-go" dock rail. The birds were in constant motion cleaning and preening. It was a nice distraction from my important thoughts.

While observing the scratching, digging and primping gulls do their thing, I was content. I don't like seagulls that much and often think of them as "flying rats", as they are rodent-like in their propensity for annoying people and eating trash. Nonetheless, they were interesting.

Proving, once again, that inspiration can strike in some strange places, the birds delivered: As the gulls on the lower rail carried on with their very deliberate cleaning efforts, another bird on the higher crossbar over the deck released a big and bold dump directly onto the back of the bird below him. (It had to be male...) I chuckled, maybe because I am male...or juvenile...or both.

Either way...I wondered how the "victim" in the "assault" felt about this incident. During the few minutes I was watching these birds, I noticed that they were very intent about their cleaning. It seemed like their life's work. Having an overhead colleague suddenly destroy all that hard work would be a little frustrating, I suspect. The lower bird may have glanced up with a cross look. I can't be sure. Seagull expressions are hard to read.

Here is where the inspiration struck me: the seagulls are US. Our lives are an endless act of "cleaning": Dirty dishes return to the kitchen. Unexpected car problems soil our bank accounts. Kids need braces and casts and new shoes. The grass grows...and we must mow it again.

Just when we think we have life squared away "stuff" happens. And we have to clean it up. This happens forever. Life is not a clean business. It requires constant maintenance. Though, no matter how diligent we are in our endeavors to keep things tidy, it's still a mess. But, it's a beautiful mess.

Life for all of its confusing, frustrating, head-shaking, fist-shaking, confounding moments of "why me?" is worth it. The tough times make the good stuff better. We need the bad things to appreciate the good. It's an undeniable relationship.

Following the "episode", the lower bird just started over. He started cleaning again. He didn't squawk or scream about it. He didn't bow his head and hide in his wing. He went back to work. It was quite dignified.

So, like the seagull, when life unloads on us, we should simply get back to work and keep moving. Life is never perfect and it never will be, but it's still pretty great. We clean what we can and keep trying and smiling and cleaning some more. This is a solid recipe for a good and happy life...and not crapping on other people trying to clean their messes is important, too...

Wasted Time.

Last night, I had to make a drive that I did not want to make. Following another long day in an already long week, I was required to travel for three hours delivering my daughter to my lovely mother's home. I had to do this when all I really wanted to do was sit on my couch. I was less than thrilled.

During our trip, my little girl was happy. She loves her grandma. She especially loves when her brother is not there. She receives my mom's undivided attention and the doting and baking and loving suits her well. So, she was in a good mood and her joy pleases me.

On my solo return trip, following a brief chat and a hug from my mom, I traveled lightly. The traffic was light and so was my mood. I love road trips. I nestled into my seat and listened to whatever music I wanted. It was an unexpected, but welcome relief from my week's worries. I like it when this happens.

As my thoughts meandered through my wandering mind, I felt the clouds lift. Too often it seems, we tend to mire ourselves in the thick mud of life's challenges. The boiling cauldron of our problems seems to require constant stirring. And stir we do. We give vast amounts of attention to what is "wrong" with life.

On rare and precious occasions, in the steamy vapor of our boiling pot of problems, we smell what's working and what's right with our world. This is nice. In the midst of life's challenges lies some gold. Always, the gold is there. We spend too much effort and attention stirring our problems and overlook the gold in the pot. Sometimes, to see it, we simply need to avoid focusing on the negative stuff.

On a lonely stretch of highway, with bare pavement and shadows of moonlight through the trees, the radio gods delivered a gift. It came in the form of the Eagles' song "Wasted Time." I love this song. One line is especially potent to me. As I sang, loudly, with no one in my truck to complain about it, I waited for some of my favorite song lyrics: "...sometimes to keep it together...you've got to leave it alone..."

I love these words. On this day, on this road, they were perfect. As I set my wooden spoon on the counter and stopped stirring my problems, I saw the smiles of my friends and family. I saw the good things I already have. I saw the soft moments when life is right. And I have plenty.

When we take a break, take a breath or sometimes take a drink, the problems fade away into their proper place. When we "leave it alone", stop stirring and listen to the heart beat of our lives. We often find that it beats powerfully with feelings of peace and love and joy. These feelings sometimes hide in the bottom of the pan, but are always accessible, if we seek them and when we need them.

Arriving back home, with a tired mind and a happy heart, I finally made it to my couch. My problems lay on the highway's shoulder, replaced by fond memories and hopeful dreams. These things are much more fun to think about. I think I'm gonna leave the other stuff alone for a little while...

Compliance.

My son mowed the lawn after being asked one, single time. I did not have to cajole, bribe, beg or threaten. This is a new development. It felt like a parallel universe, one in which my kids comply with my directions without complaint, negotiation or irritation. They just do what I say. It's a nice place to be, if only for a brief visit.

I will not be getting ahead of myself here. Perhaps an anomalous shift in cosmic forces caused a once-in-a-lifetime alignment resulting in my son's compliance. If so, I will still take it. After asking/telling him in the morning of my expectation that he mow the lawn, I left it alone. I was hopeful, but realistic. In the late afternoon, I heard the unusual sound of a chore being done. The mower sang outside of our living room window and I was pleased.

In this life, I have learned to care the right amount. Not too much, but not too little. I have achieved a balance in my expectations. I do this as protection for both myself and these people I love. A crazy and angry person I would be without this perspective. I don't want to be either.

Nonetheless, some crazy and a little angry is not always bad. I can become very clear when I need to. I don't want to simply make noise. My minions understand when I am serious and they usually respond appropriately. Knowing when to wield my sword is the trick. I will flash it with a raise of my eyebrows. I will measure my words with a heavy sigh expressing what is not said. My kids don't want me mad. They seem to enjoy me slightly aggravated, but mad is no fun for anyone. I enjoy and use their fear as a wonderful tool to get some action from them.

The evolution of parenting is a slippery road. My kids change and I don't. Sometimes I don't recognize that they have changed and my communication lacks with this new person. They are constantly becoming new. They learn new things and think in different ways as they get older. I struggle to keep up despite their reminders and "encouragement." I think I will always be a little behind. And this I don't mind.

I want to linger in their youth. Their changes unnerve me and make me uncertain and nostalgic. I want them to stay little just a bit longer than they are willing to. I can't keep up, because I don't really want to. I enjoy living in the false dream of suspended time where they will always need me to care for them: a special time where my advice is welcome and a piggy-back ride is fun and not creepy.

Well, those days are gone and new days are here. As I try to catch up while clinging to the monkey bars wanting to stay back, my grip will fail. My kids will force me, through some yelling and tears, to move with them, which, as I ponder these things, is really where I want to be anyway...

Hand-raisers.

Every day, in every room, hands are raised. These hands climb from the uncertain pockets or desk tops to do the difficult, but important things. While many secure their sweaty palms firmly in place while deliberately avoiding eye contact with the challenges we face, a special few raise their hands and say, "I'll do it." These people are our heroes.

Many years ago when my now teenage son was in kindergarten, I stood at the end of the breezeway waiting for him to leave his classroom at the end of his school day. When the bell rang and doors opened, kids scurried down the path, eager to move on to their afternoon activities.

During this melee, a little girl dropped her notebook and her papers scattered across the concrete. While the other kids laughed or made a game out of jumping over her disaster, I saw my little son's big head strolling then stopping. He took off his back pack and began picking up papers. He "raised his hand" to help.

In this moment, I understood that for all the ways that this boy would drive me crazy, he was going to be ok. His character was strong and with his hand in the air, he would change the world. I was and remain proud. And his hand is still in the air.

Raising our hands is scary. We risk our peace and security and comfort. We become "responsible" for something. We stake our time and effort and reputations on outcomes that we have limited degrees of control over. Yet, we still try. The courageous and creative minds of our innovators and educators raise their hands and think and serve and give what they have to create a better world. We can all do this.

Life is a complicated business. Many challenges exist. We have projects to do and problems to solve. And we need sharp minds and big hearts to do this. This mission is a collective one and we need more hands raised. "All of us are smarter than any of us." We are better working together with uniquely fresh ideas and perspectives as we face our issues. We all have these things. And now is the time to use them. All of us have hands and hearts. Worthy of note is the fact that the beautiful consequence of raising our hands is that we elevate our hearts, too...

Courage.

This week's column was especially challenging to get a bead on. My original idea involved my family's dinner time discussion on "courage" and I was reminded of my son's second grade talent show performance that involved him demonstrating his deep karate prowess, while some rather pingy oriental music played in the background.

He tag-teamed the martial arts with another kid and as my son moved to the back of the stage to await the other "artist", he fell off. It was fast and looked a lot like a magic trick. Amidst the gasps and chuckles, he reached his seven year old hand to the stage deck, then the other hand came up and he climbed back on. He walked straight to the middle of the stage, tightened the orange belt on his dusty black gi and bowed his best karate bow to a stunned and packed elementary school gymnasium. It was the coolest thing anyone has ever done and there has never been a more proud dad in the history of dads.

While my son's courageous act was, in several ways, impressive, it paled in comparison to the fortitude expressed by my old college buddy, Johnny B. Johnny B. died this week after a long, brutal battle with brain cancer. His struggle was well-documented and his grace and strength and love for his family were truly inspiring.

Though I haven't seen or spoken to Johnny B. since our college days together, my profound sense of loss at his passing was undiminished by our distance. Some people stick with you. Some people are so remarkably alive that they should not die. Johnny B.'s death is the world's loss. He laughed easily and made everyone around him feel good. His humor and fantastic energy were contagious and he infected many people. He was, in a world of much unkindness, very simply, kind. He was the best this world can produce.

So, this week I have struggled to bridge the gap between my son's courage and Johnny B's. I have been torn between my pride in witnessing a wonderfully memorable personal moment and understanding that my friend will no longer be witnessing these terrific things. This sadness is more than a feeling. It is almost a taste. It is tangible. I am forced to think of other things when I ponder too long on his family and the incalculable loss they have suffered. It breaks my heart.

My conflict has not been in trying to compare my son's moment and Johnny B's death. They are incomparable. My conflict has been in whether or not they

170

belong on the same page. I suppose my conclusion has been that they do, because life does not have different pages. It is a single, joyously excruciating, working document, a scroll, with nothing as simple as a page turn to separate the good from the bad. It is one. And sometimes it is too short.

Other than this, I have experienced no illuminating epiphany concerning life other than to be tremendously grateful for mine. I am grateful for my family and friends. I am grateful for each day on this earth that I have been blessed with. I am grateful to have known Johnny B. and I will be forever. I am thankful for the opportunity, at least today, to have more moments. I am thankful for all of this and much, much more.

As I worry a little bit about whether or not expressing my gratitude for my life in the wake of Johnny B's death is appropriate, I think that it is. Johnny B. was a giving, caring, laughing lover of life and I think he wouldn't mind too much. It's just the kind of guy he was.

Mark Twain said, "Live so that when you die, even the undertaker will be sorry." Well, this week, the undertaker is sorry.

Vuvuzelas and Donuts

Well, my eleven year old son, Aden, made it through another week. But not by much. It was only by the thinnest of margins and perhaps some divine intervention that allowed this to happen. He is far more confident about his survival than he should be. His vuvuzela might very well bring a sad end to this young boy. I should note, for those fortunate enough to not know, that the vuvuzela is an annoying plastic horn and it was the causal factor in me having watched most of the World Cup games last summer with the sound muted.

Aden's already dubious fate took another step in the wrong direction Sunday as I was outside working on a project for my wife that involved me missing some of my beloved/behated Seahawks game. My relationship with my home team is complicated, but I always watch them, at least until I just can't. In ways unforeseen to me, I am much like my own Dad.

As a kid, during the Seahawk season, we had the cleanest garage on the block. This was because my Dad's tolerance for the emotional roller coaster that is being a fan of this team was low. Mine is low as well. Usually after the first quarter, when it became clear that they were sucking and to avoid three more hours of pain, my Dad stopped watching. He didn't stop swearing. He just did it in the garage as he was rearranging the things that he had rearranged the previous Sunday and swept the already clean floor. It was a form of therapy for him. I, come most Sunday afternoons, find myself looking for similar distractions. Fortunately, my wife is always available to offer them. She's good in this way, maybe too good sometimes.

So, last Sunday, as I was working on the aforementioned project and deep in thought, my son snuck up behind me and blasted his vuvuzela horn. I jumped and swore at him and though I have never actually weighed a Makita worm drive circular saw, I'm sure it would have hurt had I clobbered him with it as I, very seriously, considered for a moment. He grinned devilishly and went back in the house. He is intimately familiar with my potential to do him harm and made a rare wise choice to get away from my strike zone post-haste.

Two days later, as I sat on the couch reading with my daughter, he again snuck around the corner and laid on the horn. My seven year old and I both jumped and one of us screamed. I won't reveal who it was, but I will say that it was pretty manly as far as screams go.

172

Again, the little drive-by tooter escaped any serious consequence besides some more swearing and the usual threats. The kid lives on the razor's edge and nothing good exists on either side of it or in the middle for that matter. I don't understand why he likes it there, but apparently he does.

Well, as luck or fate would have it, the tides turned on this marauding little hit-and-run artist. I have a notoriously short memory. Fortunately or unfortunately, my daughter has a long one and as my son was in the shower the other morning before school, she walked up to me with the vuvuzela in her pretty little hand and looked at the bathroom door. I knew what I had to do.

I stalked carefully to the door and silently opened it, then peeked to make sure he was unaware. Seeing that he had shampoo in his hair and was talking to himself, I knew he was indeed quite unaware. I stuck the horn in the shower stall and blew. I blew like it was my last breath. I blew hard and strong. The sweet blast could be heard by my neighbors and my sleepy, wet, warm boy was now very awake. I saw him jolt and stumble. He made some strange noises and then was silent. Even the most inviolate assailant understands that when true justice strikes, it's best just to take it. He took it and I was proud.

Perhaps the most disturbing element of this episode was my daughter's cold, satisfied eyes. This girl has some devious potential that I feel will trump my son's goofy, mischievous prankster ways by miles. I have some concerns, deep and real concerns about my future. This girl is gonna make the vuvuzela seem like a church bell and I'd better stay on the good side of this little time bomb. In fact, I think I'll go buy her a donut now. She likes donuts.

Left-hand turns.

While rifling through an old wallet the other day, I found a jewel. This wonderful little gem was tucked in a far corner of the broken zipper pocket. I remember replacing this wallet after the Velcro croaked. (Yes, I still have a Velcro wallet…and I always will…) I was shocked that this treasure did not make the transition to my new wallet. Something must have gone wrong…or I just didn't see it.

My secret little jewel is an old newspaper clipping. It may have been in an Ann Lander's column. On the worn and yellowed little slip is a quote that I like and carried around as a reminder of something good to remember. Here it is:

"I have come to the frightening conclusion that I am the decisive element in the classroom. It is my personal approach that creates the climate. It is my daily mood that makes the weather. I possess tremendous power to make life miserable or joyous. I can be a tool of torture or an instrument of inspiration. I can humiliate or humor, hurt or heal. In all situations, it is my response that decides whether a crisis is escalated or de-escalated, and a person is humanized or de-humanized."
–Haim G. Ginott

I believe I was in college when these words struck me. Though I was very far from teaching anyone anything, I liked the message. I still like the message and I view the world as a "classroom". I like the idea of personal responsibility and I like the idea that we can impact other people's lives. I also like that we can CHOOSE how we impact these lives. This has been a powerful message for me and I'm glad I got it young.

Being a typically flawed human being, my intention of living by these words has hit some speed bumps. I have "tortured" and "hurt" people in moments of haste and indifference. I have "escalated" crisis through my own fears or doubts. I willingly cop to these facts. I can do this, because I have also been good and done good things. We are a complicated, yet simple species.

My son just got his learner's permit to drive. Cruising around in the passenger seat of my truck trying my best to be my best, the lessons from my old, crusty newspaper clipping may have saved my boy some later-in-life counseling. After he turned directly in front of a car heading down the hill towards us, I had a choice. I could "hurt or heal" or "humanize or dehumanize". I wanted to scream and tell him to pull over and frankly, in my fright, I kind of wanted to punch him.

I did none of these things. I said, "That was a close one. OK, so…umm…don't turn in front of other cars." That was it. I knew he was rattled and I also knew that, in that moment, I had the power to really rattle him or play it off, "escalate or de-escalate". Gratefully, I played it off, which was no small feat for me. I was good when my son needed me to be good. We kept driving without further incident.

The lessons we learn throughout the living of our lives are many. It is important to embrace the ones which make us better. We have a duty to be better, for ourselves and for our world…and especially for a fifteen year old kid just trying to figure out a left-hand turn…

Polished.

Yesterday was a long day. It was a day filled with stress, emotion, busyness that goes nowhere, and feelings of lack and fear. These days happen. Having had enough of them, I understand that they pass. Knowing this doesn't make them fun, but does allow for a little hope. And a little hope is all we need some days...

My hope yesterday came in the form of a lively and rich conversation with one of my smart and thoughtful CrossFit members. Sometimes a conversation that takes one's mind off of auto-pilot and requires a little effort expands us. It makes us bigger and reminds us through our participation that we are already bigger and capable of big thoughts in a world that sometimes tries to shrink us to its size.

Upon my arrival home from a long day, I entered my living room to witness BOTH of my kids doing their homework on the couch. Their heads were down in focused effort as they greeted me with the obligatory, "hey, dad".

Not wanting to disrupt this lotto moment, I began quietly preparing dinner. Earlier in the day, I had marinated some pork chops, so I stepped out on our deck to put them on the grill. It was cold so I had my heavy coat on. In my pocket, I had Jimmy Buffett playing on my phone helping to keep me warm.

As I fed the dogs and flipped pork chops, my life began to feel pretty good again. Then, as I looked through the kitchen window from the deck, I saw my son chopping broccoli. This is significant in that I only had to ask him once. Normally, a task like chopping broccoli would require at least three "asks" followed by a threat...minimum. Sooo....this was nice to see.

Through the same window, at the same time, I saw my daughter practicing piano. I could only see her head over the pony wall upstairs where the piano sits, but that was all I needed. In one single frame, I had my son doing something I requested and my daughter doing something she should, without request. It was the moment when my feet came back to the ground and my world felt as perfect as it ever gets.

In life, we spend a lot of time and effort in work and worry polishing things. We dote and dance and stress and strive for things to be better. For all our efforts at scrubbing and shining, some days are just going to be dull.

Life is an untidy business. And I kind of like it that way...This morning as I took my dogs outside for their constitutionals, I stood in the darkness and fog and thought about my long-lost dad and felt like crying. Reflecting on this moment I realize that, though they may lack some of the luster we think we'd prefer, these soft, unclean moments with our soul exposed and our truth clear contain things more valuable than shine...

Lightbulbs.

A couple of days ago, I had the privilege of speaking to some 8th graders at Pacific Middle School in Des Moines, WA. My presentation was a part of my Rotary Club's vocational program series. I spoke about my path to business ownership and my day-to-day duties, what I like and don't like and the importance of doing both to have a successful business.

While preparing for my chat, besides feeling that I am probably the worst example of how to get anything done, I wanted to say something more than simply discussing the pretty mundane details of my days. I wanted to leave them a little inspired and a little hopeful.

Junior high is probably the worst years in a kid's life, at least mine were. Rife with all of the transitional challenges of growing up, these years are a boiling cauldron of fears, insecurities and uncertainties. They are miserable in ways that the kids suffering through them don't yet understand, thankfully.

During my speech, I enthusiastically chronicled my own "road less traveled" path to today. I passionately spoke of my quest for some level of fulfillment and my need to move forward which often involved taking risks. I, as much as anything, wanted to communicate that it really doesn't matter what anyone one does, as long as it makes them happy. Of course, I ruled out drug lord and hobo as potential employment options, but it was pretty wide open from there.

"Everyone is a genius. But if you judge a fish by its ability to climb a tree, it will spend its life believing it is stupid." –Albert Einstein

I referenced this quote as a foundational principle necessary to finding a proper career path. Self-belief and trusting that little voice, which knows the truth, is vital to a good life. Understanding that we already have what we need to succeed is an important recognition. Some of us come to this late and some of us don't ever come to this. As kids, it is beautiful thing to know. I wish more people knew this.

Another quote I mentioned (I use a lot of quotes, because I think they make me sound smarter than I really am) was Thomas Edison's: "I've not failed. I've just found 1,000 ways how not to build a light bulb." I used this to illustrate that failure is important to finding success. We learn and we grow and we try again. This is life. Mistakes happen. Corrections happen. Forever this pattern continues. Being afraid of a making a mistake is perhaps the most dastardly, limiting and diabolical fear we possess. We were born to screw up. It's what we do. So what? Get better. Be better. Learn from it. Move on.

While reflecting on the things I said to these kids and the things I didn't say, I came to a remembered realization that life is built in a moment: a simple moment when we, as kids or grown ups, "get it". We understand where we belong and begin our journey to getting there. My own path is worn with ruts and potholes and deep, soggy puddles of bad choices and magnificent screw ups. My life is pretty normal.

Through my mistakes, I have learned many ways how not to build a light bulb. Sometime the contrary truth is more powerful than getting it right the first time. Failing leaves an imprint that is often unforgettable, but rarely unforgivable.

"Don't ask yourself what the world needs. Ask yourself what makes you come alive. And then go and do that. Because what the world needs is people who have come alive."

This was my last pilfered bit of insight. I don't know who said it, but whoever it was truly is a genius to me. This is a liberating idea. It frees one to explore the infinite ways to construct a light bulb or a life and truly being alive is the best thing there is.

As my own search for illumination continues, I will keep tinkering and changing and fixing and trying, with a hope that the light will shine. This is living. And it's good.

Lives.

While taking an unexpected side trip up to Capitol Hill in Seattle the other night, I recognized many old landmarks that I hadn't seen in several years. As a little kid, my earliest memories involve riding in the car with my Dad on these streets while visiting my baby brother in the hospital. I always enjoyed these trips. I looked forward to seeing my Mom and brother and cruising around with my Dad. It was a special time. My Dad and I would always eat a late dinner at Burger King on our way home. As I drive by BK today, the smell of a Whopper still reminds me of this time in my life.

Following our little unplanned excursion, my wife and I drove home. Trekking back through the same streets that were so long ago traveled by my Dad and I, I thought about the many different lives we lead during a single lifetime. Visiting my Mom and brother as a child is a very distinct life to me. It sits alone in my memory and remains a guardian to this age. A high fence has been constructed around this memory isolating it from other memories, thereby, preserving it.

It is hard to reconcile the fact that I am the same person today that I was when I lived some of my other lives. Violations bordering on atrocities were committed by the same shell of skin and bones typing these words. Magnificent stupidity was common place. I am not proud, but that was a different life. It wasn't me...really...I'm better than that...really...

Each single life involves a certain schizophrenic evolution. We must try on different shoes, be different people and wander for a bit before we can settle in. I have worn different shoes and hats and wandered. For this, I am grateful. I harbor a tremendous fear of not living. I am not afraid of dying. But, I am afraid of NOT trying to have my greatest life, as defined and designed by ME. So, with this in mind, I will enter the next personality phase with a grin and a hope that in the subsequent years I can feel better about these years than I do about some others. There were some rough ones.

As I glance over at my nine year old daughter, I cannot help but smile. She got braces today. Braces are a big deal. They signify that a new age is coming. They represent a change. She is entering a new life of her own. And, by extension, so am I. I hope the years are kind, though, I suspect they will not be. I am going to be in it deep with this little firecracker. I can only hope to conjure up some of my other lives to lend a hand, some were wiser than I feel right now and I'm going to need all the help I can get...and I will be very pleased if my memories of this time one day rest as fondly in my heart as the evenings I spent riding shotgun with my Dad visiting my brother and waiting for my cheeseburger...

Vacuum.

Around 11 o'clock last night I was awoken by a high-pitched wail shattering any appropriate peace in the neighborhood. I was thinking it might be some weird car or house alarm. The sound was steady and out of place. My sleepy mind could not imagine what could make this annoying noise at this unfortunate hour...until it did: my son.

I threw on some shorts and ran out the front door, jerked the plug from our outside electrical socket and quieted the devil vacuum that my son was using to clean his car...at 11 o'clock at night. I then unleashed a string of loud and creative profanity as I grabbed the offending device from his startled hand. My yelling at him may have been more disruptive than the vacuum, but I was mad. His late-night project was over, as was my restful slumber. I crawled back into bed, very awake with anger. That was then...

This morning I made my boy a cinnamon roll for breakfast. I heated and buttered it with great care and I peeled him an orange. Last night's venom was long forgotten. I think this is how life works. We get mad and then we sleep and forgive. No residual impacts lingered this morning between my son and I, at least as far as I could tell. Though I suspect he won't be doing much late night vacuuming any time soon, which is fine by me.

The lesson I see here is that sometimes things matter very much, then don't. Nothing lasts except the things we want to last. I don't want to be mad at my son, so it couldn't last. I want to love him and this always rises, even when he does something stupid. With this insight, especially in an increasing sensitive and self-critical world, we can let ourselves off the hook. It's ok to get frustrated and reactive on occasion. Sometimes events warrant this response. It's human and humans are naturally irrational, hasty and imperfect. It's just the way it is and we are.

So, with last night's debacle now living only in memory, I move on with a story. The interesting stories of our lives are the ones when things didn't work out perfectly. We laugh and shake our heads and remember fondly events that, at the time, shook us. Again, this is just more interesting than the boring, mundane, colorless moments when everything works out right. Of these stories our lives are made and perhaps by appreciating the truth and beauty in our imperfections we can liberate ourselves from debilitating and unfun idea that we need to be perfect...and this is perfect...

Untethered.

Last night I took my first "actual" shower in seven days. My son and I spent a few days traveling around the state, fishing, eating beef jerky and bathing in the lakes and rivers on our path. It was great. We were untethered and unshaven and unconcerned. During our trip, I came to one glaring conclusion: I don't vacation enough.

Through four simple days of driving the back roads, we reconnected to some of our human roots, as father and son and fellow wanderers of this earth. These connections are important. The road has a special way of connecting us to these things. Exploring the world through a windshield provides a unique perspective. Having complete sanction of when and where we stop is powerful and liberating. It reminds us of what it feels like to truly be FREE.

In a life encumbered by "stuff to do", this is an important thing to remember. We ARE free. We can choose how our time is spent. It is easy to create imaginary cages where we are bound by duty to do what we don't want to do. But, these cages are illusions. Certainly, we must work and provide and contribute to the commerce of our households, but we don't have to do this in a cage. We can choose to open our cell door any time we want. This can occur through a bold act of revolt and changing our world or we can simply change our minds. Both work.

A road trip with a beloved fifteen year old boy is a great way to change a mind. Potential and possibility live in the tar and gravel two-laners spidering in all directions of our great country. Like a country song, the tires hum and the wind blows through the open windows with smells of sage and pine and lake grasses. Worries evaporate in our slip-stream and we get lighter. Burdens are removed and replaced with the truth that we already have it all.

I don't vacation enough. Because of this, I forget these things. I get tense and uncertain and crabby. My illusory burdens drive my life. I begin to feel like passenger in my life, instead of the conductor. A relatively unglamorous, brief, but beautiful excursion shifted me back into the driver's seat. I like being there. It's where we all belong.

As I sit with a cup of coffee on my couch planning my day, my mind looks back to a moment standing by the shoreline of a mountain lake with my son by my side and my fishing pole in my hand. As the sun began to set over the trees and shimmered off the cool, glassy water, I believed in my son and God and myself.

And I knew that I have all that I need. We all have all that we need. We just need to remember this.

Unsentimental.

Well, the kids are back at school. This event seems to be lacking some of the significance of years past. I'm not sure why. I don't feel jaded or like I'm becoming unsentimental about these things. But, I just don't really care that much that they're in new classes with new teachers, learning new things. I kind-of care, but am not wrapped up in it. I am happy they're out of the house. I'm happy they have some structure and get to see their friends each day. But, all-in-all, I'm pretty underwhelmed by all the to-do.

Historically, the first day of school provokes feelings of nostalgia and near-weepy sentiments about the passing of time and my kids growing up and my slow-crawl to the grave. This year I just don't feel it. This is neither good nor bad. It just is.

I guess it feels like life. Time passes and we feel and don't feel and care and don't care and do and don't do. Some days we drive the boat and some days we simply drift in the current and watch the water flow around the rocks and eddys. Some days we make the weather and some days we sit in our lounge chairs and observe it.

As the world spins madly through the hours and minutes and years of our lives, sometimes we must step off the ride. Occasionally, it is necessary to let it spin without us. Being a non-participant allows us to just check it out, without the urgency to contribute. In these moments, our paths become more clear and our purpose more inspiring.

While it seems a bit odd that I have chosen a relatively significant time to sit on the bench and catch my breath before getting back in the game, but maybe we don't pick this time. Maybe this time picks us. Perhaps some cosmic clairvoyant sense measures these things and picks our time to ride the pine. I'm not sure what the metrics are which determine when we need to take a break, but when I get to sit for a few minutes, it sure feels right.

So, this morning I will sit and watch. I will do this after I wake my son, yell at him to get out of the shower, remind him to bring the stuff he is trying to forget. I will wake my daughter, make her breakfast, get yelled at by her for reasons I will likely never understand, then take her to school, wish her a wonderful day and tell her I love her.

I guess that as the world spins we must spin with it. Our little intermissions are allowed only in our minds. We are duty-bound to live our lives. Each day.

And, all things considered, this is not such a bad thing. Life is a pretty fun game to play...

Surrender.

With the cool mist of an early August morning breaking the sleepy grip of my night's rest, I see my world in my yard and understand that it's a good place to be. As the sun begins to crack through the tree tops to my east, a sense of possibility and potential shines on the swing set sitting quietly on my lawn. An empty swing with rusty chains and a dew-covered seat is a good reminder that I have much. I have important things.

Drinking my coffee, gazing at the dry grass and flowers in bloom, I take stock of my life. As my dogs wander through the yard, peeing of every shrub and fixture, I only feel the good things this morning. The worries of bedtime and stresses of yesterday have been erased and replaced with a new dawn. It's fun when this happens: a simple moment of peace and contentment.

While waiting for my coffee to brew, I stood in my living room looking out the window at water and trees and sun-capped mountains. My daughter slept on the couch and I looked at her, too. Snuggled in her favorite purple blanket, her sleepy peace was reassuring. She's getting too big for the little couch she was sleeping on, but her face in slumber was as it has always been. And it has always brought me comfort.

Through the hustle and bustle of the business of life, these moments are sometimes hard to shake from the tree. Distractions distract and urgency is urgent. With much to do, plan, think and be, it's easy to miss a morning of profound and necessary quiet. It's important at these times to surrender. To let go and just let the good feelings be. In the race to arrive at a "better" place, these mornings are easy to miss, but when we don't miss them, we see that they are the "better" place and we already live here. This is worthy of some regard...

Weeds.

The other day I picked the weeds which live in the sidewalk in front of my wife's office. I hate these weeds. I hate the weeds that clutter the sidewalk more than I hate picking them. And I don't like picking them much at all.

Picking weeds from the sidewalk cracks is a crappy job, however the results are satisfying. At least, they are to me. I have what some might classify as a "perversion" about untidy weed growth. I am largely untidy throughout much of my life, but I cannot tolerate weeds in a flower bed or an untrimmed lawn. It makes me uneasy and slightly annoyed in a place that is rarely revealed. It is my place and my perversion and since I'm the one doing the weed-picking anyway, it shouldn't matter too much to anyone else that it exists at all.

Landscaping is my therapy. My most important and profound thoughts sprout while out of doors, in motion. I have solved a lot of problems walking behind a lawnmower. I think more clearly with spongy earplugs muffling the noise of my world. I meditate and ponder and mull over my life and what it all means.

My most significant insight occurred several years ago when I realized that I will never really KNOW anything. I was weed-wacking at the time. My understanding involved understanding that I will never understand. And that answers don't exist that are as sharp and clean as a freshly edged curb line.

I found, and still find, this idea liberating. It frees me from the disappointment of my ignorance about things. As more days pass on my life's calendar, I don't really think anyone else knows that much either. Lots of people try to fake it and speak with great certainty about stuff they don't know a damn thing about. I find this humorous and unfortunate in the same breath.

"If people ever find out what's really important in life, there will be a shortage of fishing poles."- Sign in a Northwoods bait shop.

This is as true a truth I have ever witnessed and I will take it as perhaps the only one I will ever see. Life confounds and contradicts and puzzles. Many truths are true, even contrary ones, but I claim this one for myself.

During my weed-picking meditation, I considered whether maybe some parallels could be drawn between the weeds which grow in the sidewalk and other things in life. We see them without the clear recognition that we don't like them, but we don't like them anyway. They trouble us in ways and in places that we feel more than we see. They burden us and undermine us and are insidious little creatures of discomfort. This sense is intuitive and sometimes illogical, but also true, and can serve to release us if we acknowledge it and act.

All matters may not be as simple as picking weeds from the sidewalk, but most are not that complicated either. We know them as we feel them. Seeing them is the trick, but picking the little devils is where the magic is made.

"Everything has a time and we have time for everything" –Mosca, borderline crazy man in Puerto Viejo, Costa Rica, 1994.

This is a second truth I just remembered. It's now time to finish picking some weeds...or begin...

An Ordinary Sunday Morning.

On an ordinary Sunday morning with a late spring sun peeking through the high clouds, my buddy Dave and his wife and young son were driving through the sweet sage and early corn-sprouted fields of eastern Washington. They were making a store run for coffee and beer and water for our holiday weekend camping crew. On the lightly travelled two-lane country road, they were making a regular trip on a regular morning; a morning like many other mornings.

Ahead in the distance, an anomaly broke the ordinary scene: the road was littered with debris and a woman was walking around frantically and talking on her phone. Approaching the site, it was clear that an accident had happened. Dave stopped the car. In speaking with the woman, it was discovered that the other vehicle had careened into an irrigation canal.

Seeing the SUV in the water and no passengers in the water, it was clear that people were still in the car. Dave jumped in and swam to the back of the vehicle and he heard voices, including a child's scream. In the frigid and swift current, Dave dove beneath the water to try to unlock the back hatch. He tried to unlock doors and as the car was still barely afloat, but air was present, he debated busting out a window and whether or not doing so might compromise the already delicate buoyancy and cause the car to sink faster.

Eventually, emergency vehicles arrived and a lot of talking happened. Frustrated by the lack of action, Dave got in the water again, this time with a hook and cable and tried to attach the car to the line. Again, in the cold, quick current with trained personnel standing on the banks of the canal, Dave dove under the water and searched for a secure hold. He found what he could and swam to shore. He was shaken and bleeding from crawling around the sharp, bent metal in the dark water. He did the best he could. In a moment he was unprepared for, he acted. He was just going to the store when circumstances called him to act and he did.

Four people died: a mother, a father, and their two children aged three and seven.

Obviously, this was the worst possible outcome and against all the hopes and wishes and prayers, it came true. And this idea is at the core of any insight I have gained as the result of this tragedy. Sometimes, in spite of our best efforts and our highest hopes, our greatest wishes and most sincere prayers, bad things happen.

Despite his will and his strength and his blood, Dave could not save those people. He just couldn't. A bad thing happened. On an ordinary Sunday morning in the soft fields and cold water off of a tar and gravel country back road, a bad thing happened. Through fate or folly, bad things happen.

This is little or no solace the families left behind or to my friend who dove in the water and heard the voices. I suspect he will hear those voices forever. My only condolence and the only redeeming element in the circumstances for him that I can see is that he ACTED. While many others stood on the safe shoreline and waited for someone else to DO IT, he DID IT. This is not a small thing. This is a big thing and in fact, might be the biggest thing there is. And for this, I am more proud of my friend than my words can express.

Life happens and bad things happen. When they do, choices are made and the most significant choice is whether or not to act. I respectfully submit that in our actions we are revealed. Outcomes are sometimes unfair, unjust and make no logical sense, but happen just the same.

As they always do, tragedies force us to face the real world where the bad things happen. In doing so, a greater awareness of our own fickle mortality stares us down. Oddly, in these hollow, dark eyes we see light. This light is changes us. We see the value of a sunrise and a cheeseburger and a blade of grass. We see more and this more is truth. We see life for what it is. And it is beautiful.

Uneventful.

I cleaned my kitchen this morning. I did this while warming some cinnamon rolls in the oven for my kids to enjoy on a cool and drizzly morning. Pandora radio played as I scrubbed some pots and pans and wiped down the counters. I performed some bathroom monitoring duties to ensure no conflicts regarding this valuable space. My beautiful offspring came down stairs well-coifed and ready for their days. After breakfast, my son drove himself to high school and I drove my daughter her middle school. All in all, it was a pretty typical, uneventful morning. Just the way I like it.

In looking back on my early days, I remember sitting at our kitchen table eating my breakfast cereal as my dad drank his coffee while working on a crossword puzzle and KJR radio played. After finishing my Count Chocula, I would stroll into the living room and position myself and favorite blanket over a heat register and watch cartoons. My dad would come into the living room to put his work boots on before leaving the house. This ritual was a staple of my days for many years and it's what I remember most and what I love remembering best.

In my life I have seen some fantastic places and visited some exotic lands full of new and beautiful experiences. In doing these things, I have realized that I like home better. I like my family better. I like soft mornings listening to music and loving my kids better.

It's easy in the busy, stressful, challenge-laden lives many of us live to look for an escape. We look forward to a big vacation or a big change with grand hopes that it will provide some relief. There's a tendency, I think, to believe more in explosions and events as the path to joy than the mundane dailies. I believe we miss something with these thoughts. We can overlook our days. And we have some good ones. These days pass and we will miss them when they're gone.

In examining the days of my life, I am always warmed by the simple ones; breakfast with my dad, playing cribbage with my son and buddies, eating ice cream with my daughter, sharing a couch with my wife. These wonderful things happen every single day.

While I enjoy a vacation or event as much as the next guy, I always look forward to coming home and mowing my lawn or helping my kids with some homework. These are the days of our lives. They are finite and they are precious and they are worthy of regard. There is much beauty in the simple and real moments of our days. The non-event IS the event. The ordinary IS the extraordinary and when we look back on the pages of our lives, I think we will know this as truth...OR we can accept this as truth now and enjoy each day a little bit more with this understanding...

Fish Farts.

"I have seen the fish fart underwater before…and watched the bubbles rise…" I have no idea what this means. My dad uttered this phrase countless times as I was growing up and I never knew what it meant. He would look very profound and philosophical when he said it, so I took it to be a collection of weighty words too heavy for my young mind.

Now that I am older, I still have no clue what in the hell it means. Nonetheless, my ignorance did not prevent me from positioning a wise and thoughtful look upon my own face as I dazzled my son with these same words.

My thirteen year old son, Aden, furrowed his brow, shook his head and walked away. He gave me a rather confused, if not outright contemptuous, look as he left me standing in the dining room being awesome. His "look" is a pretty common one and I fear that it is no longer "a" look, but is becoming just how he looks. But, maybe he just looks that way around me.

While I remain puzzled about the meaning behind my dad's words, what is more mysterious to me is why I chose to repeat them. I never understood them and still don't. As I ponder this riddle, my only explanation is that "I had to." My dad made me. He framed me and shaped me and I am a product of his "tutelage."

Often this does not make me too happy. My dad was a flawed man. He was stubborn and impatient and sometimes unhappy. He was hasty and intolerant. I remember these things when I find myself being stubborn and impatient and many more things that I am not proud of. It is easy for me to find things to feel bad about and we all have plenty. However, as we often get our parents' less desirable traits. We also get the good ones.

My dad was funny in his own, sometimes unfunny, way. My friends and family will certainly attest that my funniness is usually not really that funny. This doesn't matter to me. Like my dad, I am often my own best audience. I can amuse myself pretty easily. Also, like my dad, I enjoy kids and play and "Smokey and the Bandit." I like a good steak and a beer with my buddies. I like cutting and splitting wood and fishing. My dad gave me these things, too.

My dad gave me many things and now I am giving my son many things. He will curse me for some and bless me for others and I have no control over what he takes and/or values. He is his own man and he's a good one.

But, in the years ahead (many years ahead, I hope), when I overhear him repeat my dad's words to his son and looks at me in disbelief that these words actually fell out of his mouth, I will simply shrug my shoulders and give him a compassionate smile that says, "I know, buddy, I couldn't help it either...blame Grandpa..."

Mondays and Fridays.

"I think it's kind of mean that Monday is so far from Friday, but Friday is so close to Monday." –My eleven year old daughter, Helena.

These simple, yet astute, words made me turn my head in a discount double-check maneuver with a "what did you just say?" look on my face. When the dim bulb of my awareness finally lit in recognition that these were some interesting words, I was surprised and proud.

I was surprised first, because I had never considered the Friday/Monday relationship in this way. I was surprised second, because my daughter was the one who surprised me this this idea. I was proud that I was surprised.

On a Sunday night while already lamenting the following morning, my little girl said these profound words. Most of the free world shares this sentiment on a Sunday night. Songs have been written about Mondays, not kind ones, and a collective lack of enthusiasm surrounds this day. Mondays really do feel mean sometimes. I get it.

My daughter surprised me with her words mostly because it was a new way of surprising me. During her years on this earth, beginning with day one, she has surprised me: She has surprised me about the differences between little boys and little girls. (Besides the obvious one…) She has surprised me with her independence and strength. She has surprised me with her personal development in every way, every step of the way. Mainly, she has surprised me with the understanding of how much a father can love a daughter.

With this in mind, perhaps I should not have been surprised. She has been surprising me for a long time. However, this was a bit different. I could actually relate to her statement in a new way. It was an intellectual understanding, not an emotional one or one of perspective. This is new.

Now, the "mouths of babes" have a history of revealing truths, often unintentionally. The distinction here is that my girl "got it". She knew what she was saying and as pedestrian as the idea may seem, to me, having experienced every step of her evolution, I know this is different and significant.

I'm not sure if I should be happy or scared that my eleven year old daughter is inching closer to being my intellectual equal. She is a kid. I am a full-grown, well-read, experienced-in-the-ways-of-the-world, educated American man. She is a little girl. But, she's also more. And this is the part that will challenge me.

Well, sometimes there is nothing to be done. So, I will steel myself and my self-esteem for the inevitable changing of the guard. I will prepare myself to ask my daughter questions that I don't know the answers to, but she does. I will pass her the torch of whatever brightness I possess. And I will take the light from her torch to brighten my own. I will do all of this with pride and dignity...after all...I lit her damn torch in the first place!!!

No chicks.

I began last week with a sense of trepidation, but also opportunity. My wife was leaving town for a few days and I was being left to care for our kids. Solo. Well, I've been doing this for a while, so I wasn't too concerned, but since my daughter recently seems to be migrating closer to the womb than further away, I was a little worried. Her "mommy-love" has resulted in my becoming a bit of an outcast, except when she wants me to serve her. To face this challenge I, in my typical glass-half-full fashion, framed my wife's absence as an opportunity to connect with my girl, though I knew that this connection would likely involve some yelling and probably some tears.

As luck would have it, the benevolent gods intervened and in a rare, but not unwelcome act of mercy, delivered a savior: my mom. On a sunny Saturday morning, my angel of a mother scooped up my little girl and carried her away for a five day vacation filled with the good stuff that only grandmas can provide. This development left the boys home alone.

This does not happen very often. On a daily basis, we stand as easy targets for our dominant women to steamroll. Our more mellow natures get bulldozed by the intensity and volume of our ladies. We share this position at the back of the line in our home. We suffer in silence, but not alone.

Now, this golden chance to be the true masters of our domain was upon us!!! What were we to do??? Short answer: whatever the hell we want!!! (This is my quoted response to my son asking the question, "What are we gonna do?") And that's exactly what we did.

We walked to the Farmer's Market. We ate crappy food. We sat around on separate couches and watched bad TV. We went to the movies. We did a little yard work. Then, we went golfing. We ate more crappy food and watched more TV sitting on our designated couches. We were at peace in a peaceful home. And it was nice.

Too infrequently do I get the chance to just "hang out" with my son. He is fourteen and has his own program which, as far as I can tell, mainly involves playing video games and cruising around town on his longboard eating ice cream sandwiches. He has these things mastered. Another task he has become quite proficient at is avoiding any work I ask him to do. Here, he really excels, too.

Last weekend, without any outside schedule makers dictating our obligations, we had a chance to find some common ground or common couches, as it were. And it was awesome. We laughed and didn't yell very much, with the notable exception being his frustration while golfing, which doesn't really count, because, to my understanding, you're supposed to yell after shanking yet another drive. I think it's in the rules. Lots of swearing is also required.

It was really nice connecting with this man-child who is rapidly becoming more man than child. He's not only a good kid, he's a good guy. Being a good guy is an important attribute, if not the most important. It felt great to be reminded that my son is a good guy. As a dad, I spend a lot of time being a dad and not as much time being a pal. We were just pals. I didn't sweat him for leaving his socks on the living room floor, maybe because they were next to mine...but no conflicts distracted us from enjoying our time together. We hung out as buddies and it was awesome.

Well, that ship has sailed. The girls are now home and back to forcing me outside to fake being busy in the yard and my son has sequestered himself in his room. But, it was good while it lasted. When detailing our adventures with my wife, she smiled and shook her head in awe at our lack of productivity. Well, rather than try to explain, I will just chalk this up as another Mars-Venus thing. I can share this page of my life with my son and, with a knowing nod to this marvelous boy, understand that it was pretty cool.

No man's land.

Firmly nestled in the no man's land between the Christmas and New Year holidays, I ponder the year past and the year ahead. While polishing off the last of the Christmas cookies and peanut butter balls, I look forward to turning the page on what was and optimistically craft promises to complete last year's unfinished work next year. I enjoy this time. I like a page turn.

Whoever set up the calendar was a genius. Allowing for this little neutral time in between holidays was a good move. We need a couple of days to decompress from the Christmas craziness. We also need to tighten the bow on last year's business before shutting it away for good. It is during this brief purgatory that we are our most hopeful. Resolutions to do and be better, eat healthier, exercise more, work harder, be more thoughtful partners and parents inspire us. This hope is alive and as we enjoy leftover turkey and ham sandwiches with stuffing and gravy, we KNOW that next year will be "the one". This is a good time.

With a calm certainty, we anticipate a new future, filled with stuff we don't have. More money, more time, greater joy and career fulfillment await us. When the clock strikes 12, we will be different in the ways we want to be different. Sometimes this holds true, sometimes not, but this doesn't matter to us right now. What matters is the possibility.

The belief in possibility is probably the most valuable of human beliefs. We (usually) maintain an unwavering faith that life, as good as it may or may not be, will "get" better. Here is where we stumble sometimes. Life doesn't "get" better. Life is "made" better. Action is required. Doing something different is required. Movement is necessary to move. So, while making my annual list of dreams and goals, I am including some actual action in the process. A wish remains a wish without action. Fantasies are not arbitrarily fulfilled simply because we hope they will be. Dreams come true because we make they come true.

While I enjoy the lustful ideas of winning the lottery or being super-fit without exercising and eating properly, I understand that they are foolish wishes. It is fun to dream them, but relying on them as a life strategy is doomed to fail. Knowing this, I must take great heed and make great efforts to first define and then calculate a plan. This is where I sometimes struggle. I like the dreaming part, not necessarily the planning. But...I do it anyway, because my fear of not doing it and my desire for good outcomes is greater than my capacity to keep my head in the sand. For this, I am thankful.

Included in my list of goals, and maybe the cornerstone of them, is a commitment to serve my world better. I resolve to serve my wife and kids better. I resolve to serve my community better. I, through prodigious study, have come to understand that this is where my own happiness lies. Giving liberates me. Giving the best things I have frees me to enjoy any gift I receive. And, in 2013, I hope to earn plenty of them...after I finish off this turkey and maybe have another chunk of homemade almond roca...

Someday.

Yesterday, I did something I rarely do. I completed all of the items on my "to-do" list. Granted, some of the items included: eating bacon, drinking water and sleeping. Nonetheless, I did not have any carry-overs. I always have carry-overs. I am a procrastinator. I put off the things I don't really want to do. I am a genius at making excuses and justifying and copping out of my obligations. I am a master at making myself feel better about my mediocre performance. Well, yesterday that changed. I did what I said I was going to do...and not all of it was fun.

A couple of things inspired this productivity: The first was heat. I was feeling some serious heat about WHEN certain tasks would be completed. And, trust me, my wife can really stoke a fire. It gets hot around my house when she ramps us the bellows. Even with my expert excuse making capabilities, I was running short and time was running out, so I did what I knew I inevitably must do anyway. The next thing that inspired me to move was an idea that I encountered at a seminar last week. This idea was about "someday". Being a procrastinator, I have clung to the idea of "someday" as my life raft. "Tomorrow", "later" and "at some point" are analogous to "someday". The trouble with these ideas is that they exist only as ideas. They are fantasy. They don't exist in the real world. There is only today.

This fairly abstract concept took some time to get through my gate keepers which insulate me from acknowledging my failures. Eventually, this idea became comforting. Allowing that someday doesn't exist creates some urgency in "doing something" today. I am prone to lean on "someday" as validation for what I haven't done yet. However, "I will do it" is NOT the same as actually "doing it." This is a dangerous habit and it has not served me well. I have missed opportunities and compromised my success in important ways. I have undermined my good intentions and capacity for delivering on them through simple inaction. I am not proud to write these words, believe me. But, being an excuse making human being, I can always forgive myself and I do.

I forgive myself because the idea of today being the only day that counts is not new to me. I read a lot. Some of what I read is important books written by important people (whatever that means). In reading these books, once in a while, I will stumble across a profound thought that I recognize as a familiar friend.

Occasionally, I find that a smart person will share an idea that I thought, on my own, at some point in my life. It is here that I live in the company of giants. I have independently thought important thoughts and, because of this, I must be important, too. Sooooo, if I can think the same important thoughts that people I admire think, then by extension, I can achieve what they achieve. This only difference is "doing" it, whatever "it" is. This comforts me. I am not a lost cause. There is hope. And that hope is today.

Many, many years ago, I used to carry around a little notebook in which I would write down quotes and/or book passages that I found interesting, inspiring...or just funny. While weeding out some of my excess junk, I stumbled across my little notebook in a thread bare box of miscellaneous old photos and beer coasters. In my little book, I found some jewels.

Most of the time, I kept these words as my little secret treasures, unless the rare opportunity to impress a weird chick with a quote might get me some action presented itself. Again, this was exceedingly and painfully rare (honey...sweetheart). But the words still live as a time capsule to what I was thinking back then.

One particular quote from Ernest Hemingway's "For Whom The Bell Tolls" strikes me as appropriate to my new way of thinking and demonstrates that it is actually an old way of thinking. The quote is:

"So (what) if your life trades its seventy years for seventy hours. I have that value now and am lucky enough to know it. And if there is not any such thing as a long time, nor the rest of your lives, nor from now on, but there is only now, why then now is the thing to praise and I am very happy with it."

Granted the circumstances were different for the character in this context. He was going on a mission to blow up a bridge that he knew would likely result in his own demise. So, while this is not a small distinction, there are still parallels to be drawn.

We are all facing an "imminent" demise. We don't know when it will be, but it will be, certainly. This is why "someday" is a dangerous illusion. Postponing life today is postponing life and sometimes never getting around to living it. Now is the only thing we have. Today is the only palette we can paint with. We cannot paint with tomorrow. We can only act today. Today is the only day we have. It is only here that we can do anything about our lives. This being so, then today is the thing to praise....and I am very happy with it.

Lucky.

While walking around the supermarket the other day, I saw an older, kind of chubby guy wearing a pair of blue and white striped coveralls. They weren't the working type of coveralls. They were all leisure. He reminded me of my dad.

As a child of the seventies, I was privileged to witness many dubiously awesome fashion choices in my household, not the least of which was my dad's pair of blue and white striped coveralls. Watching this brave man in 2015 strolling down the aisles, a memory hit me:

I was 4 or 5 years old, shopping with my dad at the old Tradewell store on Pac Hwy (Dollar Store now) and as we were waiting in a long line, I got bored and was fidgeting, standing behind by pops. As my eyes searched for ways to pass the time, I noticed that my dad had a small hole in the rear end of his cool coveralls. Apparently, my dad went commando.

From this hole at eye level, several fine hairs presented themselves. Not being blessed with much foresight at this delicate age, I chose to pull these small hairs. I only remember a smack in the head and didn't see much of the coveralls after this incident.

I laughed at this memory as I pushed my cart and recognized that my legacy of poor choices began early. Reminiscing about the old Tradewell years, it's worth noting that this is the same store that I, in another brilliant moment, managed to get my arm trapped behind one of the sliding entry doors. I recall placing one foot on the activation pad and my hand on the edge of the door. Apparently, I stepped too hard on the pad and the door opened, sucking my entire arm between thick panes of glass. Several people were required to extract me from this predicament. Again, I was with my dad and I'm sure he entertained thoughts of getting me tested or just leaving me behind...

So, these fun little stories played in my head as I stood in line waiting to buy my groceries the other day. As usual, I picked the shortest line. The guy in front of me had a few things, but being an experienced line-picker, I predicted a pretty quick run. I was wrong. The guy in front of me was paying with assistance checks. Every three items required a long transaction to process the checks. I stood and shuffled and looked around, much the same way I did moments before plucking my dad's butt hairs.

This time, though, I had some thoughts. I was not in a hurry and I was lifted by fond memories of my wonder years. So, all I felt was lucky. I was not impatient with the man having to take time to pay for his supplies. Several people behind me moved to other lines. I stayed. I was grateful that I did not have to use assistance checks to purchase my things. As I remembered my life and my dad, I was happy waiting.

When the checker eventually moved on to my items, he apologized for the wait. I shook my head and said I it was no problem. I meant it. I imagined the guy in front of me knowing that he was holding up the line and feeling a "way" about this. I felt for the guy. He was a worker. I could tell by his boots. He was buying diapers and formula and fruit and meat. He was just a guy who needed a little help. All I could offer was patience. On a different day, I may not have had that to give. But on this day, I had it and I knew I had other things, too. I understood these "other things" and I still feel lucky...

The Freshman.

This morning I dropped my fourteen year old son, Aden, off for his high school orientation. He will be a freshman at Mount Rainier High School, my alma mater. As I am prone to do, I became a bit melancholy after leaving him at the doorstep to another stage in his life. Driving down the hill to coach my 9 am CrossFit class, I knew that I was entering another stage of my life as well.

As I get older, I recognize less and less the passing of time. My own milestones are further apart than they used to be. The only nominally significant tell is my hair. As I watch it diminish in some spots and grow in others, I am reminded that I am, indeed, aging. But for the most part, my kids' little evolutions provide the most powerful evidence of life moving on.

Reflecting on my son's first day of kindergarten (where I drove away crying like a baby), I thought about where we have been, where we are and where we are going. I have seen this boy through everything. From butt-wipes and baby teeth to hobbies and interests and ideas, I have been there offering my perspective, whether he wanted it or not. We have grown together through our time shared.

A couple of weeks ago, my boy and I took our annual road trip around the state. We fished, camped, ate crappy food and talked. On a dusty back road with our windows down and music up, I realized that our conversations have changed. These changes mirror HIS changes. His questions and thinking have changed. What he cares about is different. "Hey, Dad, I was thinking...." are words that always pique my interest, because I never know what is going to come next. I am always interested to know what he is thinking. When he shares his thoughts, which is not as common as it used to be, I am always intrigued. He is contemplating some important stuff and I am glad that he will occasionally include me in his quest for understanding.

I often describe having kids as being the "best pain in the a#s there is." They frustrate and confound and annoy. They make messes and inconvenience and compromise our sleep and peace. They also enlighten us to what truly matters in life: they do. We will sacrifice all that we have to provide for them. We will give things we didn't know we had to support and encourage them to learn and grow and be happy.

Dropping my son off at high school made me feel old. My own long-lost years of beautiful youth stared me down and smiled. I smiled back. Life is life. It moves on, whether we like it or not. I am choosing to like it. I can't help it. Watching my son take new steps towards his own great life is pretty fantastic. Seeing him developing into a man of worth and kindness is an equitable exchange for every minute of lost sleep and every lost hair I endure. In fact, it's the fairest deal I have ever found.

Friendly Apparitions.

Last weekend was busy. My son had a wrestling tournament, which tends to consume an entire day, and my daughter needed serving prior to this event. I was up early on a Saturday morning navigating my various duties. I was also traveling solo as my wife was out of town. I had much to do in a limited time, but despite some obligatory screaming from my girl and the standard last minute fire drill exercise from my late-running son, I managed to avoid any of the big, potential disasters lurking around each corner. I handled my business and carried on with a light heart and clear mind. It's nice when this happens.

Following my busy bee morning, I began the twenty-five mile trek to my son's tournament. On the freeway heading south, a heavy fog shrouded the lanes of travel. The fog was thick, but not dangerous. I could see my lane and the others fine, but the distractions off the highway were invisible. A cocoon of white mist canceled the eye-noise of ancillary commerce and busy people doing busy things. Traffic was light and courteous. It was a nice drive.

Sometimes in life, moments of brief, but meaningful peace and contentment will capture us in their magic. These moments when time slows and the world seems right are precious. They are not entirely rare, but they can be hard to see though the noisy distractions when life's chores and worries seem to pile on high.

For a few golden minutes, I drove with no care for the distractions, but a deep care for the life I was living and the people in it. I felt like a kid in a living room fort: I knew that other people were in the room, but I was warm and quiet in my own thoughts. I reflected and looked forward and enjoyed the fog. I had all that I needed. I lacked nothing. My drive was a nice surprise and good medicine. In a few silent, but glorious moments, I cured the ailment I didn't know I was afflicted with. A friendly apparition haunted my soft spots and I healed.

So, during our perpetual quest for righteous riches and high regards, it's a good thing to remember that a foggy Saturday morning drive with a full tank of gas is a fine thing, too...

Hard things.

Life is full of hard things. Work, kids, money, fear, hope, relationships and change all serve to challenge us in ways that stretch us, sometimes uncomfortably so. The confounding element of hard things is that they are often also the RIGHT things. Doing the right thing can be hard. For this reason, it may be even more important to do them.

The other day my eleven year old daughter dropped a jar of raspberry jam on her foot. The jar exploded when it hit the ground and her foot at the same time resulting in a nasty gash. My girl barely winced. She comforted my very "wincy" wife as the depth of this gruesome little injury became known. She didn't flinch in the emergency room during the anesthetic shots or the stitches. She's a tough girl in ways that gratefully don't often reveal themselves. She handled a hard thing with a stoic acceptance of events and provided comfort to her mother and me. It was a proud moment for me which alleviates many concerns about her capacity to handle the hard things this life will invariably deliver to her. She's gonna be fine.

Life is like this. Hard things happen and we choose a path. We rise or shrink with them. We allow them to diminish us and hide from the truth or we accept them and forge a new path with a new truth. We recognize the truth as the right thing but it takes some serious balls to face the truth as a hard thing and act anyway.

These moments define us. They shape us and change us. It is during these times that we grow. Hard things force us to be more and when we ARE more, we BECOME more...forever. This is a valid result for our efforts in navigating life's hard things. Extending ourselves, logically, extends us. We are bigger. And while hard things don't always feel good, surviving them does. This is why in the face of the hardest things this life presents us, a speck of hope always lives in the truth that things will get better, if we just keep moving.

"If you're going through hell, keep going..." –Winston Churchill
Good advice and good reminder that hard things end. The rain stops and the streets dry. The grass grows and sun warms the new skin of our new life as a survivor of hard things...

Spaces.

While on vacation last week, I had the fortunate opportunity to stumble across Steven Tyler's autobiography. For anyone living under a rock for the past thirty years and who may not know, Steven Tyler is the front man for the legendary rock band, Aerosmith.

In full disclosure, I am always lured by sordid rock star stories of gratuitous and rampant drug use and groupie sex, so that was my first attraction. But as I read this book, I was struck by the insight and interesting perspectives from a genuinely unique and thoughtful guy. Even without the drugs and sex, this was still a pretty fascinating book.

One re-occurring idea that resonated with me was the significance of spaces. In his story, Steven, kept coming back to an idea about the spaces between the notes and what they say. The power of a pause and the timing of notes or words shape the message. The spaces create the meaning. The words are the "what". The spaces between them are the "why".

I find this idea compelling and true in more contexts than just a song. In life, what is not said is often most important. The strength of silence is powerful and somewhat unnerving if one happens to be on the business end of a prolonged and deliberate silence.

Growing up, my Dad was a man of few words. He was old school and not fond of much expression. Thusly, when he spoke, I listened. On the very rare occasions that I would screw up, I got yelled at. My Mom was always the first in line, but Dad would sometimes follow up with his thoughts about my behavior, if my Mom's yelling was insufficient.

However, when my crime was grievous enough my Dad was silent. I knew I had really stepped into some deep sh*t when he was quiet. This was not good. I really wished he would just yell at me instead of quietly gazing at me with a "look". His look was loud and said much more than his words could have. I hated the "look,"

Nowadays, I get the "look" from my wife. And so, the power of silence is alive and well in my life.

Significant spaces create the moment. The true depth and meaning of words is found in between their spaces. This is an interesting phenomenon. Much is made of intonation and rather garish displays of verbal circus tricks, but for my money, a well-placed and well-timed silence is more effective and important than whatever happens on either side of this space.

In our life, we are faced with much noise. From all directions, we are bombarded by the cacophonous whine of the world. Now and then, we find some peace and this peace is in our silence. It is the empty, yet full, spaces between the notes of our life that create our song. And it's a pretty good song when we slow down...and listen to the quiet...

Fourteen.

On April 3rd, 2013, my son, Aden turned fourteen years old. At 6:45 AM, on this day, I loud-whispered, "Happy Birthday, buddy!!!" The rest of our house slept as he replied, "thanks, Dad" in a voice deeper than mine. What the hell happened?!?!

This is a largely rhetorical question, as I know what happened, but what happened is ripe with implication and deep with sentiment…at least to me. My little boy grew up is what happened. It is what it should be. Little boys grow up. It's what they do, at least in a fair and just world.

I grew up…mostly…and now it is my son's time. I understand this logically, but as always my emotions lag a little behind. My head knows he's growing up, but my heart wants him to stay little. I miss him needing me for something besides my wallet.

I miss his squeaky little frog voice chiming out oddly articulate questions about mature ideas. It was in his early questions, of which there were many, that I came to know that this kid was special. He had a unique curiosity about things and a mind whose wheels rarely stopped spinning. It is this curiosity that has inspired me and driven me crazy, sometimes at the same time.

As he has grown and answered many of his own questions, it seems like his list is only growing longer. The more he knows, the more he realizes how little he knows. I understand this very well. I get smarter and dumber all the time.

Of my many contributions to my son's life, I think my perspective about these types of questions will be my most valuable. I "get" these questions and I "get" that sometimes satisfying answers are hard to come by. And I think this is OK.

I think that the value of a question is more significant than a clean and tidy answer. All knowledge begins with a question. From the question, many elements merge and meld and form a shape. From the question more insight is gained than any answer can provide. A good question spawns more good questions…forever. The question has the power and my son has powerful questions. And for this, I am grateful.

So, as I fondly reflect on my time watching this kid of mine grow up, I am happy and sad at the same time. I cried as I left him for his first day of kindergarten. I taught him to ride a bike and cook a good burger. I have read to him and taken him to countless soccer practices. I have made him laugh and I have seen him barf. I have heard him sing Johnny Cash songs in the shower and

70's songs from his old car seat. I have been victimized by his viola, oboe and, more recently, bassoon. We have fought and we have fished. I have tried to teach him kindness and math, though we're about maxed out on my math knowledge. I have hugged and kissed and spanked him. He is my son.

He will be my son forever. And I will be his dad. I look forward to sharing his life for as long as we have. I look forward to sharing all that I possess. Parenting is sometimes an ugly business. But sometimes, too, it is beautiful. What is often overlooked and lives as a little secret is the fact that our kids teach us more than we teach them. And I look forward to all the great things I will learn from my boy's questions. He's a great kid and he's my son.

Doing Dishes.

After picking my son up from school yesterday, we/he decided it was a good day to burn the left over branches from a cherry tree I cut down that had been a bit of an eye sore in our yard since last autumn. So, burn we did. The sun was out and a light breeze fanned the smoldering coals into a pretty decent little fire.

After a few minutes of clipping branches into the appropriate size for our fire pit, my son got bored. This is not unusual. I saw him begin to waver. I have seen this before and I know the signs. I warned him, encouraged him and yelled at him. To no avail, he went into the house because he was "hungry", once again, leaving me to do the heavy lifting.

As my window was closing on this project and I had to go to work, I admonished him with an expectation. I expected the project to be complete before I returned home. He sat in his desk chair, eating his bagel and with zero enthusiasm said "ok". I was not optimistic.

Alas, upon my arrival back home the yard was clean and he had actually done what I asked. It doesn't usually work this way and I was pleased. Following his hard work, he apparently felt worthy of a reward and walked down the street to get a soda from ABC Grocery. I don't like that he loves soda, but I do like that he walks around town to get it.

I like that he "lives" in our community. He knows people and chats and visits and buys. I regularly get updates on his visits from my friends about his travels. People like him and I like this. As parents we see ALL sides of our kids. We see the good and the bad. It seems our kids often reserve their worst behavior for their parents. I recall hearing an "expert" on parenting pine that when our kids act up/out, they feel safe and secure enough to express, fully, all aspects of their character and emotion. Some days, I think maybe my kids feel a little too safe and secure, because they often express more than I want to deal with.

I stumbled across some words the other day that reminded me of my contribution to my kids' behavior:
"It doesn't matter how strong your opinions are. If you don't use your power for positive change, you are, indeed, part of the problem." -Coretta Scott King

I have strong opinions and regularly express them. My results are not always positive. As I suspect most parents do, I often feel unqualified to teach my kids anything and that I truly am "part of the problem". I see them reacting in haste and frustration. I see them being impatient and just not very nice. These characteristics are mine. I, also, see them being kind and I hear about how polite and well-spoken they are. These traits are mine, too. Some imperfect balance is being sought and hopefully, found. Being mindful of my influence, I simply try to do the "right" things, whatever the hell they are...

While standing in my kitchen doing the dishes this morning, I glanced out the window at the sunrise colors on the mountains across the water and almost began to cry. As I listened to some happy Jimmy Buffett music and heard the busy sounds of my family scurrying around, I was overcome by gratitude. I had a sense that things were right and good. In that simple moment of recognition, I truly and deeply felt love for the life I have and the people in it.

For all of life's challenges and struggles, the sun still came up and shone on the mountains. Many things change, but the important things like a sunrise and the love of a family are constants and make all pain and worry and fear worth it. This is nice to remember, and may be the most important thing to remember...the sun always rises...

Hard to say...

The older I get, the more uncertain I have become about many things. Proving this point, I'm not even sure if this is a good thing or a bad thing. I often find myself perched on the fence about lots of different issues and/or ideas. I don't like declaring a position. And, I typically don't trust people who are quick to take a strong position. I have been either blessed or cursed with the capacity to see multiple potential answers to questions. My wishy-washiness is not a lack of courage to stake a claim and own my opinion. I merely have lots of opinions and can see issues from different viewpoints.

Over the years, I have managed to frustrate my old buddy, Dan, with my standard response to his seemingly simple questions: "Welllll....it's hard to say..." I reply and I'm pretty sure he has wanted to punch me hard upon hearing, once again, my lack of commitment to any position.

I found my defense in a quote I read the other day:

"The whole problem with the world is that fools and fanatics are always so certain of themselves, and wiser people so full of doubts." - Bertrand Russell

Eureka!!! This is it!!! This establishes that I am NOT the problem with the world. This is good to know as I was beginning to worry. Many of us can rest easy with this knowledge. It is not necessary to pick sides on everything. Most issues are more complicated than they are presented to be. That's why it's important to be wary of words that sound too good to be true. They usually are. Living in this world is not a simple business and what is "right" is rarely clear.

Sometimes, however, "right" is very clear. In these moments, it is very important that we speak up. Our voices are necessary to drown out the loud, but wrong ones intent only on creating havoc and distracting us from the truth. Justice is found in our spoken words.

While much of my water is muddy, some is not: the other morning I walked into my daughter's bedroom playing my favorite song from our recent trip to Hawaii on my iPhone to wake her. She smiled and covered her head with her favorite fuzzy purple blanket; the other night, I sat with my son discussing his high school experience and I saw his mind exploring the awesome potential of his future; this morning, I delivered coffee to my wife as she lay cozy in bed, listening to our daughter practicing "Silent Night" on the piano.

In each of these moments, I knew without a shadow of a shadow of doubt that I loved my family so very much. And in a world of so much uncertainty for me, it feels good to have something to know for sure...

PS: This week's column is dedicated to my friend, Nancy Warren. She was much more certain than I, but lived as an example of kindness and truth and love. She was more than simply human; she was an "experience". Her spirit was vast and infectious and her heart as big as her smile. The world lost a good one...

People we love.

This morning one of my wonderfully goofy 6 am CrossFit girls made me love her. When she looked at me with hope and fear as she asked if we could play her iPod during the workout, I was moved. There was really nothing special about this moment, but 6 am on a weekday morning our standards of love may be unique. As I shook my head and smiled and plugged in her device and Prince came blasting out, I felt love for a person and an ordinary moment in time.

This is not unusual. I feel this way often. My life is filled with people who create moments in which a love can happen. The people we love are made in the moments we share. They change with the times and places of our lives. We can and do love many people, if only for a brief moment. This is ok. The duration of the love is not important. The connection is what matters. I don't understand how or where or when these connections occur and why sometimes they do and sometimes they don't. I do understand that it's nice when they happen. They remind us that we're connected and make us feel good about life. They tell us the truth that life is pretty good.

While parking my truck at the grocery store the other day, an old black guy and I met in the lot as our vehicles parked side-by-side. We walked across the pavement toward the store together chatting about the recent storm as the autumn sun shone on our path.

Upon entering the store, we went our different directions with wishes for a good day and grins. I loved this man in this moment. For 30 seconds, we connected as human beings and our lives were moved in some infinitesimal degree by this. It mattered.

We can feel love for people at any time. We don't choose the times we feel this way. These moments seem to choose us. We can love in a grocery store line. We can love at the gas pump. We can love while walking our dog or doing the dishes. We can love as a memory, as a fantasy, or in a dream. These feelings can surprise us with their power and they resonate long after the moment has passed. It's a good hangover to have.

Sunset.

The day began with a nice sunrise. It remained a good day throughout, minus some expectedly unexpected violations. Overall, it was a good day. This may not seem remarkable, but in its lack of remarkability is the magic. A pretty ordinary day is always extraordinary.

Through the course of our lives we wake each morning with a chance: A simple chance to do and be what we want. We have friends and opportunities and choices. All of these beautiful things determine our life.

This morning, following the nice sunrise, another rising took place, this one not as nice: my daughter woke up in a "mood." Her moods are quite volatile and with only the most delicate precision I know to proceed. Using my unfortunately well-rehearsed dad-magic, I was able to avert a serious crisis. I managed to find her shoe and concoct an acceptable lunch. Disaster avoided.

While scurrying my girl out the door for school, I noticed my son's lunch sitting on the table. It was pretty pitiful. He had some cookies, crackers and fruit snacks. All garbage. Since he forgot his meager fixins', I took it upon myself to gather some actual sustenance and deliver it to his school before his lunch period, though I later discovered that he received during his last class of the day. Pacific Middle School fail….whatever…

The rest of the day, I taught my CrossFit classes and mowed my lawns and picked my father-in-law from the airport. I had lunch with my wife and cleaned my kitchen and I know how absolutely boring this all is and I don't care. It is my life.

It is all my life and it is all beautiful. Without much pomp or haberdashery, I live my life. And I like it that way. I enjoy my kids' "moods" and my wife's "wife-ness". I like mowing the lawn and cleaning my kitchen, because these hours are my life. And they are passing.

Our hours pass. This being the case and life being life, I understand that certain things must be done. The lawn needs to be mowed, regardless of how I feel about it, so enjoying it lets me enjoy it. The kitchen is a mess and needs to be cleaned up, so I now have a choice to be frustrated about having to clean it or turn on some music and slip into the task with good thoughts and maybe some Jimmy Buffett. This is a choice. I choose well and for this I am proud.

Following a late dinner, the server arrived with the check and informed me that our bill had been paid by a friend. It was in this moment that I was, again, reminded of the good people in my life. Friends that will "anonymously" pay the tab are treasures. And I have many. I am proud to have them and I am proud to have earned them.

As my family and I drove home from dinner, a wonderful spring sun began its descent behind the mountains. In this moment, I knew that this day was the best one I will ever have...and I hope the same for tomorrow...

Two Pains.

Last week, I checked a to-do off of my list. After several months of dancing with emotions which ranged from annoyed to outraged, I spent an hour out of my day and cleaned up a crappy looking property in my town. The area outside of our closed Mexican restaurant, Lago Azul, has become a magnet for trash and blowing leaves and bad feelings regarding loss and potential and lack and disappointment and hope. It's been ugly and represented ugly things to me. In short, it bugged me.

While doing my little clean-up and feeling a little indignant and self-righteous about my efforts, I conjured up words of service and community and difference-making. In fact, I wrote a whole different column in my head while raking some leaves.

While feeling the heat of my own hands patting myself on the back, I remembered that I had been annoyed and outraged for a long time before I took any action. I stand as a pinnacle of nothing, except maybe procrastination. Eventually, I got around to it, which is nice, but stand as a testament to civic action and community improvement, I cannot.

Personal development genius, Jim Rohn stated that in life "we must all suffer from one of two pains: the pain of discipline or the pain of regret." I largely believe this to be true. As I reflect upon my long-suffering relationship with the shabby lot in my town, I see that had I the discipline to address the issue earlier, I would have saved myself several months of bad-feelings.

This is a good lesson for many things. Jim also mentions that "discipline weighs ounces, but regret weighs tons..." I get this message. The weight of an unfinished obligation is heavy. It is way better to simply suck it up and do it, than to worry about it. Life is littered with these chores. Knocking a few of them off the list is time well spent. A mind free of this weight is a mind free to think important things. And life is way more fun thinking important things that we like to think about than beating ourselves up over unfinished business. So, as the great philosopher, Nike, says, "Just Do It." We rarely regret this...

Twelve.

I have an alarm set on my phone for 3:30 pm. I didn't set this alarm. I suspect my daughter set it to remind me to pick her up from school back in the days when I used to walk over to the elementary school every day and walk home with her. I keep this alarm because the reminder note says "Love you". This alarm has been on my phone for many years and will not leave until my phone dies or I do.

Today is my daughter's twelfth birthday. As I reminisce on this day twelve years ago, I recall standing stiff-legged behind my wife as she hunkered over the hospital bed like a cavewoman while our slimy little bundle of joy came into this world. Everything changed in that moment. As I cut the umbilical cord, it was as if I somehow attached it to myself, but instead of me feeding my baby life, she fed me.

We love these damn kids so much, yet they drive us so mad. My daughter is a complicated one. Our relationship is a complicated one. Her moods shift between indifference to outright hostility. None of which bothers me in the slightest (most of the time...). This is because I love her regardless; regardless of her being nice or polite or kind to me. I know that she loves me, but I also know that I love her more. This is the way it always is. Parents love their kids more.

Now, I love my parents very much, but my kids are different. It's a different love and it's a love that I don't expect to receive from my kids. They don't have it. They can't. I hope they get it and then "get it", but until then I will just be happy loving them more without condition.

A couple of days ago, I bought my baby girl a necklace that I was excited to give to her on her birthday. As she opened it this morning, she smiled and placed it back in the neat little felt pocket it came in and said, "I like it, but I don't really wear jewelry". And so it went. I smiled and poured her some juice. I was unfazed by her indifference. I have come to expect it. But, that's the beauty of true unconditional love; the gift of giving something that I knew was kind of special was really a gift to me. I knew it meant something, independent of her response. I felt good anyway, because I love her more.

So, on this birthday, I am reminded of the many ways that I was "born", too. My girl has touched me and taught me and sometimes tortured me, but I am different because of her. I understand important things. I know how much love is possible. And I know how much forgiveness is possible. And patience. And frustration. And giving when I don't feel like it. She has taught me more than I can teach her and I am proud to love her more. She is the sunbeam that lights the sometimes dim path of my life and she sheds a beautiful light...

Night Dive.

Several lifetimes ago, I drove to Costa Rica with a couple of buddies. We slept in my 1986 Vanagon with each other's feet in our faces. We ate cheap street tacos and drank cheap beer. We wore flip flops and board shorts and occasionally a t-shirt. We gave away sunglasses and books and cassette tapes to the street kids hanging out at the many border crossings we passed through. We met locals and expats and drank and ate and laughed with them. We were tan and happy and free.

On Isla de Utila, off the coast of Honduras, we took a scuba diving certification class. For five days, we swam around the warm Caribbean waters under the "watchful" eye of our "instructor", Eddie, a man of dubious credentials. On several occasions, eyebrows were raised in regards to Eddie's teachings...but, we didn't die, so it worked out.

Following our daily lesson, we would head to the local beach bar for a few Port Royals and to say "hi" to our "pet" tarantula which lived beneath the weathered planks of the palapa. He would pop out through a knot hole and was a furry little reminder of how far away we were from home. With our damp trunks and salty bodies, we ate plantains and pork tacos and drank beer and talked and read and wrote. It was a special time indeed.

The highlight of this experience was the night dive. On the final evening of our stay, we rode with Eddie and crew offshore and as the sun went down, we dove. We had little lights illuminating the phosphorescence and the corals and fish. It was sublime. It was exciting and peaceful in the same moment. I've found that the best moments are like this.

As Eddie signaled that it was time to surface, we drifted out of the depths into a magical scene of sky and water and stars. The only light pollution was the universe and a white canvas of possibility sang from heaven as we slowly skulled ourselves back to the boat.

This was one of the finest moments of my life. As I lay back, gently pushing the warm waters, gazing at the stars, I realized that world is indeed a wonderful, mystical, and powerful place. It was a beautiful moment and I knew that I was beautiful to be a part of it. I was fully alive and understood that my life contributed to all life and that this mattered...

I recently read an article discussing the loss of this feeling for men. Our wanderlustfully curious, bold and brave spirits begin to shrink at some point in life's journey and this shrinks us. It confounds us and makes us uncertain and unhappy and wondering what the hell happened.

When we are no longer simply driven by our quest or hunger or boredom or gas tank, and other schedules determine our days, we become unsettled, looking to scratch an itch. The article described in great detail these feelings and how denying the force of them poisons us and the killing of this spirit can destroy our lives. When we no longer feel in control or inspired or excited, this spirit dies and we die with it.

Gratefully, the key remedy to turning things around is simply recognizing it: When we see it, we can fix it. Everyone has their own itch and knows how to scratch it. We know this in the part of our spirit not yet diminished. And we always have some of this beautiful, little fire burning inside of us, waiting for us to add a few drops of gasoline.

So, while I can't turn back the clock's hands and swim weightlessly through the Caribbean Sea in the dark, I can look and my own hands and know that they did this thing, and many other things too, and they were driven by a spirit that still lives. This spirit lives in all of us...always...

TMI.

While browsing the various mostly meaningless post updates on my Facebook "news" feed the other day, I raised my eyebrows a few times. It seems that as folks become more comfortable with this relatively new technology, they are, too, becoming more comfortable exposing parts of themselves that should maybe remain covered. Don't get me wrong, I enjoy seeing pictures of my friends' kids and some of the pictures of their dogs, if the dog is doing something cool. I like reading about their lives and the fun little tidbits of humanity that make me smile. I like the inspirational stories and the funny memes. I like much of my Facebook experience.

I don't like all of it. I don't like negative stuff. This judgment is subjective and the lens I pass my judgment with is scratched and dented and bent from my own experiences. Now that I have qualified any subsequent comments, I will say that I don't friggin' get it. I do not understand how people can share some of the things they share....so publicly. I am often awed by either how secure or stupid people are.

From gun control to abortion to super-personal family issues, extreme view points and traumatic experiences are passed along with a click of the finger presumably without a thought to where it's going. I don't like extreme viewpoints. I don't like extreme viewpoints, extremely. I understand this contradiction and don't really care. It is because of this that I can be a little lenient when faced with an especially offensive post, even if I cannot comprehend not only why someone could think that way, but why they would want to share it.

Again, through my lens, I am very aware of the vast and varied eyeballs that will see my words and form an opinion of me based on them. It is important, to me, that I represent myself if not favorably, at least accurately. As I know many of the people I shake my head about, some pretty closely, I wonder where I missed some of these pieces of their personalities or character. I wonder who the hell some of these people are and why they would want the world to know about their dirty laundry or dirty soul. I suppose they just feel so strongly about things that I don't feel so strongly about that they need to get it off their chests. With this in mind, I will try to be forgiving when I read things that make me want to do something else.

My Facebook experience makes me really glad that it was not around when I was younger. I have said some monumentally dumb things that I am very happy were delivered to a pretty limited audience. Young people are dumb. Teenagers are stupid. Their perspective on the world is so limited that the thoughts they think lack sense to a more experienced eye. As harsh as this judgment may sound, it is not without a certain reverence, and maybe some jealously, about being able to view the world with young eyes. I see words that I may have said at that age and am glad that I thought them then, but am glad I moved on...mostly...

The old adage, "It is better to remain silent and thought a fool, than to open your mouth and remove all doubt", is a truth. It is a truth that I have come to understand, like most things I come to understand: the hard way. My hope is that the novelty of our "information" age will wear off and we can return to private stuff remaining private. I suspect that this lesson will be learned the hard way, too. My hope is that this technology can bring us closer, not divide us more. My wish is that we can share our different perspectives in ways that do not isolate us or change our friends' minds about who we are. We are all united in our common humanity and the roots are too strong and deep to be compromised by a few crackpot comments. We have all said things we wish we had not. Now, our words will survive longer than we will. Here, it is important to remember that we are more than our words sometimes belie. This is a good thought for me to keep on hand....and please keep sharing the funny pictures...I always like a funny picture...

Sin and Waffles.

About 1 pm on a Tuesday afternoon, I walked by my son's bedroom and instead of being annoyed by the fact that he was still asleep, (which did not surprise me since when I woke up at 5:30 am he was still milling about the house) I was moved nearly to tears. I was awe-struck by his goodness, intelligence-both emotional and intellectual, his humor and his heart. As I stood and looked at my sleeping boy, I truly and deeply felt the special love that only a father can have for a son. It was nice to be reminded of this feeling.

Through the chaos of life, things get overlooked. For a time, since my son is pretty low-maintenance (certainly compared to my daughter), I have neglected to do the little special things that let him know how valuable he is to me. Simple gestures of my love and recognition of him as a great kid didn't happen. Well, after seeing my sleeping boy and feeling the feels, I committed to acknowledging him in my standard, humble way: food.

Later that night, I asked him if he would like some waffles and bacon for breakfast the next day. He said sure. So, the next morning, I made him waffles and bacon. As I fried the bacon, I thought about my own dad and the legacy he left me. I also thought about the legacy I have left for my son and I embarked on a complicated conversation with myself.

My dad had two primary forms of expression: silence and anger. He also had great humor and an elephantine loyalty to his family. I examined my own default behaviors and found much of my dad. I was proud of some and not proud of others. The "sins of the father" truly do pass down generationally. There is no shame or blame in this, only the clear understanding that we do the best we can with what we have and we can only know what we know. And though the cost of these sins can be expensive, they don't define a heart.

Gratefully, I am not too late to mitigate some of the impacts of my haste and sharpness and silence. My son is not built yet. He's getting close, but I trust I still have some influence and I also trust that plenty of my good bits have made it through the sieve. Watching him walk the world with grace and kindness and strength, I am proud in the knowledge that I contributed to this as well. Sins be damned.

In an uncertain world, a few precious people live as anchors keeping us safely moored as the tempest swirls around us. Our kids and parents are these anchors. They remind us that we can love and are loved and that we have generosity and a selfless devotion to ensuring their peace and happiness. And though the tornados swirl and the thunder claps, making us afraid of both the dark and the light, we can sometimes find our own peace and happiness by delivering a plate of waffles and bacon to a late-sleeping teenage boy. Bacon is always a pretty good gift...

The things we love the most...

My daughter played "Frosty the Snowman" on the piano last night. As I watched and listened and smiled, I saw my little girl as a young woman and was happy and sad at the same time. Time moves swiftly. It seems she was just beginning kindergarten, then I blinked, and she's now in seventh grade. I guess life is just like this.

My son drives himself each morning to his college classes. As junior "running start" student, he attends both college and high school classes. In my wallet, I keep an old picture of him as a toddler with big dark eyes and little teeth, grinning and standing on a box in his small sneakers. Our feet are now nearly the same size, though his are hairier. Though I love him all the way through, I miss his bald-feet days.

In a world filled with much strife and struggle, I always return home to these beautifully annoying creatures. I care much about others and wish good things for everyone, but my heart and soul lives with my family. I think it's this way for everyone lucky enough to have a family. Much posturing surrounds global events with incendiary language and provocative stances, but I suspect a lot of this outrage is phony. Most people reserve true love for their families and true hate for those who would harm them.

Life is a personal business. We all live in a certain sized bubble and while we're connected more and more through technology, I don't think our bubble sizes change that much through these exchanges. We love who we love the most...the most. I believe this is as it should be. It's where we begin. It's the foundation upon which we can stand and share ourselves with others. Without a firm base life is slippery. Family is our safe haven we can always return to following our journeys. I think this is true for every human being.

Media seems to enjoy creating division and conflict and has been successful in telling a part of the story. People are different in some ways, certainly. Culturally, we do things differently. We think differently and act differently. But, I don't think we FEEL differently. And this, I believe, is an important thing to consider. The heart of humanity is in the heart, not the mind. And I refuse to believe that a mother or father in any land loves her/his kids less than I love mine. We are connected here. It's humanity's foundation.

It's also a place to start. From here, leading with our tremendous capacity for love, the good people can and will create a better world and, gratefully, there are many more good people than bad. The bad people just make more headlines. Trusting that others are capable of great love allows for possibility. Hate and fear eliminate possibilities.

While the challenges we face are complicated ones, they are not impossible. They are not even new. Throughout history, bad people have done bad things. This is and will always be true. So what? They don't define all people, just bad people. They are unique in their badness. They only represent themselves. And they are few compared with all the good people. Knowing this, I am not afraid of them.

I am afraid of my son making a dumb, irreversible choice. I'm afraid of my daughter's young heart being hurt. These are my true fears. These unnerve my heart. While I am not indifferent to the sad things happening to other good people, I have tremendous faith in them being temporary. I have tremendous faith in the resilience and compassion of good people and know that we will prevail through any atrocity. Good people are survivors. Bad people are not.

Comforted by this faith and understanding that all of life is temporary, I'm going to enjoy all of the brief moments in my kids' temporary childhoods and leave the rest of the noise to the people who think it means something…I'm too busy loving what I love most…

Slurpee day.

A few weeks ago my son was in the kitchen pilfering through the cabinets searching for the largest container he could find. It happened to be "Bring Your Own Cup" day at 7-11 for slurpees and he was gearing up. He found an obscenely over-sized pitcher and smiled. I shook my head and told him that his selection was a stupid choice, because: he couldn't drink that much slurpee; it was wasteful; and I was trying to help him "not be THAT guy." He responded with, "Well, Dad, I appreciate your efforts, but I AM that guy..." And he was out the door with his slurpee trough.

Several hours later, walking past the kitchen, I spied the slurpee urn half-filled with melted colored sugar water and felt validated. But, so what? I was right, but I knew I would be right from the start. My son probably knew I was right, too. He didn't care. It didn't matter and doesn't matter. Sometimes, a kid's gotta do what a kid's gotta do. No lecture from me, no matter how valid, can override the simple need to be a jackass sometimes. I understand this well, probably too well.

We possess, as human animals, a certain need for self-destruction. We know the right things to do, but sometimes need to do the wrong things. I'm not sure where this need comes from. I suspect it's just a minor form of rebellion. We spend much of our lives doing what we should do. We punch the clock and drive kids and make snacks and pay bills. Our schedules are full of responsibilities, obligations and chores.

"On the whole human beings want to be good, but not too good, and not quite all the time." –George Orwell

Once in a while, we need to raise a figurative (usually) middle finger to the world and claim a day for bad choices. We stay up too late, drink too much, eat too much, sing too loud, cuss, dance and laugh. We take instead of give. We are selfish and feel no guilt about this. We earned this selfishness.

The next day, we wake with foggy heads and a clear heart. The itch was scratched. We remind ourselves that we are not simply meal-makers and check-writers. We still have the capacity for irreverence and self-expression and fun. We are whole human beings.

These little revolutions take different shapes, but yield the same spiritual outcome. We return to center. We find our balance. A late night spent laughing

232

with friends is therapy and is as necessary to our well-being as proper sleep and water.

So, I'll forgive my little slurpee glutton and understand that being "THAT guy" once in a while is the right guy to be. In fact, I probably wouldn't like him as much if he was never "THAT guy." I'm a sucker for the untidy, imperfect, yet beautiful people which give the world its color. I get it, buddy. I get it...

Dancing in the mud.

This morning I received two text messages: One came from my wife notifying me that a friend of ours had delivered her baby. The second one came from a best friend notifying me that his mom had passed away.

As I often do, I have been trying to find some understanding about the events and how they are connected and how they are distinct. I have discovered many obvious distinctions: One family is preparing to welcome a new member into the fold. They are cleaning and smiling and eating in anticipation of their lives changing in many wonderfully unknown ways. At the exact same time, another family is mourning and with the sleepless eyes of grief trying to imagine life without their loved one in it any more. Here, the contrast between events is clear.

What is similar is that life will never be the same for either family. Yesterday was the last day of "before…". Life is changed and will be changed forever. We cannot go back to before.

Reflecting on these things as another summer wanes into autumn, I feel grateful to be passing my time with the people in my life. I don't have many things, but I have many friends. My life is rich with characters. Unique, caring, funny and generous oddballs surround me always. They give my life its color. They validate my choices; the good ones… and the bad ones. Laughter is healing magic and we laugh a lot. In this way, we heal each other. Friends and family are the most valuable assets anyone can have.

As I sit looking out my living room window to the waters of my youth contemplating the day's events, I have no clear answers. Life is a miracle of contradictions. It confronts and confounds and makes no sense and perfect sense in the same breath.

A single geometric insight stands alone as a vital understanding. It is this: The whole "circle of life" thing is garbage. Life is not a circle. It is a line; an often shaky, uncertain and spastic line leading us from the cradle to the grave. We do not return back to where we started from. (With the possible exception of needing diapers and if/when this happens to me my son is firmly secured as "wipe-boy". He knows this and is not thrilled.) Time that passes is gone. Life travels in one direction only. This thought does not dishearten me. It inspires me. It slaps me in the face with the certain awareness that my own opportunities to enjoy my life are limited to the time I have left. Whatever the hell that is. And I would be a fool to waste a moment of it.

With this in mind, if it starts to rain today, I will simply turn my palms up, tip my head to the sky, and dance in the mud. There is nothing to gain and everything to lose by doing something else.

Not a tree.

Last fall, my son told me he was thinking about joining his high school swim team. For the previous couple of years, he wrestled. I liked wrestling and was a little disappointed that he was considering jumping ship. I, also, being a typical dad somewhat protective of my boy's fragile teenage ego, remembered the great line from the book, Sh#t My Dad Says, ""**You can't swim. Son, you're a good athlete but I've seen what you call swimming. You look like a slow kid on his knees trying to smash ants."** So, I had some concerns but supported whatever he wanted to do. I'm glad I did. He had a great time. He made some good friends and didn't drown.

I'm proud of this kid. He is pretty fearless. He tries new stuff. These are good qualities that will serve him well. Life is not a script. It rarely follows a predictable path. It weaves and wanders with many unforeseeable events shifting the stream's channel. Being able to adjust course and navigate new waters is vital to being happy.

Sometimes these things are circumstantial. Events happen that make us move. Sometimes, though, these things are just how we feel. They lack explanation and often understanding, but they drive us as powerfully as a hurricane. They are the storms that only we can feel. In these storms, we make choices. We choose to act or to stay put. I'm glad my son is willing to risk uncertainty and take on the challenge of new things. He does so with genuine effort and an interest in exploring different opportunities. Not everything works out awesome, but he is undeterred. He just changes course.

Success consists of going from failure to failure without loss of enthusiasm.
-Winston Churchill

Life rarely works out the way we plan it. We have control over many things, but not all. The single most defining characteristic of people that succeed in spite of circumstances is enthusiasm. Enthusiasm enrolls others in our journeys. Enthusiasm makes the necessary persistence possible. We infect others and ourselves with this contagion.

If you don't like how things are, change it! You're not a tree. -Jim Rohn

This is beautiful idea: the option of changing course is always available to us. We can change anything and everything, anytime we want. We can change our jobs, our homes and our minds. This awareness is liberating. We float this river for an undetermined length of time. Our days are our currency and frivolously wasting this precious tender on things we know aren't serving us, bettering us or making us happy is silly and wrong. We have a single chance at life and with this in mind, exploring, thinking, caring and creating joy for ourselves and the world that surrounds us just seems right. With the absurd notion that we are truly free to do and be what we want, even the ridiculous makes sense...it's fun when this happens...

Of hands and hearts.

The other day I helped a buddy pour some concrete. After we were finished, I looked at my hands. They were nicked and dusty and sore. I saw new wounds and old scars. I'm not sure I've ever really looked at them before, certainly not with any more than a cursory glance. They tell quite a story. Our hands are with us every day of our lives. They are a time capsule of our experiences and they are special.

As children, our hands hold our mothers' hand during our first walk into elementary school. Then, they let go and we begin a new journey. Our hands play paddy-cake and peek-a-boo and cribbage. Mine have thrown balls for friends and dogs, thrown tantrums and a few punches. They have held my babies and fishing poles and beer cans. They have wiped tears and bottoms. They have comforted and scolded. They have raised a finger behind my dad's back when I was mad as child and they shaved his face as he was dying of cancer. We live our lives with our hands.

I have a wonderful scar from the ONE time I was the kindling holder while my cousin, Shelly, was the kindling chopper. We were young and I bled a lot. I have scars on three knuckles from an old skateboard crash. I have another scar on my right index finger from a broken window handle from a 1980 diesel Rabbit. I have many more that I don't remember.

Our hands are windows into our past. They tell the tales of good and bad days. They represent our best and our worst. With them we have healed or hurt. We talk with them and through them. We hug and wave or put them in our pockets and they speak.

We bruise and scrape and callous our hands through the living of our lives. They are connected to our hearts and may in fact, represent the nearest living evidence of the memories we hold in our hearts. For this reason, looking at my hands and thinking of where they've been and what they've done, I can believe that nothing was in vain. I have worked and tried and explored and lost and won. I've lived and my hands reveal this truth.

Entering the post middle-age era of my life and really feeling no closer to an "answer" than I ever have, I am comforted by these hands of mine. They just show up and keep showing up for whatever this wonderful world presents in front of them. They still work and hold the things I love. They are not perfect, but I like their flaws. They're good hands.

Hands represent hope and possibility. They act on our ideas. They are the vehicles driven by our hearts. With good hands and good hearts, anything is possible...I like this thought...

The Primary Objective.

I've heard it said that the hardest thing to write is a simple, true sentence. I believe this. It is much easier to add words and use literary magic tricks to convey a thought than it is to strip it down to a simple truth. The conservation of words while preserving the integrity of the idea is a skilled art. This is true for words, but also for life.

It is easier to complicate life than it is to simplify it. We subtract by addition in the process of establishing this contrary truth. We add "stuff". We add more obligations, tasks and goods which only serve to clog the machine. Our schedules, minds and garages are full of this stuff, which makes it difficult to enjoy a clear, simple and true thought or park a car.

Ernest Hemingway addressed his writer's block by beginning with one true sentence. He believed that if he could write this one sentence, it would breed others. I think he was right. Drawing another parallel between words and life, by stripping away the noise and peeling back the burdensome layers of complicated, but often extraneous clutter, we get closer to where we want to be. We unblock our lives. This is liberating and peaceful and right.

"The more you strive to be sensible and serious and meaningful, the less chance you have of becoming so. The primary objective is to laugh."- John D. MacDonald's character, Travis McGee, in the novel, Free Fall In Crimson.

This idea is also liberating. In our quest to be responsible and sensible and reasonable, we lose things. We also diminish our chances of finding the things we are looking for. We search for peace, but manifest our own chaos. It's a crazy and confounding system.

For most of us, the end of our lives will be a non-event. We will simply slip into the great waters and drift away. Certainly, those close to us will mourn, but most of the world will just keep on keepin' on. The neighbor's TV will still turn on and the 7-11 store down the street will still sell slurpees. Not much will have changed by our end.

With this in mind, Travis McGee's philosophy makes much more sense. Since one day we will simply be gone, today is an important day. It is a day to enjoy and it is a day to remember and embrace a life philosophy in which "the primary objective is to laugh". The world is less for all of our seriousness. It deserves our joy...we deserve our joy...

Busted Lawnmower.

Yesterday, I took my lawnmower to a repair guy. Today, I picked it up. My lawn mower has been broken for quite a while. This has been a challenging time for me. While driving the 20 minutes for its retrieval, I was slightly giddy. I love my lawnmower. I love mowing lawns. I love the smell of gasoline and freshly-mowed grass. My brief walks behind my mower always return me to center. I become grounded as my worries fall to the land and are shredded and flung into the catcher bag. It is my meditation in motion.

For these reasons, I just mowed my lawn in the rain. With high expectations, I fired up my newly fixed mower and made a clean and straight first line to use as a reference for subsequent clean and straight lines. The first pass is critical to a decent mow job.

About round three, some barely detectable sputtering started. "NO!!" I not-so-silently screamed (among some other words unfit for print). The maladies had returned. The mower revved and stalled and finally quit. I started it again and it ran, albeit reluctantly, for the rest of my task. I finished, but not with the same flourish I had begun with. I was slightly frustrated, but mostly deflated.

In a post-mortem evaluation of my response to my mower's dying breaths, I found no satisfying answers. Disappointment happens. Let downs happen. Frustration and struggle happens. These things are life. Understanding that my reaction to lawnmower issues is uniquely weird and uniquely mine and are likely a thin comparison for "real" problems, I still believe that parallels can be drawn between a sputtering lawnmower and a sputtering life.

For example, both sap our energy and enthusiasm. They strip us of our faith and our confidence. And both leave us weary and worn and wondering what to do next. One redeeming element of tough circumstances is that they force us to ask the hard questions. Under the spotlight of a challenge we must decide a path or choose an action. Usually, these actions change us. And usually for the better.

So, acknowledging that my set-back with my damn lawnmower is more emotional that physical, I will move forward. Maybe try to get it fixed "for real". Maybe buy a new one. Either way, a faulty mower is an easy problem to remedy. As for my life, the same principles apply: Fix what's broken. Or create a new one. Either way, living with what is not working doesn't work and is not an option.

With this in mind, I look very forward to the warm, summer sun shining on my bare shoulders as I mow my lawn. I will walk slow and straight and not deviate from my course. I will let the mower erase my fear and doubt and I will be happy. And being happy is about the best reason to do anything.

Card Dealers.

On a Tuesday morning, a lovely friend informed me that she was pregnant. (NOT mine!!) She is a married mother of three equally lovely little girls, including a fine set of twins. This announcement was made with some hesitation, as a certain degree of trepidation sometimes accompanies grand announcements. Overshadowing the trepidation were the feelings of love and hope and joy that only new babies can inspire.

On a different Tuesday, another lovely friend informed me that he had cancer. While the prognosis was about as good as any cancer diagnosis could be, it's still cancer. The feelings of fear and uncertainty leak into even the most logical of outcome potentials.

On different Tuesdays, very different events unfolded. Different conversations inspired different feelings. During each breath we take, conversations like these occur. New people are born and old people die and not-old people die. The world keeps spinning through these conversations and events.

And though the world moves on, it is changed, because we are changed. We are changed when we hear certain words and we feel certain things. Minute shifts in our perspectives and awareness move us differently. These shifts change how we think and care about things. We are forever changing, often imperceptibly, in very real ways. Conversations change us and how we see and feel about our world. This changes how we act, if we use them appropriately.

While talking to my buddy about his diagnosis, he was realistic, but philosophical about his circumstances. He said some words that remain with me "Someone else deals the cards and we have to play them." These words instead of diminishing hope inspired it. Instead of resignation, I felt empowered.

In another life, I spent some time at card tables. Being an unsuccessful gambler, I am familiar with the strong feelings that a crappy dealer can provoke. After being kicked off of a Pai Gow table for expressing my feelings about a particularly shady dealer, I remember being a little sad. I was sad not because I could no longer play, about that I was happy, as I was losing my can. I was sad, because I acted like an ass. The dealer does not pick which cards come off the deck, yet I took the bad cards personally and lost my temper and some degree of dignity.

In this lesson, the enduring message is that circumstances are rarely personal and even though we are affected personally, we are only lost when we give control to circumstances instead of focusing on our response to them. Our response defines us. Bad things happen and good things happen. They always have and they always will. Maintaining some composure and dignity and faith goes a long way towards preserving and/or creating favorable outcomes.

While I support hating the cards we are dealt from time to time, I also recognize that once certain cards are dealt, we must play them. We cannot fold and start over. In these times, it is our response that determines a bust or a win. And, played right, we can walk away from even the lousiest hands with a win...

Old dogs and men.

Last night, after a longer than normal day of work and meetings and just "stuff", I opened my front door to let my dogs outside. Being uncomfortably familiar with my old dog, Diego's, digestive patterns, I knew we were treading in some dangerous waters. For this reason I was surprised when I opened the door and had to call for him to come downstairs. Normally, he is waiting desperately panting and prancing at the door trying to hold things together. This night was peculiar. He sulked his way down the stairs and seeing his head hanging while very deliberately avoiding any eye contact with me, I knew the score.

As I walked up the stairs I saw the first signs confirming my suspicions. Shredded napkins, broken eggshells and pork rib bones told the story of his dumpster dive. Entering the kitchen, all doubt and hope was erased. The garbage can was tipped over and picked through with the indelicate touch of a frenzied badger. Thoughts of simply killing my dog entered my head. Then, they left...much quicker than normal. Weird.

Usually, I hold a grudge. The fact that I say "usually" indicates that this is not the first time my dog and I have danced to this song. Diego has tormented me for years. His exploits in digging, escaping our yard, stealing, chewing, farting and otherwise disrupting the simple, happy existence I try to live is a truly impressive catalogue.

In the past, his indiscretions were met with swift and clear justice. Cause and effect. He knew the price of his choices and, apparently, was willing to pay it. He owns no poker face and his body language speaks louder than words. I can always tell when he has been up to something devious. And I've responded. That's what's strange about this evening.

After letting him outside and surveying his damage, I did nothing besides clean up his mess. This surprised both of us. As I opened the door to let him back in the house, he sat in the rain at the edge of the driveway reluctant to meet his consequences. I called him and he sat. Eventually, I had to move his direction to force his hand. He crept towards me tensely anticipating his punishment which never came. I just didn't have it in me.

I don't know where my need for vengeance has gone, but it's gone. My only explanation is that I'm old. Diego's old, too. We have played this game many times and are just weary of it. He's my buddy and I'm his buddy and for all my bluster, he knows it. I know it, too.

At a certain age, dogs and men simply stop caring about stuff that seemed important when we were younger. No meaningful outcome will come from punishing Diego these days. He doesn't care. The tasty rib bones are worth the risk and he'll accept whatever comes his way. There is no way to fight this. He wins. And I'm ok with that. We seem to have achieved an uneasy truce. In this truce, there is truth.

Diego and I have shared life. Like all relationships, we have battled and struggled and loved. Tired of the battles and struggle, all that's left now is love. The clear and present fact of our mutual mortality softens us. There are more days behind us than ahead of us and this knowledge is liberating. Time has a unique way of defining priorities. We care less about some things and more about some other things. This is true for men and dogs...and probably everything else, too...

Ceiling Fans.

As I stepped out the front door this morning, I suffered many mixed emotions, none of them good. The half-frozen, sleety rain whipped through my several layers and I felt nothing but despair. (No poetic intent here…it just happened) I don't like the cold and rain separately, but I especially don't like them in combination. The unfortunate fact that the rear window of my truck was busted out last week did not comfort me physically or emotionally. The day was dark and so was I.

In circumstances such as these, when the depths of my S.A.D-ness slices deep, as it did this morning, I have, out of a sense of necessity and desperation, developed several techniques for softening the blows. These coping mechanisms include: listening to island music and visualizing warm places. I try to remind myself that the pain is only temporary as I count the calendar days until spring.

This morning a fond memory arrived as an old friend in my mind as a savior from this somewhat depressing morning: Many years ago, in one of several lifetimes I have lived, a couple of buddies, Scott and Jason, and I took a road trip to Costa Rica. It was filled with adventure and fun and lots of stories. It was also hot. Real hot. A lot hot. And one night was especially smokin'. So much so, in fact, that I wrote about it then. This thought is what saved me this morning. Here is the story of a night many years ago written in a molten motel room in Merida, Mexico:

"I lie here in the soft bed of our cheap motel room. My back sticks, moistly, to the tainted yellow sheets. The ceiling fan above ticks noisily along as its breeze seeks to tame this brutal night. I see the lightly tanned skin of my stomach keep time with the beat of my heart. The sickly sweet humidity sweats hungrily through my dim awareness as I try to sleep. My roommates shift restlessly in the damp tropical heat, savoring each delicious draft the over-worked fan delivers. We lie, each alone in our thoughts to explore the possibilities of our lives. Each one is presented certain circumstances, through fate or folly, and must decide on a path. We all have, more or less, decided on this sauna to attempt to sleep in, for better or for worse.

I'm sure in the grand scope of life poorer decisions have been made by all, but it makes one think about how we came to this decision and whether possibly this decision is representative of other decisions and the fact that no matter how fast and noisily the fan sings, sometimes it's just going to be hot."

I was and am warmed by this memory. It is nice to know that memories like this exist. They are good and necessary. They remind and bring peace and perspective. Many more chilly days await and I think it's worthwhile to keep my little jewel a little closer to the surface. Even the most miserable of days don't stand a chance against a dank and steamy Mexican motel room with a screaming ceiling fan.

To quote from "Three Day Blow", the best final line of any Hemingway story: "It was a good thing to have in reserve." Damn right.

Double Standard.

While enjoying dinner the other evening with my family, I began questioning my 17 year old son on his dating prospects. My queries were fairly innocent and well-intentioned...for the most part. However, as I am prone to do, my tone shifted a bit and may have turned a little on the creepy side. "Is she HOT??" was likely been the question that pushed my 12 year old daughter over the edge.

With the insightful awareness that only kids (and maybe only girls) of a certain age possess, she looked at me with her pretty green, judgy eyes and asked, "Dad, how would you feel if the dad of a boy I was interested in talked about me that way?" Well, I was caught and we both knew it. My only "defense" was that things are different for boys and girls. I understand that this reasoning is faulty and borderline sexist, but as a father, I know that it is also true.

I tried to back out of my comments, in that my intentions weren't as creepy as they may have sounded. I understand all too well the power of nicer-smelling gender on a young man. Through my years occupying space on this earth, I have forgotten many things. I have not forgotten the beautiful feelings associated with my initial forays into the cauldron of "dating" relationships. In our youth, these experiences can awaken our confidence and self-esteem during a special time when both can be exceedingly fragile and rare. This is what I want for my son. Even if it did sound a little creepy.

For my daughter, I want her protected from the inevitable pain that comes with these relationships. She is my flower. I don't care about the certain evolutionary benefits of experiencing a little heartache. I want her in a cocoon safe from pain. As her protector, I want her protected. Unfortunately, I also want her to have a brave and thriving life. I understand that this courage is forged with some degree of hurt.

I also understand that this contradiction holds no logic. But, I think within a father's heart no logic is available when it comes to protecting his daughter. I understand my son. I don't understand my daughter. When my son gets injured, I can look up from my book and say "You'll be fine. Rub some dirt on it." And go back to reading. With my daughter, I want to fix it. I need answers. "How did it happen? Who did it?" And begin formulating a pay-back strategy. Again, I recognize the double-standard. But, I can't apologize for it.

A daughter captures and takes residence in a special place of a dad's heart. It is a place reserved only for them. In this place live emotions that only the father of a daughter has access to. These emotions drive us crazy and make us stupid. We contain levels of love that we cannot comprehend and a biblical capacity for violence when imagining someone hurting our girls.

So, as the years move on, my daughter and I will struggle and battle with my need to protect her. She will win. But, I will win, too. She will become all that I wish for her to be, in spite of, or maybe because of the obstacles I present. Perhaps, a father's relationship with a daughter is the first testing ground for how to deal with the irrational, stubborn, open and guarded, hasty and fool-hearty souls of men. If this is the case, then my girl has a bright future, because she owns me and I'm a disaster. She may even thank me for this one day...ahhhh...one day...

Deep Waters.

My daughter doesn't like to write. She's not super-fond of reading either. In fact, the entire scope of language arts is only grudgingly accepted as a necessary evil. As an avid reader and a lover of words for many years, this troubles me. I know the beauty and power of well-crafted words and I don't want her to miss it.

Through the years, this has caused some conflict. My natural instinct is to educate (annoy) and encourage (harass) her exploration into the lovely world of literature. I've read to her since she was born and bought her books and ranted and raved about the joys of a good story. She doesn't care. She'll read when she has to or when she finds a book she REALLY likes, but she is, beyond that, grossly indifferent.

My girl has had a phone for a couple of years and, with this, the true impact of her ambivalence punches me in the face on a regular basis. Spelling errors, weird sentences, and a complete lack of care light up my text box every day. My typical response is "READ A BOOK!!!"

The other day, I sent my flower a message gilded with love and sarcasm. In my haste, I forgot a word. This was an important word and its absence completely screwed up the note. My precious sunshine responded with "Read a book." I was shocked and shamed and proud. I don't know why we, as parents, like it when we see ourselves in our kids. Perhaps it's some validation that they do ACTUALLY listen to us and that we possess some nominal degree of influence, in spite of much evidence to the contrary.

This is both an inspiring and a frightening thought. I want my kids to be better, much better than I am. However, since I am only armed with a rusty and busted set of parenting tools, I don't know how to help them beyond just digging harder with my broken shovel. I think this is not an uncommon challenge. We know what we know and we carry our parents' goodness and "other" with us, as they carried their parents'...and so on...and so on...

The waters of familial goofiness run deep and the legacies passed along are often ones that belong in a grave. But, life doesn't work that way. We are stunted and flawed by long-dead relatives' influence. We are also enlivened and blessed, for that which often seems to be a weakness is sometimes a strength. We get the good stuff, too.

"Eventually, all things merge into one, and a river runs through it. The river was cut by the world's great flood and runs over rocks from the basement of time. On some of the rocks are timeless raindrops. Under the rocks are the words, and some of the words are theirs. I am haunted by waters."
— Norman Maclean, A River Runs Through It and Other Stories

We cannot escape our past. Even the one we didn't live. It lives with us. I'm not sure if this idea completely lets us off the hook for our failings, but it does soften the sometimes crushing and paralyzing flaws which can erode our self-esteem. It's not ALL our fault and I say this not as a cop-out, just a fact. Plenty IS our fault, just not all. We can stop blaming ourselves for every single thing we DON'T possess and we can rejoice in the things we do. And while we are "haunted by waters", we are also lucky. We got the good things, too. Now, we "haunt" our children with them...and so it goes...forever...and it's pretty good...

The Cold Swim.

The other night I drove my truck down to the marina in my hometown. As the bright orange sun lit the water, then fell behind the mountains, I cracked a twenty-four ounce "lemonade" and cried.

I cried because I had just learned that one of my oldest and best friend's dad had passed away. I cried for my friend. I cried for his mom and family. And I cried for myself.

When the people we love are struck by loss, so are we. We share their loss with them and we have our own loss, because we loved the person, too. In ways that we don't often acknowledge or maybe even understand, we love a lot of people. We love them because they are good and kind and they make us better.

My buddy's dad, Ken, was a living, breathing reminder of my history. His passing has hit me hard on many levels. Naturally, my heart broke for his family first. Then, I just felt sad and old and knew that another page had turned on this story of my life.

Beginning around 1985 until 2000 or so, I spent an uncomfortable amount of time with Ken's stuff. From his house and boat to, most significantly, his son, I was a sometimes reluctantly welcomed fixture around his life. Being the kids we were, his son and I had some monumental screw ups. When these happened, we knew the consequences would not be good. We, no doubt, frustrated and more likely infuriated Ken on more than one occasion. But, I cannot help but think that on the soft, warm summer evenings, when we would tie up the boat in front of his house at dusk and swim to the beach, he was proud.

Being a dad myself now, I understand that providing opportunities for our kids to grow and test and experience life is a primary duty. Ken understood this, and though it always cost him something, sometimes his time and always his money, he paid the toll for our experiences. It was not cheap. In fact, I believe he may still hold the Washington state record for most boat starters purchased in a six year time frame.

He paid this because he cared. There is no other reason that I can think of. He rarely even used his boat. He effectively gave it to us and in doing so taught us about responsibility, again "consequences" helped with this lesson. But, more importantly, he taught us how to be good fathers. His expectations were high and though I had my own dad, Ken's example and impact on my life were profound.

These lessons, unfortunately, we usually understand too late. Too late to say the word, "thanks." My life was defined by these years. I was shaped by sunsets and cold water swims in from the boat. And my gratitude for these years is beyond measure.

So, as I sit in my truck and stare out at the cold waters of my youth, I see and feel the page turned and I understand clearly that the pages turn without asking us. We give no sanction as to when they turn. Life simply moves on. It's what it does. I see the walkers and boaters and know that the world keeps spinning and the clock ticks forward in spite of my wish to turn it back.

Today, I will be sad. Tomorrow, I will wake up and take my son to school and make my daughter breakfast. Tomorrows come until they don't. So, I will appreciate the ones that I have and will give what I have to the people I love. And in the cold moments ahead in my life, when I travel warmly back in my mind to sunburnt shoulders and salty skin...and much more, I will say, "Thanks, Ken". It mattered.

The Broken Wingman.

For the past several weeks, I have sensed that something might be special about this year's Seattle Seahawks' season. Since I have been a fan of this team for as long as it has existed and have seen it all, I believe myself to be a bit clairvoyant about these things.

As a kid, I watched their games with my dad and have many fond memories of him yelling and swearing, then climbing out of his recliner to go clean the garage when they sucked too bad for him to watch any further. To this day, my old friends still text me, asking if I am "cleaning the garage, yet" when my team is crapping the bed. Gratefully, this year, my garage remains a mess.

Being excited about my Seahawks' season and their potential to do something special (this is NOT A JINX!!), I have been very mindful of sharing this year with my fourteen year old son, Aden. I know that I would love to have some memories with my dad enjoying a good team, though, frankly, I don't mind remembering his anger and frustration either.

With my Seahawk sense unusually, yet cautiously, optimistic, some time ago, I began deliberately planning to watch the games with my boy. I skipped going to buddies' houses. I skipped going to the bar. And on one occasion, I skipped actually going to the game to sit with my kid and share a special time.

For weeks, I have hoped and wished and performed my silly little rituals ensuring a successful Seahawk season. And my son sat next to me as happy as I was. Well, the time has come for the big game and while I was preparing to cement a rare and wonderful father/son memory in to my canon of great moments in my life, my wife informed me that Aden was planning on going to his buddy, Rick's, house to watch the game.

Needless to say, I was stunned, but I also didn't completely trust my wife with this important information. I needed to talk to my boy immediately. Upon my query, my son confirmed that he was, in fact, going to Rick's. So, there it was. My son, my favorite male human being on earth, my little buddy and my wingman riding shotgun as we travel the back roads of our shared life, dodging potholes and loose gravel on the corners, was ditching me for his buddy ON SEAHAWK SUPERBOWL SUNDAY!!

My response to his confirmation was a leer followed by the mumbled words, "Benedict Arnold", as I left the room to sulk. He shrugged, indifferent to my pain and replied, "Hey, it's his birthday." "I hope it's a good one, traitor," I whispered continuing my walk away.

So, it's a done deal. What could and should be, won't be. This, I believe, is called "life". I have struggled through my share of disappointments and I will handle this one. I should probably not be surprised. My son, on a daily basis, reminds me that he is inching his way closer to the front door on his way out of it forever. For this reason, perhaps, my reaction to his betrayal was a little overboard. I'm simply not ready for him to go. My recognition of this moment's imminence scares me. I am unprepared.

Well, with this in mind, I will try to not be so harsh on my little turncoat. It's my problem, not his. A man's gotta do, what a man's gotta do. He's gotta go to his buddy's birthday. So it goes. I will still enjoy the big game plenty without him. I will swear and yell and drink beer. I will be with my old buddies, raising our glasses on the good plays and shaking our heads and screaming at the bad ones. And, if things get too ugly, I can always go clean the garage, just like my old man. I suspect I will also leave the door unlocked for my son to return home after his stupid party...and for all days after that, as well...

Open Windows.

I hate the end of summer. I am never ready for it to end. This has been a weird week. It seems as though summer is finished and I never had a chance to say "goodbye". It just left me. I needed some closure and got none. While I *will* hold out hope for a few more summer-ish days, I *will not* hold my breath. I know better. This ain't my first rodeo.

In times like these, two equally natural responses occur for me. The first one is to become annoyed and petulant and try to fight it. The second is just to sit back and take it. I can't change it, so I might as well accept it.

As I returned home from work this evening, the sun was setting across the water and a light breeze rustled the yellowing leaves on my cherry tree. In this breeze, I smelled fall. I smelled peace and transition and my youth. I smelled the mellow change of the season and I remembered that I like fall.

While I am always a "summer guy", I like the wind-down that autumn allows. I like cool mornings and fog on the water. I like blowing leaves and not having to pick weeds in my flower beds. Fall is a season of reflection. In the shorter days and chilly nights, autumn brings us inside; inside of our homes and inside of ourselves. Nature gives us permission to grab a blanket and sit on the couch with a warm drink and feel ok about it. In these moments, the hard edges of life soften. The busy world slows and we can remember the things that are important to remember.

My wife and daughter are leaving in the morning for a week-long trip to New York. In a last gasp, last chance effort to scrape the last good bits of summer from the bottom of the pan, my son and I were planning on heading to eastern Washington. However, as "the best laid plans of mice and men oft go awry", our plans have gone awry. The weather is going to suck over there, too. It seems I cannot get a break.

Well, as I sit in a chair next to a slightly cracked window, in the soft breeze I can still smell fall. Summer may be over and I am not unhappy with it. Response phase two is kicking in solid.

I have heat and food and hope. I refuse to bitch about the weather. My son and I will hang out, maybe go see a movie or buy him some new socks. We can do whatever we want. The world is ours and without any pushy and loud nine year-old female disruptions distracting us from our time together, we will savor it. We may do much and we may do nothing. It doesn't really matter. It's our time.

And if the sky darkens and the clouds burst, I will open the window and feel the cool, fresh air and be happy with the rain.

Fifteen.

My son, Aden, turned fifteen. How this happened I do not know. Time, I suppose, does this. Time and a couple of rare, but fortunate, demonstrations of parental self-discipline during those moments when I wanted to kill him myself. Kids can make us crazy and this boy is no exception. For a while, "bonehead," "knucklehead" and a variety of other "head" suffixed names became his. At fifteen, I believe we may have turned a corner. (Jinx alert here!!)

While he is still highly capable of some supremely stupid things, these incidences are increasingly rarer. His mind and heart are good. He is kind and works hard at the things he should work hard at, a notable exception being cleaning his room. He is funny and creative and thoughtful. He's smart and articulate and wise in ways that are good to be wise. He cares about the world and is shaping his role in it. It's fun being his dad.

I really like him. As parents we are probably obligated to love our kids, though I'm not sure we have to like them. Some kids are very challenging to like, even for their parents, I suspect. Liking someone may be more personal preference and choice than love. Sometimes, we can't help loving someone, even if we don't like them. I'm glad I like this boy.

As a dad I worry about my influence screwing up a pretty good kid. I can recall in great detail my own dad's successes and failures. Moments when he said or did the right things shaped me, as did the moments when he said or did the wrong things. We never know our score as a parent. Our kids keep the scorecards to themselves, though occasionally when observing them in action, we catch a brief glimpse of our influence. Sometimes this is good and sometimes this is bad. The results speak for themselves.

So, at fifteen, my son and I still have a few miles ahead of us. My hope is that we travel well: we make a few good choices and throw in some bad ones for a little color and share some smiles about both. Perfect parenting has never been my goal. I am not foolish enough to prescribe myself a destiny of failure. My only wish for my kids is joy in life. Joy will only come through the truest expression of their unique gifts, of which they are blessed with many. I hope to support this whenever and wherever I can. My place in their journey is sometimes conductor, sometimes riding shotgun. They decide where I sit. And this is ok with me...

(Sidenote: To all the other parents believing their son is the best one...you're wrong...because, I've got him.)

Tables.

During my lifetime, I have sat at many tables. I have enjoyed dinner tables and picnic tables and high-top bar tables. I have rested my elbows on various shapes and sizes and textures of tables. The single common thread connecting the tables of my life are the other people sitting at them with me.

Family and friends reside at my tables. We share a laugh or mashed potatoes or a pitcher of beer. We share our lives. Certain tables remind us and reassure us. We are safe and certain at these tables. They are a sanctuary from the harsh winds that life can blow at us. Simple peace and joy live at these tables. They're beautiful.

Through my years, I have shared many tables with many people. I have enjoyed a meal or a beer with kids of all ages. I have smiled and cried with my tablemates. These tables reflect our shared lives. Looking around the table at Thanksgiving this year, I was proud to see a wonderful and rare collection of friends who, through life and time, became family. These are the best kind of people. They are the family we choose. Through mutual decision, we tie our lives together and face the world with hands and hearts connected.

These are the special people and I am happy I have them. I know they're rare and I know people who don't have them and I feel bad for them. These people give life its color and create sound and move our hearts and minds. They are the "why?" They are the answer to our questions of purpose and meaning.

Sitting in my quiet house, I look out the window and see the raindrops melting the snow and I understand the fleeting hands of our clock and am happy and proud to know that for all the mistakes I've made and flaws I possess, I am a good friend. I have won and lost many things, many times, but my greatest treasure, my lotto ticket win, are the people at my tables. I've earned these people and they've earned me and as life continues its trek to wherever the hell it's going, this fact makes every single thing worth it. This is true for me and this is true for all of us...

A Morning.

This day belongs to the dogs. They claimed it early and aren't letting it go. The tic-tac revelry call of toenails on the hardwood floor kills any hope I have of finding my place back into the wonderful dream I was having. I don't remember what it was, but it was good.

This morning I succumb to my better nature and get up and let the dogs out. Some mornings, I don't. I can feign sleep with the best of them and have achieved some truly miraculous performances. My wife is no slouch, either. This day, she breathes deeply and slowly and throws in a twitch for good measure. I can tell she is in the zone. As I open the bedroom door, I glance back and see just a hint of a relieved smile. She wins this battle.

In the kitchen, I put coffee in the machine. This will be handy today. My dog, Diego, stares at me. I know what he wants. As I grab his leash, he knows his wish is about to come true. He jumps and twirls and bucks like a bronco. I do not.

We head out the door and onto the sleeping streets of my hometown. Roads are empty and shops are closed. Only one restaurant is open, Jack's. Every town has a Jack's. It is where the old-timers gather to drink coffee and discuss important things like politics and fishing, mostly fishing.

I walk by Jack's and one smell hits me hard: bacon. Bacon is one item that can inspire me to dance around like a Diego getting ready for his walk. The sweet, smoky goodness floats in the air like God's own aftershave. "I will be having some bacon today." I think to myself and repeat as a mantra several times over the course of this morning's walk.

Ahead, I see a light on. It is coming from the office of my friendly, local attorney, Brian. It appears that someone else was either disrupted from slumber as well, or is behind on some work...or looking to actually get ahead on some work; a foreign concept to me.

As I peek through his blinds from the sidewalk, Brian looks pretty intense and engaged in his project. I tip-toe through the planter bed and bang on his window. While I have never actually witnessed an electrocution, Brian's response is what I would imagine one looks like. His head jerked up, eyes wide, his hands instinctively clutched the arms of his chair and he shook, violently, for a couple of the longest and best seconds of my year.

I smiled and waved. He did not smile, but did wave. With one finger. I carried on. Diego and I went home, our mission complete.

This day was simply one of many days of my life. It was a morning of little consequence. It meant nothing and everything. It was life. It was my life written on the pavement. My history was scribed in worn skid marks on the sidewalks. Memories met me at every street corner and I was happy to greet them. As I returned to my silent home, I felt complete. The circle was full and, as I looked in on my sleeping children, I believed in angels and the idea that dreams really can come true.

Broken Bits.

I don't work on Tuesdays. By "don't work", I don't mean that I lie on the couch eating delicious grilled sandwiches all day. (Though, this, frankly, sounds like a pretty damn fine day...) Tuesdays are my day to pick up the pieces of my home life neglected since the previous Tuesday: Laundry gets done. Nominal housework gets done and all the running around that needs to happen happens.

Last Tuesday was a lovely day. As such, it was a yard day. Early autumn weather in this state is a crap-shoot. I happened into some good luck and did not waste it. I fired up my line-trimmer, mower and blower and chopped and raked and mowed and blew my tidy edges.

It was a day I needed. Being a yard guy, I find peace in my little "meditation-in-motion" chores. I think big thoughts, solve my problems and return to a certain center that is sometimes hard to find; it can be an elusive target.

This Tuesday was especially necessary as I am somewhat broken right now. Life, as it does, has presented me with a challenging time. I write this not to inspire any sympathy or pity. It's simply life. Gratefully, I am armed with the awareness that difficult times pass. Nothing lasts- the good or the bad. I share my brokenness not as a salacious conversation starter, but only with a hope that other broken people don't feel alone.

As I logged steps behind my lawn mower, I pondered my broken bits and while little clarity revealed itself to me, I was somewhat comforted by the understanding that I am not alone either. Though not happy about anyone else's misery, the knowledge that we all have our own pocketful of broken bits does serve to dull the sharp blade a bit.

Every one suffers varying degrees of trauma, tragedy, abuse, struggle and hardship. Parents die young, cars crash, economies turn and relationships change. These events are simply life. They are the price we pay for breathing air on this earth.

An idea spawned by the smells of fresh cut grass and 2-cycle engine exhaust is that perhaps our broken bits are the best things we have. Having our own sack of broken bits allows us to access other people's broken bits. When we truly "get it", we can connect. This empathy creates the axis for the genuine heart-to-heart human connections upon which our world turns.

Understanding our own fear, uncertainty, and conflict allows us to understand others'. And this is a good thing. It is said that: "Friendship multiplies happiness and divides grief." This division of grief is powerful and it can only exist with the understanding of our own broken bits. This little reframe on our "brokenness" suddenly makes it kind of beautiful. Not fun, but still beautiful. We can serve better and be better for those who deserve us to be better, including ourselves.

So, while the broken bits we carry in our pockets can make us uncomfortable, they may also be necessary for us to grow and give and live better lives. This idea makes those sharp little devils jabbing into our leg a little more tolerable. It is easy in our brokenness to lock the doors and close the shutters. We want to isolate and protect the unbroken bits. But perhaps we should just be sprinkling our busted little shards all over the place, so that others can have a look and maybe feel a little better about their own broken bits and not feel alone. No one is alone.

Wholly Moses!!!

While drinking my morning coffee the other day, my phone chimed, signaling an incoming text message. It was pretty early so my interest was piqued. As I checked the screen, the words "Wholly Moses" brightened the sky on this nominally dismal and dreary, overcast morning and I may have laughed out loud. I replied, "Damn. Nice."

Several years ago, my old college buddy, Jeff, and I were involved in a beer-driven challenge to name old HBO movies we watched as kids. We compiled a pretty impressive list, which I still have scribbled on the wrinkled napkin we recorded our results on.

Now, a few times a year, the light bulb will go on and a simple text with only the title of the movie will be sent. We each enjoy receiving these. Though, in all honesty, I am occasionally annoyed when he remembers a good one before me.

Nonetheless, these little notes always make me smile. I am reminded of a fun day with a good friend and I know that he is reminded of me. It's nice to know that other people think of us. That's the beauty of old friends. Anything, even old HBO movie titles, can have meaning and make us smile. These things reflect time spent and life shared.

Old friends require little maintenance. And there is tremendous comfort in knowing that my muddled and motley collection of great old friends and I will be drinking a beer and playing cribbage, sharing successes and tragedies and calling each other bad names forever. These are the good and easy relationships.

Other relationships we experience require tending; delicate attention and mindful grooming. Our kids and our spouses live here. Throughout shared lives, a million little cuts are delivered as a harsh word or an unspoken word. Tiny neglects and lack of attention to the minute variations in a heartbeat become bricks in the walls that we construct. Individually, they appear insignificant. Over time, though, these cuts or bricks compound and eventually strike an artery and the relationship bleeds out or a fortress is erected with walls too high for a man to climb.

When this happens, restitution must be paid. We must atone. It is here that we are forced to emotionally strip down in front of the classroom and stand uncovered while the pupils stare open-mouthed at our form and point and laugh. In these moments, we are built. We learn things that we could not learn otherwise.

And when we're naked, stripped bare of all ornament and garnish, we are changed. Lying exposed on the desert floor as the night animals and buzzards pick apart the carcass of our past and leave it to bleach in the sun, pride, ego, self-consciousness, filters and lenses that send us false information and all other diabolical human emotional creations evaporate. Leaving only a truth. And in this truth is the somewhat comforting understanding that endings and beginnings often wear the same shoes...

Pretending.

I walked into my house and sensed disaster...again. Opening the front door, I was met with shredded napkins and a trail of rice leading up the stairs. At the top of the stairs, my old dog, Diego, lay motionless except for his eyes. He glanced at me with sad, sick eyes and although he...again...destroyed our kitchen garbage, I did not have the heart to even raise my voice to him. He must have eaten sufficient garbage scraps to self-impose his own punishment. He eyes said that he had. Recognizing this, I muttered some profanity and went about the task of cleaning up his mess...again.

I have done this many times. I used to blame Diego for his lack of self-control. Now, I mostly blame myself. Cleaning the kitchen on this morning, I recall tossing some left-over taco meat on top of the three-quarters full garbage and thinking, "I'd better dump that or Diego will have a field day." Alas, I forgot and a field day was had. Diego and I both paid the price for my oversight. He was sick and I was scraping refried beans off my kitchen floor.

In the past, I might have dispensed some swift and uncomfortable "justice" upon Diego. I don't anymore. I understand that a dog is going to be a dog. No purposeful logic inspires his dumpster diving. He is afflicted with instincts beyond his control. It is here where Diego and I (and maybe all of us) can find some common ground.

Reading a book the other evening, a particularly impactful line slapped me in the face:
"People don't change," she said. "They grow into what they've always been. They just stop pretending, that's all." This line is from my favorite author, James Lee Burke's, new novel, The Jealous Kind.
I felt the slap, because the idea of "change" represents hope to me. And these words diminished this hope.

I read and re-read and shared these words with a couple of buddies. Their responses were similar, yet different. One replied with "Ugh..." with almost the "that's what I was afraid of" tone. The other was "Ugh"ish, but with a "so what?"-we're still ok tone. I understood both interpretations.

My first instinct, like many folks I suspect, is to steer towards the self-critical path; to identify more closely to the negative than the positive. And, as much as this is true, so is the fact that after I stew on these things for a while, I tend to reverse my position. After some searching, I find and remove the eggshell from my omelet and enjoy the meal.

These words, like all well-written words, challenge the reader to explore; to taste the words and roll them around the mouth and mind, and find the different flavors.

The hope I thought I lost was found in a new flavor I discovered in these words. "Growing into" what we've always been spun towards the positive. We ARE good, too. We're kind and powerful and beautiful. Becoming more of these things is an inspiring idea. We don't need to change. We just need to truly "be" what we already are.

Stopping "pretending" gives us permission to express these things. For all the ways we limit our expression- fear, doubt, insecurities, etc.-, understanding that we're not going to change, and we don't really need to, opens the door to the somewhat liberating idea that we're already ok. We have nothing to fear or prove. We're built and we're good and we can freely deliver on the promise of us.

So, my damn dog will be a damn dog and I will be whatever I am. He will make messes and I will make messes. We will also enjoy sitting on the deck watching the sun set over the water and know that being what we are is a fine thing to be. We don't need to change a thing...all of us are good...

Finding Words.

The other morning I woke up with an ominous sense that something was just not right. My household is one of rituals. My morning always begins with my old dog, Diego, doing his pee-pee dance at the foot of my bed hollering at me to let him outside. On this day, Diego was absent. I was unnerved by this. I have come to count on certain things and when they're not there, I get a little uneasy. I knew something was up.

Walking my slippered feet downstairs, my suspicions were confirmed. My damn dog was laying on our old green couch with his head on a throw pillow looking at me with the sad, cloudy eyes of shame and disappointment. On the carpet in front of the couch and beyond was a crime scene of dog-doo of unnatural proportion. Diego got into the garbage the night before and paid a heavy price. Unfortunately, it was a price that I was now forced to pay as well. Cleaning this disaster was not on my day's itinerary.

I felt bad for the guy. I called him off the couch to take him outside, just in case he wasn't completely empty. Though, based on the volume and distribution of his illness, this seemed unlikely. Anyway... my plans for the morning took a turn. I had not anticipated this possibility, yet here I was. I was surprised and not surprised and just kept moving; another story in the sea of stories of my life. We all have great canons of stories.

All great stories begin with the stroke of the pen. They shift from an idea or a dream into a physical form. The ink on the page represents the blood pulsing through the heart of a dream. Getting the pen to the page requires work, which is probably why so many wonderful stories go untold. Dreams require work. We must stretch and push and pull and stride forward against the wind to make our magic.

Dreams get stalled and there are moments when we can't find the words to our stories. In these moments, we must simply keep the pen moving. The words are there. Our words don't leave us. They hide, but they're always with us even when we think we've lost them. These can be difficult times. But, proving again God's absurd and sometimes cruel sense of humor, these difficult times may be the most important ones we experience.

They force us to find new words and to change our stories. We must reinvent and re-create and grow. Through this growth, we see the world differently. The world becomes new again, full of opportunities and hope and fresh blooms in the trees.

Life is funny. The unexplainable and inconceivable are the norm. We're often surprised by the truth that our plans don't always work out. When our tree gets shaken and we must make a new move or invent one, we try to fight it and we lose. We can hold-fast and set our feet and minds and we still lose. We must adapt and adjust our sails to greet the new wind. This is usually uncomfortable, but also vital to the beautiful evolution of our spirits.

Nonetheless, sometimes the clouds are dark and the days seem to begin and end with neither a sunrise nor a sunset. It's just dark. In these times, when we've lost our words, the best one can do is to hold tight to the idea that our words have not lost us... and they will find us. They always do...

Finish Lines.

Each morning I wake up and go for a walk. I contemplate my day as I take my little two-mile stroll from my house around the Marina. My little morning jaunt is more meditative than a part of any fitness strategy. It's just a walk and talk...with myself.

I try to walk around the same time of day and, as such, I tend to encounter the same people. I like this part. I see the little Asian gal jogging and stopping to do some air squats. I see "Bob", a pretty old guy that I meet "again" about every two weeks. And I see an older couple who walk holding hands and smiling and seem as happy to see me as I am them. I enjoy seeing them, though I may really just enjoy the smell of lady's perfume. It's nice...

These mornings, I am reminded of my past, consider my present, and ponder my future. I breathe in some sea air and exhale the little toxins compiled since the day before. It's a cleansing time. I take steps and think thoughts and don't think thoughts. I feel the wind or the sun or a raindrop on my face.

A thought which danced across my mind recently was my/our "destination". My thought played out like this:

A great fallacy of life is that there is a finish line, besides the grave. There is a great tendency to believe in the fantasy that upon arrival at a particular milepost in life, we will find the peace, certainty and security we seek.

This deception is diabolical in its power to create false expectations which set us up for disappointment. We never arrive. The finish line keeps moving. For every hill we conquer, another pops up in the near horizon. This fact is not meant to be depressing or disheartening. When we understand this truth we can avoid the pain of believing a lie. And I much prefer an uncomfortable truth to a happy lie.

When we know the truth, we can respond with our own truth. And our own truth while sometimes being flawed, scarred, bruised and afraid, is also beautiful. It is real and human, and the best of us lives inside of this truth.

Our doubts and fears and insecurities-all of the weird little confusions we suffer as human beings walking this earth- are where our truth lives. They are our power and they are our beauty. All these little things that scare us and shame us, also serve us. All life stories are survival tales of over-coming, of facing our fears and keeping moving. All of us.

272

On my whiteboard at my CrossFit gym, I had a couple of quotes. The first was, "Learn to love the climb." This addressed the idea that certainly fitness, but really life, is a forever climb. No finish line exists. We can always get stronger, smarter, better...forever. This idea softens the expectations of an "arrival place" and gives permission to simply enjoy the process of living life in forward motion.

The second quote was, "Comparison is the thief of joy." Certainly in the context of a gym, this quote served to disarm the tendency to define ourselves by standards other than our own; the idea that somehow we are less; that others possess something that we do not. And while sometimes it is true that others possess things we do not, it is also true that we possess things that they do not. We are all wonderfully unique and enjoy strength beyond our mind's eye.

This reminder is especially potent when the hill we're climbing feels steeper than we believe we can climb. Trusting in the power of our personal and powerful little truth changes the grade of every hill we climb and can transform raindrops into sunbeams on an early morning walk by the water...and at all other times, too...

Rocket Ships.

2016 sucked. Hard. It was without question the most challenging year of my life and maybe just simply the worst one I've ever had. I hope it dies in the dust of my history and not become a challenge to "God" to sharpen his pencil and invent new and even more painful ways to bring me misery. 2016 was enough for a while.

Reflecting upon my year, I see loss and I see gain. It's difficult in the firestorm of loss to see upsides. Having survived hard things before, I know that invariably we learn valuable things through them. We learn things we cannot learn without them. We gather materials for life after the hard thing. These things are important. We add to our catalog of information from which we can construct a better life.

When our rocket ship blows up, if we survive, we have new data about how to build a better rocket ship. This is not failure. This is success. Survival is success and learning is success. Growth is success. Though sometimes, growth is uncomfortable.

Like the lobster growing out of its shell, the exoskeleton must be shed, through deliberate and painful effort, to make room for a new, better one. This is life. I know many people living uncomfortably in a shell that no longer fits. This is sad. And while change is sometimes sad, it is not as sad as not changing. This is the saddest thing there is.

So, as I turn the page on crappy 2016, I look forward to 2017. I look forward with new eyes and a perspective gained and a fresh start. I look to the sky and see a successful rocket launch. The lessons learned were for something, not nothing. Believing this requires faith. And I have it. Learning the lessons requires believing in this faith. And I do.

In my sky, I also see other colorful and stable flying machines next to mine and if at some point during this magical journey I see yours, I will smile and wave from my rocket ship window and be happy for you. Counting down...

Made in USA - Kendallville, IN
1089785_9781539593294
04.23.2020 1102